taste of home
Contest Winning
ANNUAL RECIPES
2012

taste of home.
Contest Winning
ANNUAL RECIPES
2012

EDITORIAL
EDITOR-IN-CHIEF: Catherine Cassidy

EXECUTIVE EDITOR/PRINT & DIGITAL BOOKS: Stephen C. George
CREATIVE DIRECTOR: Howard Greenberg
EDITORIAL SERVICES DIRECTOR: Kerri Balliet

SENIOR EDITOR/PRINT & DIGITAL BOOKS: Mark Hagen
EDITORS: Sara Rae Lancaster, Michelle Rozumalski
ASSOCIATE CREATIVE DIRECTOR: Edwin Robles Jr.
ART DIRECTOR: Jessie Sharon
CONTENT PRODUCTION MANAGER: Julie Wagner
COPY CHIEF: Deb Warlaumont Mulvey
COPY EDITOR: Mary C. Hanson
EDITORIAL ASSISTANT: Marilyn Iczkowski
RECIPE TESTING AND EDITING: Taste of Home Test Kitchen
FOOD PHOTOGRAPHY: Taste of Home Photo Studio

BUSINESS
VICE PRESIDENT, PUBLISHER: Jan Studin, jan_studin@rd.com
REGIONAL ACCOUNT DIRECTOR: Donna Lindskog, donna_lindskog@rd.com
EASTERN ACCOUNT DIRECTOR: Jennifer Dietz
MIDWEST & WESTERN ACCOUNT DIRECTOR: Jackie Fallon
MIDWEST ACCOUNT MANAGER: Lorna Phillips
WESTERN ACCOUNT MANAGER: Joel Millikin
MICHIGAN SALES REPRESENTATIVE: Linda C. Donaldson

CORPORATE INTEGRATED SALES DIRECTOR: Steve Sottile
VICE PRESIDENT, DIGITAL SALES AND DEVELOPMENT: Dan Meehan
DIGITAL/INTEGRATED DIRECTOR: Kelly Paxson

GENERAL MANAGER, TASTE OF HOME COOKING SCHOOLS: Erin Puariea

DIRECT RESPONSE: Katherine Zito, David Geller Associates

EXECUTIVE DIRECTOR, BRAND MARKETING: Leah West
VICE PRESIDENT, CREATIVE DIRECTOR: Paul Livornese
MARKETING MANAGER: Katie Gaon Wilson
PUBLIC RELATIONS MANAGER: Heidi Frank

VICE PRESIDENT, MAGAZINE MARKETING: Dave Fiegel

READER'S DIGEST NORTH AMERICA
PRESIDENT: Dan Lagani

PRESIDENT, CANADA: Tony Cioffi
PRESIDENT, BOOKS AND HOME ENTERTAINING: Harold Clarke
CHIEF FINANCIAL OFFICER: Howard Halligan
VICE PRESIDENT, GENERAL MANAGER, READER'S DIGEST MEDIA: Marilynn Jacobs
CHIEF MARKETING OFFICER: Renee Jordan
VICE PRESIDENT, CHIEF SALES OFFICER: Mark Josephson
VICE PRESIDENT, GENERAL MANAGER, RD MILWAUKEE: Lisa Karpinski
VICE PRESIDENT, CHIEF STRATEGY OFFICER: Jacqueline Majers Lachman
VICE PRESIDENT, CHIEF CONTENT OFFICER: Liz Vaccariello

THE READER'S DIGEST ASSOCIATION, INC.
PRESIDENT AND CHIEF EXECUTIVE OFFICER: Robert E. Guth

COVER PHOTOGRAPHY
PHOTOGRAPHER: Dan Roberts
FOOD STYLIST: Kathryn Joy
SET STYLIST: Dee Dee Jacq

@2012 REIMAN MEDIA GROUP, LLC
5400 S. 60TH ST. GREENDALE, WI 53129

INTERNATIONAL STANDARD BOOK NUMBER (10): 1-61765-061-7
INTERNATIONAL STANDARD BOOK NUMBER (13): 978-1-61765-061-1
INTERNATIONAL STANDARD SERIAL NUMBER: 1548-4157

PRINTED IN U.S.A.
1 3 5 7 9 10 8 6 4 2

PICTURED ON THE FRONT COVER: ELEGANT CHOCOLATE TORTE, PG. 194.

TABLE OF CONTENTS

CHEDDAR-VEGGIE APPETIZER TORTE, PG. 11

HOLIDAY GELATIN MOLD, PG. 30

REFRIED BEAN SOUP, PG. 44

MEDITERRANEAN VEGETABLE PASTA, PG. 130

OVER 350
PRIZE-WINNING RECIPES & TIPS!

Every year, cooks eagerly wait for the latest edition of *Contest Winning Annual Recipes*, anticipating the compliments they'll receive when they serve the "best of the best" appetizers, main dishes, sides, desserts and more! Jam-packed with top-rated dishes from Taste of Home, the world's #1 food source, it's no wonder people keep asking for this cookbook year after year.

Now in its ninth edition, *Contest Winning Annual Recipes 2012*, serves 312 prize-worthy recipes—all honored in a year's worth of contests—and expert kitchen tips that will have you cooking like the pros in no time.

Wondering how these recipes received high honors in their respective contests? First, home cooks from all around read our request for entries and sent in their creations—the must-have dishes their family and friends ask for time and again.

Then our Test Kitchen professionals sorted through the many entries we received and prepared the most promising selections for our judging panel of experienced food editors. After much delicious sampling, the judges selected a Grand Prize winner and the runners-up.

Winners from Dozens of Contests

The contests spotlighted in this cookbook cover a wide range of recipes—snacks and beverages; salads and dressings; soups and stews; entrees; side dishes and condiments; breads and rolls; brownies, bars and cookies; cakes and pies; and special desserts. No matter what type of recipe you're looking for or occasion you're planning, you're sure to find the perfect offering in this mouthwatering collection.

For a complete list of chapters, please see the Table of Contents on page 3. Here's a quick peek at some of the yummy goodies in store:

- **GO NUTS:** That's exactly what your group will do when they try the tempting goodies showcased here—especially the simply munchable Rustic Nut Bars (p. 166). A platter of them never lasts long.

- **SOUP'S ON!** Yes, soup for you! Savor a steaming bowl of Colorful Chicken 'n' Squash Soup on page 54. Every spoonful is so comforting, it's hard to believe this homestyle favorite is good for you, too!

- **CUPCAKE CHALLENGE:** So cute and portable, cupcakes are all the rage. Turn your kitchen into your own corner bakery with an assortment of fun-to-eat recipes. We think you'll agree, Special Mocha Cupcakes (p. 180) take the (cup)cake!

- **BOUNTIFUL HARVEST:** The best part about having a garden is getting to enjoy the fruits—and veggies—of your labor. But sometimes, using up that abundance of fresh produce can be a challenge. This fresh-tasting collection features the best garden creations, including grand-prize winner Spaghetti Squash with Red Sauce (p. 124).

- **POTLUCK PLEASERS:** Does the sight of a potluck sign-up sheet make you hyperventilate? Breathe easy! Simply pick any of the crowd-winning specialties from our Potluck Pleasers contest and you're armed with a can't-fail contribution. Our panel of judges suggests Duo Tater Bake on page 152. Yum!

- **HOLIDAY BAKING BONANZA:** If there is ever a time we try to impress our guests, it's during the holidays. Present the showstopping Elegant Chocolate Torte (p. 194) and expect plenty of "oohs" and "ahhs" from those gathered around the table.

- **SLOW-COOKED FAVORITES:** Nothing beats coming home to a meal that's all ready to serve. Slow cooker fans will rejoice at this chapter brimming with simmered favorites such as succulent and flavorful Teriyaki Pork Roast (p. 112).

- **COOKIE DOUGH CREATIONS:** Admit it. We've all swiped a taste of cookie dough from the bowl. Who can resist that rich, buttery taste? A slice of Special Pleasure Chocolate Cheesecake (p. 216) lets you enjoy the decadent treat safely and deliciously.

- **EASY BREEZY BERRIES:** The jewels of summertime, sun-ripened berries are a sweet treat served at breakfast, dessert or any meal in between. Our judges couldn't think of a

MEXICAN LASAGNA, PG. 94

tastier—or prettier—way to highlight these sweet gems than in Special Summer Berry Medley (p. 32).

- **FIX IT WITH FIVE:** You'll give a "high-five" to these fast-to-fix recipes. Effortlessly transform just five ingredients into scrumptious, time-saving dishes. Go ahead and let people think you invested a lot of time and work into making the Grand Prize winner, Chocolate-Cherry Ice Cream Pie (p. 190).

- **LAST-MINUTE LUNCHES:** Brown is the new black when it comes to lunch—brown bag lunches, that is. And thanks to these speedy selections (you *must* try Onion Beef Muffin Cups on page 90), you can cut down on both time spent in the kitchen and money spent buying lunch.

- **FUSS-FREE HOLIDAY FARE:** Stress less this holiday season by keeping the menu delicious, but simple. No-fuss Chocolate Coconut Candies (p. 172) prove it is possible to make your own holiday goodies and still stay in a merry mood.

- **LOVE THAT LASAGNA:** Did someone say lasagna? Grab a fork and dig into the very best layered noodle creations. Worth It Lasagna, our judges' top pick featured on page 100, is just one of the tempting recipes you can try. Choose from traditional, Southwestern spins, meatless versions and more.

- **MEATLESS MAIN DISHES:** Tired of the same old Meatless Monday menu? Get out of the rut with these veggie-laden favorites. The winning recipe, Lemony Vegetables and Pasta on page 120, is as pleasing to the eye as it is to the palate.

- **FANTASTIC FROZEN DESSERTS:** Frosty and refreshing, frozen desserts offer a luscious and versatile way to cool off a warm day. When the votes were tallied, incredibly rich Chocolate Peanut Butter Dessert (p. 222) was the winner with our panel...we're pretty sure it will be with yours, too.

- **FAMILY REUNION BUFFET:** Sure it's great to catch up with aunts, uncles and cousins, but family reunions are also about the food—those time-honored recipes that bring back childhood memories. Make a few new memories with Almond-Filled Butterhorns (p. 140) and this chapter's other family-approved treats.

- **EXPRESS ENTREES:** Even your busiest nights can include a home-cooked meal. Easy Chicken Potpie on page 86 and other in-a-flash main dishes make it simple to have dinner on the table in mere minutes.

- **HOLIDAY BREADS:** Celebrate the season with a selection of yeast and quick breads. A traditional Swedish Tea Ring (p. 70) really wowed our group. One bite of this nutty, glazed sweet bread and you'll understand why.

- **SOUTHWESTERN SPECIALTIES:** Enjoy a taste of the Southwest without leaving home. Packed with authentic spices and flavor, Marvelous Chicken Enchiladas (p. 104) turn any night into a fiesta.

- **BOUNTIFUL BRUNCH:** Why head to a restaurant for brunch when you can treat family and friends to a delicious late-morning meal at home? You'll be absolutely smitten with the individual Florence-Inspired Souffles on page 76.

- **CRISPS AND COBBLERS:** Pass up the cake and pie! This chapter is dedicated to easier-to-prepare and faster-to-bake crisps and cobblers. Indulge in spoonfuls of freshly baked desserts, including our winning entry, Peach Blackberry Cobbler (p. 204).

- **GUILT-FREE GRILLING:** Get the grill fired up while you keep fat and calories down with the too-good-to-be-true options from our Guilt-Free Grilling contest. Incredibly juicy and bursting with flavor, Zesty Turkey Burgers (p. 44) bust the myth that healthy alternatives are bland and boring.

- **SLIMMED-DOWN THANKSGIVING SIDES:** Turkey Day doesn't have to leave you feeling stuffed. Swap out a few of your heavier traditional dishes for these lightened-up versions instead. Sweet Potatoes and Apples Au Gratin on page 136 will have you going back for seconds. We promise!

- **GREAT CAKE MAKEOVER:** Have your cake and eat it too with these trimmed-down finales. Our judges agreed Coconut Cream Dream Cake (p. 176) wins the prize for swapping out fat and calories without sacrificing any of the decadence.

- **QUICK BREAD CREATIONS:** Quick breads are versatile, easy and suitable for a variety of occasions. Try Parmesan Herb Loaf (p. 148) as an ideal sidekick to soups, salads or any entree.

- **LIGHTEN UP:** "When food tastes this good, it's easy to eat healthy!" That's what our judges declared when they tried the winner from our "Lighten Up" contest, Mediterranean Vegetable Pasta.

- **APPLE APPEAL:** So flaky and bursting with juicy cinnamon flavor, Apple Turnovers on page 212 just may become the apple of your eye...and the star of your fall dessert lineup!

ALMOND-FILLED BUTTERHORNS, PG. 140

PG. 14

PG. 9

PG. 10

SNACKS & APPETIZERS

When a snack attack hits, calm cravings with this irresistible collection of tasty bites. Grilled Feta Quesadillas, Baked Egg Rolls and Roasted Cumin Cashews are just some of the can't-be-beat party pleasers found here!

PG. 15

Goat Cheese 'n'
Veggie Quesadillas

Prep: 55 min. Bake: 5 min.

Sara Longworth, Bristol, Connecticut

The roasted veggies and goat cheese make this an elegant party option. We love to top the crispy, melty wedges with our favorite salsa for an extra kick.

✓	This recipe includes Nutrition Facts.

  1 **small eggplant, peeled, quartered and cut into**
    1/2-inch slices
  1 **medium zucchini, cut into 1/4-inch slices**
  1 **medium sweet red pepper, chopped**
  1 **medium onion, chopped**
1/4 **cup chopped ripe olives**
  2 **garlic cloves, minced**
  2 **tablespoons olive oil**
  1 **tablespoon lemon juice**

1/2 **teaspoon chili powder**
1/2 **teaspoon cayenne pepper**
  1 **tablespoon minced fresh cilantro**
1/2 **cup crumbled goat cheese**
  8 **whole wheat tortillas (8 inches)**

1. Place the first six ingredients in an ungreased 15-in. x 10-in. x 1-in. baking pan. Combine the oil, lemon juice, chili powder and cayenne; drizzle over vegetables and toss to coat. Bake, uncovered, at 400° for 35-40 minutes or until vegetables are tender, stirring once. Stir in cilantro.

2. Spread 1 tablespoon goat cheese over one side of each tortilla. Place two tortillas, plain side down, on an ungreased baking sheet; spread each with 2/3 cup vegetable mixture. Top each with another tortilla. Repeat. Bake at 400° for 5-10 minutes or until golden brown. Cut each quesadilla into six wedges. Serve warm. **Yield:** 2 dozen appetizers.

Nutrition Facts: 1 wedge equals 171 calories, 8 g fat (2 g saturated fat), 7 mg cholesterol, 191 mg sodium, 20 g carbohydrate, 3 g fiber, 6 g protein.

Baked Egg Rolls

Prep/Total Time: 30 min.

Barbra Annino, Galena, Illinois

Chinese take-out can be high in sodium, fat and calories, so these crispy appetizers are a nice alternative. Whenever my husband craves a take-out egg roll, I make these instead.

 This recipe includes Nutrition Facts & Diabetic Exchanges.

1-1/3 cups chopped fresh broccoli stir-fry vegetable blend
   1 cup shredded cooked chicken breast
4-1/2 teaspoons reduced-sodium soy sauce
   2 teaspoons sesame oil
   2 garlic cloves, minced
1/2 teaspoon ground ginger
   8 egg roll wrappers

1. In a small bowl, combine the first six ingredients. Place 1/4 cup chicken mixture in the center of one egg roll wrapper. Fold bottom corner over filling; fold sides toward center. Moisten remaining corner with water; roll up tightly to seal. Repeat with remaining wrappers and filling.

2. Place seam side down on a baking sheet coated with cooking spray. Spray tops of egg rolls with cooking

spray. Bake at 425° for 10-15 minutes or until lightly browned. Serve egg rolls warm. Refrigerate leftovers. **Yield:** 8 egg rolls.

Nutrition Facts: 1 egg roll equals 140 calories, 2 g fat (trace saturated fat), 16 mg cholesterol, 315 mg sodium, 21 g carbohydrate, 1 g fiber, 9 g protein. **Diabetic Exchanges:** 1 starch, 1 lean meat, 1 vegetable.

Orange and Jicama Salsa

Prep/Total Time: 25 min.

Cheryl Perry, Hertford, North Carolina

Tiny cubes of crunchy jicama and ripe juicy oranges make for a change-of-pace salsa. Adjust the amount of jalapeno pepper to best suit your taste.

✓ This recipe includes Nutrition Facts & Diabetic Exchange.

   6 medium oranges, peeled, sectioned and chopped
1-1/2 cups cubed peeled jicama
1/4 cup chopped red onion
1/4 cup chopped sweet red pepper
   2 green onions, thinly sliced
1/4 cup minced fresh cilantro
   1 tablespoon lime juice
   2 teaspoons chopped seeded jalapeno pepper
1/2 teaspoon sugar
1/8 teaspoon salt
Baked tortilla chips *or* scoops

1. In a large bowl, combine the first 10 ingredients. Serve with chips. Refrigerate leftovers. **Yield:** 4 cups.

Editor's Note: Wear disposable gloves when cutting hot peppers; the oils can burn skin. Avoid touching your face.

Nutrition Facts: 1/4 cup (calculated without chips) equals 22 calories, trace fat (trace saturated fat), 0 cholesterol, 20 mg sodium, 5 g carbohydrate, 1 g fiber, trace protein. **Diabetic Exchange:** Free food.

Sweet Berry Bruschetta

Prep/Total Time: 20 min.

Patricia Nieh, Portola Vally, California

I've made this recipe by toasting the bread on a grill at cookouts, but any way I serve it, I never have any leftovers. The bruschetta is sweet instead of savory, and guests enjoy the colorful and tasty change.

✔ This recipe includes Nutrition Facts & Diabetic Exchanges.

10 **slices French bread (1/2 inch thick)**
5 **teaspoons sugar,** *divided*
6 **ounces fat-free cream cheese**
1/2 **teaspoon almond extract**
3/4 **cup fresh blackberries**
3/4 **cup fresh raspberries**
1/4 **cup slivered almonds, toasted**
2 **teaspoons confectioners' sugar**

1. Place bread on an ungreased baking sheet; lightly coat with cooking spray. Sprinkle with 2 teaspoons sugar. Broil 3-4 in. from the heat for 1-2 minutes or until lightly browned.

2. In a small bowl, combine the cream cheese, almond extract and remaining sugar. Spread over toasted bread. Top with berries and almonds; dust with confectioners' sugar. **Yield:** 10 pieces.

Nutrition Facts: 1 piece equals 92 calories, 2 g fat (trace saturated fat), 1 mg cholesterol, 179 mg sodium, 14 g carbohydrate, 2 g fiber, 4 g protein. **Diabetic Exchanges:** 1 starch, 1/2 fat.

Grilled Feta Quesadillas

Prep/Total Time: 20 min.

Jacqueline Correa, Landing, New Jersey

Tangy feta cheese and traditional Greek ingredients make this a deliciously different appetizer that's perfect for parties.

✔ This recipe includes Nutrition Facts & Diabetic Exchanges.

3 **ounces fat-free cream cheese**
1/2 **cup shredded reduced-fat Mexican cheese blend**
1/3 **cup crumbled feta cheese**
1/2 **teaspoon dried oregano**
4 **flour tortillas (6 inches), warmed**
1/4 **cup chopped pitted ripe olives**
2 **tablespoons diced pimientos**
1 **green onion, chopped**

1. In a small bowl, beat cheeses with oregano until blended. Spread 3 tablespoons of cheese mixture over half of each tortilla; top with olives, pimientos and onion. Fold tortillas over.

2. Using long-handled tongs, moisten a paper towel with cooking oil and lightly coat the grill rack. Grill quesadillas, uncovered, over medium heat or broil 4 in. from the heat for 1-2 minutes on each side or until golden brown. Cut each quesadilla into three wedges. Serve warm. **Yield:** 12 wedges.

Nutrition Facts: 1 wedge equals 62 calories, 3 g fat (1 g saturated fat), 6 mg cholesterol, 198 mg sodium, 5 g carbohydrate, trace fiber, 4 g protein. **Diabetic Exchanges:** 1/2 starch, 1/2 fat.

Cheddar-Veggie Appetizer Torte

Prep: 25 min. **Bake:** 30 min. + cooling

Barbara Estabrook, Rhinelander, Wisconsin

There is always a line behind this quiche-like torte at our family gatherings. The wedges are easy to eat as finger food.

1-1/3 cups finely crushed multigrain crackers
1/4 cup butter, melted
   2 cups (8 ounces) shredded sharp cheddar cheese
   1 small zucchini, finely chopped
   5 small fresh mushrooms, sliced
1/3 cup finely chopped red onion
1/4 cup finely chopped sweet red pepper
   1 tablespoon olive oil
   1 carton (8 ounces) spreadable garlic and herb cream cheese

   4 eggs, lightly beaten
   2 tablespoons crumbled cooked bacon
   2 tablespoons grated Parmesan cheese

1. In a small bowl, combine cracker crumbs and butter. Press onto the bottom of a greased 9-in. springform pan. Sprinkle with cheddar cheese. In a large skillet, saute zucchini, mushrooms, onion and red pepper in oil until tender. Spoon over cheese.

2. In a large bowl, beat cream cheese until smooth. Add eggs; beat on low speed just until combined. Stir in bacon. Pour over vegetable mixture. Sprinkle with Parmesan cheese.

3. Place pan on a baking sheet. Bake at 375° for 30-35 minutes or until center is almost set. Cool on a wire rack for 10 minutes.

4. Carefully run a knife around edge of pan to loosen; remove sides of pan. Serve warm or chilled. Refrigerate leftovers. **Yield:** 16 servings.

Golden Ham Croquettes

Prep/Total Time: 30 min.

Peggy Anderjaska, Haigler, Nebraska

Neighbors happened to drop in the first time I made these and just loved them. A tasty favorite, these croquettes are often part of our family dinners.

      3 tablespoons butter
  1/4 to 1/2 teaspoon curry powder
  1/4 cup all-purpose flour
  3/4 cup milk
      2 to 3 teaspoons prepared mustard
      1 teaspoon grated onion
      2 cups coarsely ground fully cooked ham
  2/3 cup dry bread crumbs
      1 egg, beaten
      2 tablespoons water
Oil for deep-fat frying
CHEESE SAUCE:
      2 tablespoons butter
      2 tablespoons all-purpose flour
  1/4 teaspoon salt
Dash of pepper
 1-1/4 cups milk
  1/2 cup shredded cheddar cheese
  1/2 cup shredded Swiss cheese

1. In a saucepan, melt butter; stir in curry powder and flour. Gradually add milk. Bring to a boil; cook and stir for 2 minutes or until thickened. Remove from the heat. Stir in mustard and onion; add ham and mix well. Cover and chill thoroughly.

2. With wet hands, shape mixture into 10 balls. Roll balls in bread crumbs; shape each into a cone. Whisk together egg and water. Dip cones into egg mixture; roll again in crumbs.

3. Heat oil in a deep-fat fryer to 375°. Fry croquettes, a few at a time, for 2 to 2-1/2 minutes or until golden brown. Drain on paper towels; keep warm.

4. For the cheese sauce, melt butter in a saucepan; stir in flour, salt and pepper until smooth. Gradually add milk. Bring to a boil; cook and stir for 2 minutes or until thickened. Reduce heat. Add cheeses; stir until melted. Spoon over croquettes. **Yield:** 5 servings.

Hawaiian Cheese Bread

Prep: 15 min. Bake: 25 min.

Amy McIlvain, Wilmington, Delaware

My mother's friend brought it to a party at work, and after one bite my mom knew she had to have the recipe. Simple and fast, this mouthwatering loaf is a hit with everybody.

      1 loaf (1 pound) Hawaiian sweet bread
      1 block (8 ounces) Swiss cheese
      3 slices red onion, chopped
  1/2 cup butter, melted
      3 garlic cloves, minced
      1 teaspoon salt

1. Cut bread diagonally into 1-in. slices to within 1 in. of bottom. Repeat cuts in opposite direction.

2. Cut Swiss cheese into 1/4-in. slices; cut slices into small pieces. Insert into bread. Combine the onion, butter, garlic and salt; spoon over bread.

3. Wrap loaf in foil. Bake at 350° for 25-30 minutes or until the cheese is melted. Serve the bread warm. **Yield:** 16 servings.

Butter Dips

Prep: 25 min. **Bake:** 15 min.

Elaine Norton, Lansing, Michigan

I like these bread sticks because I can whip them up in a hurry if company drops in unexpectedly (which happens often since my husband is a minister). Most folks are amazed that a recipe this easy can taste so good!

✓ This recipe includes Nutrition Facts.

2-1/2 cups all-purpose flour
    1 tablespoon sugar
3-1/2 teaspoons baking powder
1-1/2 teaspoons salt
    1/2 to 1 cup shredded sharp cheddar cheese
    1 cup milk
    1/3 cup butter, melted

TOPPINGS:
Sesame seeds, garlic, onion *or* celery salt

1. In large bowl, combine the flour, sugar, baking powder, salt and cheese; add milk. Stir slowly with fork. When dough clings together, turn onto well-floured surface. On a floured surface, knead gently 10 times. Roll dough into 12-in. x 8-in. rectangle.

2. Cut dough in half lengthwise with sharp knife, then into 16 strips. Place butter in a 13-in. x 9-in. baking pan. Dip both sides of strips in melted butter. Place two rows in pan. Sprinkle with topping of your choice. Bake at 450° for 12-15 minutes. Serve immediately. **Yield:** 32 breadsticks.

Nutrition Facts: 1 serving (1 stick) equals 65 calories, 3 g fat (2 g saturated fat), 8 mg cholesterol, 188 mg sodium, 8 g carbohydrate, trace fiber, 2 g protein.

Cucumber Tea Sandwiches

Prep: 30 min. + chilling

Kimberly Smith, Brighton, Tennessee

My children wanted to plant a garden, and we ended up with buckets of cucumbers. When I tired of making pickles, I came up with these pretty little sandwiches. We made 200 of them for a family gathering, and everyone wanted the recipe.

    1 package (8 ounces) cream cheese, softened
1/4 cup mayonnaise
    1 tablespoon snipped fresh dill
    1 tablespoon lemon juice
1/2 teaspoon Worcestershire sauce
1/4 teaspoon salt
1/8 teaspoon cayenne pepper
1/8 teaspoon pepper
    2 large cucumbers, seeded and chopped
1/2 cup chopped sweet red pepper
1/4 cup chopped onion
1/4 cup pimiento-stuffed olives, chopped
1/4 cup minced fresh parsley
  12 slices whole wheat bread
Cucumber slices and fresh dill sprigs, optional

1. In a small bowl, combine the first eight ingredients; beat until blended. Stir in the cucumbers, red pepper, onion, olives and parsley. Cover and refrigerate for up to 2 hours.

2. Remove crusts from the bread; cut each slice into four triangles. Spread with cream cheese mixture. Garnish with cucumber slices and dill sprigs if desired. **Yield:** 4 dozen.

Catfish Spread

Prep: 20 min. + chilling

Edna Carter, West Point, Virginia

Whenever we have a fish fry, we begin the meal with this dip. My children and grandchildren love it, and it gets rave reviews at picnics and potlucks. Someone always requests the recipe.

> ✔ This recipe includes Nutrition Facts.

- 1 **pound catfish fillets**
- 2 **teaspoons water**
- 2 **packages (8 ounces *each*) cream cheese, softened**
- 2 **packages (5.2 ounces *each*) garlic-herb cheese spread**
- 4 **green onions, thinly sliced**
- 1/2 **cup minced fresh parsley**
- 1 **tablespoon lemon juice**
- 2 **teaspoons Worcestershire sauce**
- 1/8 **teaspoon garlic powder**
- 1/8 **teaspoon cayenne pepper**
- Dash paprika
- 1 **can (6 ounces) crabmeat, drained, flaked and cartilage removed**
- 1 **can (6 ounces) small shrimp, rinsed and drained**
- **Assorted fresh vegetables**

1. Place catfish in a 2-qt. microwave-safe dish; drizzle with water. Cover and microwave on high for 4-6 minutes or until fish flakes easily with a fork. Drain and discard cooking liquid. Using a fork, flake fish into small pieces; set aside.

2. In a large bowl, beat cream cheese and cheese spread until smooth. Add the onions, parsley, lemon juice, Worcestershire sauce and seasonings and mix well. Stir in the crab, shrimp and catfish. Cover and refrigerate for at least 2 hours. Serve spread with vegetables. **Yield:** 5 cups.

Editor's Note: This recipe was tested in a 1,100-watt microwave.

Nutrition Facts: 1 serving (1/4 cup) equals 117 calories, 9 g fat (5 g saturated fat), 57 mg cholesterol, 226 mg sodium, 1 g carbohydrate, trace fiber, 8 g protein.

Roasted Cumin Cashews

Prep: 15 min. **Bake:** 50 min. + cooling

Martha Fehl, Brookville, Indiana

Kick up parties and get-togethers a notch with these well-seasoned snacks. They're sweet, salty, crunchy...and oh, so munchable!

✓ | This recipe includes Nutrition Facts.

- 1 egg white
- 1 tablespoon water
- 2 cans (9-3/4 ounces *each*) salted whole cashews
- 1/3 cup sugar
- 3 teaspoons chili powder
- 2 teaspoons salt
- 2 teaspoons ground cumin
- 1/2 teaspoon cayenne pepper

1. In a large bowl, whisk egg white and water. Add cashews and toss to coat. Transfer to a colander; drain for 2 minutes. In another bowl, combine the remaining ingredients; add cashews and toss to coat.

2. Arrange in a single layer in a greased 15-in. x 10-in. x 1-in. baking pan. Bake, uncovered, at 250° for 50-55

minutes, stirring once. Cool on a wire rack. Store in an airtight container. **Yield:** 3-1/2 cups.

Nutrition Facts: 1 serving (1/4 cup) equals 145 calories, 10 g fat (2 g saturated fat), 0 cholesterol, 477 mg sodium, 10 g carbohydrate, 1 g fiber, 4 g protein.

Pina Colada Slush

Prep: 10 min. + freezing

Alisa Allred, Vernal, Utah

For a special treat on a steamy day, try this fruity cooler. I'm asked to bring it to family gatherings all year long, so I always keep a batch or two in my freezer.

✓ | This recipe includes Nutrition Facts.

- 3 cans (6 ounces *each*) unsweetened pineapple juice
- 2 cups water
- 1 can (10 ounces) frozen non-alcoholic pina colada mix
- 1 tablespoon lime juice
- 1 tub sugar-free lemonade soft drink mix
- 6 cups lemon-lime soda, chilled

1. In a large bowl, combine the pineapple juice, water, pina colada mix, lime juice and soft drink mix; stir until drink mix is dissolved. Transfer to a 2-qt. freezer container. Freeze for 6 hours or overnight.

2. Remove slush mixture from the freezer 45 minutes before serving. For each serving, combine 1/2 cup slush mixture with 1/2 cup lemon-lime soda. **Yield:** 12 servings (3 quarts).

Editor's Note: This recipe was tested with Crystal Light lemonade soft drink mix.

Nutrition Facts: 1 cup equals 115 calories, 1 g fat (1 g saturated fat), 0 cholesterol, 20 mg sodium, 26 g carbohydrate, trace fiber, trace protein.

Spicy Breaded Chicken Wings

Prep: 25 min. **Bake:** 25 min.

Barbara White, Katy, Texas

Everyone really loves these spicy chicken wings! They taste just like fried chicken but are better for you because they're baked. The seasoned breading is so tasty, we even enjoy them without the dipping sauce. Try the recipe using chicken drumettes instead.

1 egg
1 tablespoon water
2/3 cup dry bread crumbs
1 teaspoon onion powder
1 teaspoon dried basil
1 teaspoon cayenne pepper
1/2 teaspoon garlic salt
1/2 teaspoon paprika
10 whole chicken wings
DIPPING SAUCE:
2 tablespoons ketchup
2 tablespoons honey
1 tablespoon Worcestershire sauce
1/2 teaspoon hot pepper sauce

1. In a shallow bowl, beat egg and water. In another shallow bowl, combine the bread crumbs, onion powder, basil, cayenne, garlic salt and paprika.

2. Cut chicken wings into three sections; discard wing tip sections. Dip chicken wings into egg mixture, then coat with crumb mixture. Place in a greased 15-in. x 10-in. x 1-in. baking pan. Bake at 425° for 25-30 minutes or until juices run clear, turning every 10 minutes.

3. In a small bowl, combine the sauce ingredients. Serve with chicken wings. **Yield:** 6 servings.

Sausage Wonton Cups

Prep/Total Time: 30 min.

Shirley Van Allen, High Point, North Carolina

Here's a tasty hot appetizer for all those holiday parties that feature fun finger foods and quick bites. I have made this recipe several times, and it always disappears so fast. Best of all, it's really easy to prepare but looks like you fussed.

 This recipe includes Nutrition Facts & Diabetic Exchanges.

4 Italian turkey sausage links (4 ounces *each*), casings removed
1 can (15 ounces) tomato sauce
1/2 teaspoon garlic powder
1/2 teaspoon dried basil
24 wonton wrappers
1 cup (4 ounces) shredded Italian cheese blend

1. In a large skillet, cook Italian turkey sausage over medium heat until no longer pink; drain. Stir in the tomato sauce, garlic powder and basil. Bring to a boil. Reduce heat; simmer, uncovered, for 8-10 minutes or until thickened.

2. Meanwhile, press wonton wrappers into miniature muffin cups coated with cooking spray. Bake at 350° for 8-9 minutes or until lightly browned.

3. Spoon sausage mixture into cups. Sprinkle with cheese. Bake 5-7 minutes longer or until cheese is melted. Serve warm. **Yield:** 2 dozen.

Nutrition Facts: 1 wonton cup equals 68 calories, 3 g fat (1 g saturated fat), 15 mg cholesterol, 270 mg sodium, 6 g carbohydrate, trace fiber, 5 g protein. **Diabetic Exchanges:** 1/2 starch, 1/2 fat.

Appetizer Tortilla Pinwheels

Prep: 20 min. + chilling

Pat Waymire, Yellow Springs, Ohio

A friend in Arizona gave me this simple starter recipe. Besides being attractive and tasty, the pinwheels can be made ahead of time and sliced just before serving, leaving you time for other party preparations.

✓ This recipe includes Nutrition Facts.

1 cup (8 ounces) sour cream
1 package (8 ounces) cream cheese, softened
1 can (4-1/4 ounces) chopped ripe olives
1 can (4 ounces) chopped green chilies, well drained
1 cup (4 ounces) shredded cheddar cheese

1/2 cup chopped green onions
Garlic powder to taste
Seasoned salt to taste
5 flour tortillas (10 inches), room temperature
Fresh parsley for garnish
Salsa

1. In a large bowl, beat the first eight ingredients until blended. Spread over the tortillas; roll up tightly. Wrap each with plastic wrap, twisting ends; refrigerate for several hours.

2. Unwrap; cut into 1/2-in. to 3/4-in. slices. (An electric knife works best.) Discard ends. Garnish with parsley. Serve pinwheels with salsa if desired. **Yield:** about 4 dozen.

Nutrition Facts: 1 serving (3 each) equals 180 calories, 11 g fat (7 g saturated fat), 33 mg cholesterol, 305 mg sodium, 12 g carbohydrate, 2 g fiber, 5 g protein.

Marinated Mozzarella

Prep: 15 min. + marinating

Peggy Cairo, Kenosha, Wisconsin

I always come home with an empty container when I bring these cheese cubes to a party. Not only is the appetizer popular with guests, it can be made ahead to free up time later. I serve the bites with party picks for a festive look.

 1/3 **cup olive oil**
 1 **tablespoon chopped oil-packed sun-dried tomatoes**
 1 **tablespoon minced fresh parsley**
 1 **teaspoon crushed red pepper flakes**
 1 **teaspoon dried basil**
 1 **teaspoon minced chives**
 1/4 **teaspoon garlic powder**
 1 **pound cubed part-skim mozzarella cheese**

1. In a large resealable plastic bag, combine the first seven ingredients; add cheese cubes. Seal bag and turn to coat; refrigerate for at least 30 minutes.

2. Transfer the marinated mozzarella cheese cubes to a serving dish or platter; serve cheese cubes with toothpicks. **Yield:** 8-10 servings.

Parsley Pointer

To keep fresh parsley in the refrigerator for several weeks, wash the entire bunch in warm water, shake off all excess moisture, wrap it in a paper towel and seal it in a plastic bag. For longer storage, remove the paper towel and place the bag in the freezer. Break off and crumble the amount you need for recipes.

Chorizo Bean Dip

Prep: 25 min. **Bake:** 20 min.

Elaine Sweet, Dallas, Texas

With zesty flavors and tempting toppings, this Mexican dip is always a hit. I serve it with extra-thick tortilla chips for some serious scooping!

✓ | This recipe includes Nutrition Facts.

- 1 **pound ground sirloin**
- 1/3 **pound uncooked chorizo *or* bulk spicy pork sausage**
- 1 **medium onion, chopped**
- 1 **envelope taco seasoning**
- 2 **cans (16 ounces *each*) refried black beans**
- 1 **cup (4 ounces) shredded Monterey Jack cheese**
- 1-1/3 **cups salsa**
- 2 **cans (2-1/4 ounces *each*) sliced ripe olives, drained**
- 2 **cups guacamole**
- 6 **green onions, thinly sliced**
- 1 **cup (8 ounces) sour cream**
- 1/2 **cup minced fresh cilantro**
- 3/4 **cup jalapeno-stuffed olives, sliced**
Tortilla chips

1. Crumble beef and chorizo into a large skillet; add onion and taco seasoning. Cook over medium heat until meat is no longer pink; drain.

2. Spread the beans into a greased 13-in. x 9-in. baking dish. Layer with the meat mixture, cheese, salsa and ripe olives. Cover and bake at 350° for 20-25 minutes or until heated through.

3. Spread guacamole over the top. Combine the green onions, sour cream and cilantro; spread over guacamole. Sprinkle with stuffed olives. Serve immediately with tortilla chips. Refrigerate leftovers. **Yield:** 48 servings.

Editor's Note: Wear disposable gloves when cutting hot peppers; the oils can burn skin. Avoid touching your face.

Nutrition Facts: 1 serving (1/3 cup) equals 78 calories, 5 g fat (2 g saturated fat), 12 mg cholesterol, 292 mg sodium, 4 g carbohydrate, 1 g fiber, 4 g protein.

Northwest Cherry Salsa

Prep/Total Time: 15 min.

Margaret Slocum, Ridgefield, Washington

Among the 50 fruit trees on our place are five cherry trees—and I like to use every bit of fruit that doesn't get eaten right off of them. This recipe is one of my favorites.

 | This recipe includes Nutrition Facts & Diabetic Exchange.

- 1 **cup fresh *or* frozen pitted dark sweet cherries, chopped**
- 2 **tablespoons chopped fresh basil**
- 1 **tablespoon finely chopped green pepper**
- 1 **teaspoon lemon juice**
- 1/4 **teaspoon Worcestershire sauce**
- 1/4 **teaspoon grated lemon peel**
- 1/8 **teaspoons salt**
Dash hot pepper sauce

1. Combine all ingredients; refrigerate at least 1 hour. Serve as a condiment with chicken, turkey or pork. **Yield:** 3/4 cup.

Nutrition Facts: 2 tablespoons equals 22 calories, 0.5 g fat (0 saturated fat), 0 cholesterol, 59 mg sodium, 5 g carbohydrate, 0 fiber, 1 g protein. **Diabetic Exchange:** 1/2 fruit.

PG. 25

PG. 27

PG. 30

SPECIAL SALADS

Topped with veggies or fruit…featuring greens or pasta…enjoyed as an entree or side dish…salad's great versatility gives it mass appeal. The variety featured here definitely won't disappoint!

PG. 22

Tropical Fruit Salad

Prep/Total Time: 15 min.

Teri Lindquist, Gurnee, Illinois

When I needed a speedy salad for a luncheon recently, I used what I had available and everyone loved it! Light, fluffy and full of fruit, this salad could double as a healthy dessert. You can also tuck it into kids' lunch boxes for a school-day treat.

> ✓ This recipe includes Nutrition Facts.

    2 cans (15-1/4 ounces *each*) mixed tropical fruit, drained
    1 can (11 ounces) mandarin oranges, drained
    1 medium banana, sliced
    1 cup miniature marshmallows
1-1/2 cups (12 ounces) vanilla yogurt
    1/4 cup flaked coconut
    1/4 cup slivered almonds, toasted

1. In a large salad bowl, combine the tropical fruit, oranges, banana and marshmallows. Add yogurt; toss gently to coat. Sprinkle with coconut and almonds. Refrigerate until serving. **Yield:** 6 servings.

Nutrition Facts: 3/4 cup equals 290 calories, 6 g fat (3 g saturated fat), 6 mg cholesterol, 56 mg sodium, 59 g carbohydrate, 3 g fiber, 5 g protein.

Mango Jicama Salad

Prep/Total Time: 20 min.

Doreen Dineen, Freeville, New York

I'm always looking for recipes with out-of-the-ordinary ingredients, like mango and jicama. When I couldn't find a salad using those ingredients, I ventured out on my own to create this crunchy, slightly sweet medley and citrus dressing.

> ✓ This recipe includes Nutrition Facts.

    1 cup julienned peeled jicama
    1 cup chopped peeled mango
1/4 cup dried cranberries
    1 green onion, thinly sliced
1-1/2 cups torn mixed salad greens
DRESSING:
    1 tablespoon olive oil
    1 tablespoon orange juice
    1 tablespoon lime juice
Dash salt and pepper

1. In a small bowl, combine the first four ingredients. Divide the greens between two salad plates; top with jicama mixture.

2. In a small bowl, whisk the dressing ingredients; drizzle over salads. **Yield:** 2 servings.

Nutrition Facts: 1-3/4 cups equals 199 calories, 7 g fat (1 g saturated fat), 0 cholesterol, 82 mg sodium, 36 g carbohydrate, 6 g fiber, 2 g protein.

Avocado Chicken Salad

Prep/Total Time: 20 min.

Karlene Johnson, Mooresville, North Carolina

It doesn't matter what type of outing I'm headed to—all my family and friends request this chicken salad with a twist. I sometimes serve it in a pita for a grab-and-go lunch.

✓ This recipe includes Nutrition Facts.

> 1 medium ripe avocado, peeled and cubed
> 2 tablespoons lemon juice, *divided*
> 2 cups cubed cooked chicken
> 2 cups seedless red grapes, halved
> 1 medium tart apple, chopped
> 1 cup chopped celery
> 3/4 cup mayonnaise
> 1/2 cup chopped walnuts, toasted
> 1/2 teaspoon ground ginger
> Lettuce leaves, optional

1. In a small bowl, toss avocado with 1 tablespoon lemon juice; set aside. In a large bowl, combine the chicken, grapes, apple, celery, mayonnaise, walnuts, ginger and remaining lemon juice. Stir in avocado. Serve chicken mixture on lettuce-lined plates if desired. **Yield:** 5 servings.

Nutrition Facts: 1-1/2 cup equals 546 calories, 44 g fat (6 g saturated fat), 62 mg cholesterol, 252 mg sodium, 21 g carbohydrate, 5 g fiber, 19 g protein.

How To Remove an Avocado Pit

To remove the pit from an avocado, first cut the washed avocado in half lengthwise, cutting around the seed. Then, twist halves in opposite directions to separate, and slip a tablespoon under the seed to loosen it from the fruit.

Popcorn Chicken Salad

Prep/Total Time: 25 min.

Teresa Wilkins-Reckard, Monroe, Indiana

Here's a perfectly portioned salad that's great for everyday lunches. I can mix up the dressing at home, then pick up enough salad ingredients at the store to last for several days. Variations are easy to make, too.

- 1 cup frozen popcorn chicken
- 2 tablespoons mayonnaise
- 4-1/2 teaspoons honey
- 2-1/4 teaspoons white vinegar
- 1-1/2 teaspoons Dijon mustard
- 1/8 teaspoon sesame oil
- 2 cups torn leaf lettuce
- 1/2 cup fresh snow peas
- 1/2 cup canned bean sprouts, drained
- 1/2 cup mandarin oranges, drained
- 1/2 cup chow mein noodles

1. Bake chicken according to package directions. Meanwhile, for dressing, in a small bowl, whisk the mayonnaise, honey, vinegar, mustard and oil until smooth.

2. Divide lettuce between two plates; top with the peas, bean sprouts, oranges, chicken and noodles. Drizzle with dressing. **Yield:** 2 servings.

Grilled Three-Potato Salad

Prep: 25 min. **Grill:** 10 min.

Suzette Jury, Keene, California

Everyone in our extended family loves to cook, so I put together all of our favorite recipes in a cookbook to be handed down from generation to generation. This recipe comes from that particular cookbook. It is a delicious twist on traditional potato salad.

✓ This recipe includes Nutrition Facts.

- 3/4 pound Yukon Gold potatoes
- 3/4 pound red potatoes
- 1 medium sweet potato, peeled
- 1/2 cup thinly sliced green onions
- 1/4 cup canola oil
- 2 to 3 tablespoons white wine vinegar
- 1 tablespoon Dijon mustard
- 1 teaspoon salt
- 1/2 teaspoon celery seed
- 1/4 teaspoon pepper

1. Place all of the potatoes in a Dutch oven; cover with water. Bring to a boil. Reduce heat; cover and simmer for 15-20 minutes or until tender. Drain and rinse in cold water. Cut into 1-in. chunks.

2. Place the potatoes in a grill wok or basket. Grill, uncovered, over medium heat for 8-12 minutes or until browned, stirring frequently. Transfer to a large salad bowl; add onions.

3. In a small bowl, whisk the oil, vinegar, mustard, salt, celery seed and pepper. Drizzle over potato mixture and toss to coat. Serve warm or at room temperature. **Yield:** 6 servings.

Editor's Note: If you do not have a grill wok or basket, use a disposable foil pan. Poke holes in the bottom of the pan with a meat fork to allow liquid to drain.

Nutrition Facts: 3/4 cup equals 191 calories, 10 g fat (1 g saturated fat), 0 cholesterol, 466 mg sodium, 24 g carbohydrate, 3 g fiber, 3 g protein.

Shrimp Salad-Stuffed Avocados

Prep/Total Time: 15 min.

Suzanne VanAlstyne, Petoskey, Michigan

My husband's favorite way to enjoy avocados is with this idea. When I needed a quick main-dish salad for my book club, I just tripled the recipe and got raves! For a tasty switch, try it with imitation crab.

- 1/2 pound cooked medium shrimp, peeled and deveined, coarsely chopped
- 1/2 cup chopped celery
- 1/4 cup chopped onion
- 3 tablespoons mayonnaise
- 4-1/2 teaspoons capers, drained
- 1 tablespoon minced fresh parsley
- 2 teaspoons Dijon mustard
- 1-1/2 teaspoons lemon juice
- 3/4 teaspoon dried tarragon
- 1/4 teaspoon seasoned salt
- 1/8 teaspoon pepper
- 2 medium ripe avocados, halved and pitted

1. In a small bowl, combine the first 11 ingredients. Spoon the mixture into the avocado halves. Serve immediately. **Yield:** 4 servings.

Tricolor Pasta Salad

Prep: 1 hour + chilling

Benjamin & Sue Ellen Clark, Warsaw, New York

This colorful salad is hearty enough to be a light meal in itself. It's a great make-ahead dish, since the full flavors of the herbs and veggies need a little time to blend.

This recipe includes Nutrition Facts.

- 2 packages (12 ounces *each*) tricolor spiral pasta
- 2 packages (16 ounces *each*) frozen California-blend vegetables, thawed
- 2 pints grape tomatoes
- 1 large zucchini, halved and thinly sliced
- 1 large yellow summer squash, quartered and thinly sliced
- 1 large red onion, finely chopped
- 1 block (8 ounces) cheddar cheese, cubed
- 1 block (8 ounces) Monterey Jack cheese, cubed
- 2 packages (4 ounces *each*) crumbled tomato and basil feta cheese
- 1 bottle (16 ounces) Italian salad dressing
- 3 tablespoons minced fresh parsley
- 1 tablespoon minced fresh basil
- 1 teaspoon Italian seasoning
- 1 teaspoon seasoned salt
- 1/2 teaspoon pepper
- 1 can (3.8 ounces) sliced ripe olives, drained

Grated Romano cheese, optional

1. Cook pasta according to package directions. Rinse with cold water; drain well. In two large bowls, combine the California vegetables, tomatoes, zucchini, yellow squash, onion, cheeses and pasta.

2. In a small bowl, combine the salad dressing, parsley, basil, Italian seasoning, seasoned salt and pepper. Pour over pasta mixture; toss to coat. Stir in olives. Cover and refrigerate for 8 hours or overnight.

3. Toss before serving. Serve with Romano cheese if desired. **Yield:** 36 servings.

Nutrition Facts: 1 serving (3/4 cup) equals 157 calories, 10 g fat (3 g saturated fat), 15 mg cholesterol, 405 mg sodium, 11 g carbohydrate, 1 g fiber, 5 g protein.

Special Sesame Chicken Salad

Prep: 30 min. + chilling

Carolee Ewell, Santaquin, Utah

With its refreshing mix of crunchy peanuts, tangy dried cranberries and mandarin oranges, this colorful pasta salad is a definite crowd-pleaser. Water chestnuts and a teriyaki dressing give this entree an Asian flair.

✓ This recipe includes Nutrition Facts.

   1 **package (16 ounces) bow tie pasta**
   1 **cup canola oil**
 2/3 **cup white wine vinegar**
 2/3 **cup teriyaki sauce**
 1/3 **cup sugar**
 1/2 **teaspoon pepper**
   3 **cans (11 ounces *each*) mandarin oranges, drained**
   2 **cans (8 ounces *each*) sliced water chestnuts, drained**
   2 **cups cubed cooked chicken**
1-1/3 **cups honey-roasted peanuts**
   1 **package (9 ounces) fresh spinach, torn**
   1 **package (6 ounces) dried cranberries**
   6 **green onions, chopped**
 1/2 **cup minced fresh parsley**
 1/4 **cup sesame seeds, toasted**

1. Cook pasta according to package directions; drain and place in a very large bowl.

2. In a small bowl, combine the oil, vinegar, teriyaki sauce, sugar and pepper. Pour over pasta and toss to coat. Cover and refrigerate for 2 hours.

3. Just before serving, add the remaining ingredients; gently toss to coat. **Yield:** 22 servings (1 cup each).

Nutrition Facts: 1 serving (1 cup) equals 302 calories, 16 g fat (2 g saturated fat), 11 mg cholesterol, 358 mg sodium, 32 g carbohydrate, 3 g fiber, 10 g protein.

Raspberry Greek Salad

Prep/Total Time: 20 min.

Carine Nadel, Laguna Hills, California

An interesting combination of sweet and salty flavors gives this Greek salad an interesting spin. The tart chewiness of the dried cranberries makes a wonderful complement to the salty feta cheese. I often take it to work for lunch.

- 2 packages (6 ounces *each*) ready-to-use grilled chicken breast strips
- 1 package (6 ounces) fresh baby spinach
- 1/2 pound sliced fresh mushrooms
- 1 medium cucumber, peeled and sliced
- 4 plum tomatoes, seeded and sliced
- 1/2 cup crumbled feta cheese
- 1/4 cup chopped Greek olives
- 1/4 cup dried cranberries
- 1/4 cup chopped red onion
- 1/3 cup raspberry vinaigrette
- 4 whole wheat pita breads (6 inches), cut into quarters and warmed, optional

1. In a large salad bowl, toss the first nine ingredients. Just before serving, drizzle salad with vinaigrette; toss to coat. Serve the salad with pita bread if desired. **Yield:** 8 servings.

Next-Generation German Potato Salad

Prep/Total Time: 30 min.

Mary Shivers, Ada, Oklahoma

My quick-cooking German-style potato salad is a keeper for family reunions. Balsamic vinegar and crisp bacon give it a special and different flavor.

✔ This recipe includes Nutrition Facts.

- 4 pounds small red potatoes, quartered
- 10 bacon strips, chopped
- 1 large onion, chopped
- 3 tablespoons chopped celery
- 2 tablespoons chopped green pepper
- 1 tablespoon all-purpose flour
- 1 tablespoon sugar
- 1 teaspoon salt
- 1/2 teaspoon pepper
- 1 cup water
- 1/3 cup white balsamic vinegar

1. Place the potatoes in a Dutch oven and cover with water. Bring to a boil. Reduce heat; cover and simmer for 15-20 minutes or until tender.

2. Meanwhile, in a large skillet, cook bacon over medium heat until crisp. Using a slotted spoon, remove to paper towels. In the drippings, saute the onion, celery and green pepper until tender. Stir in the flour, sugar, salt and pepper until blended. Combine water and vinegar; stir into vegetable mixture. Bring to a boil; cook and stir for 2 minutes or until thickened.

3. Drain potatoes and place in a large serving bowl. Pour dressing over potatoes. Add bacon and toss to coat. Serve warm or at room temperature. Refrigerate leftovers. **Yield:** 14 servings.

Nutrition Facts: 3/4 cup equals 197 calories, 10 g fat (3 g saturated fat), 11 mg cholesterol, 298 mg sodium, 24 g carbohydrate, 2 g fiber, 4 g protein.

Apple-Brie Spinach Salad

Prep/Total Time: 30 min.

Rhonda Crowe, Greenwood,, Nova Scotia

In the summer, I don't like to prepare large, heavy meals, so I make salads. I'm always on the lookout for new and interesting recipes, and this one is a winner with my guests.

 This recipe includes Nutrition Facts.

    4 **large apples, cut into 1/2-inch wedges**
    4 **tablespoons maple syrup,** *divided*
    8 **cups fresh baby spinach**
    1 **round (8 ounces) Brie cheese, cubed**
1/2 **cup pecan halves, toasted**
DRESSING:
1/4 **cup apple cider** *or* **juice**
1/4 **cup canola oil**
    3 **tablespoons cider vinegar**
    1 **teaspoon Dijon mustard**
    1 **garlic clove, minced**

1. Place apples on an ungreased baking sheet; brush with 2 tablespoons syrup. Broil 3-4 in. from the heat for 3 minutes. Turn; brush with remaining syrup. Broil 3-5 minutes longer or until crisp-tender.

2. In a large salad bowl, combine the spinach, cheese, pecans and apples. In a small saucepan, combine the dressing ingredients; bring to a boil. Pour over salad; toss to coat. **Yield:** 10 servings.

Nutrition Facts: 3/4 cup equals 242 calories, 16 g fat (5 g saturated fat), 23 mg cholesterol, 176 mg sodium, 21 g carbohydrate, 3 g fiber, 6 g protein.

Layered Summertime Salad

Prep/Total Time: 30 min.

Betty Fulks, Onia, Arkansas

Luscious layers of pasta and veggies make up this super summer salad that can be made ahead for picnics and deck parties. It makes enough to feed a crowd.

✓ This recipe includes Nutrition Facts.

    2 **cups uncooked gemelli** *or* **spiral pasta**
    1 **cup mayonnaise**
    2 **tablespoons lemon juice**
    1 **teaspoon sugar**
1/2 **teaspoon garlic powder**
1/2 **cup sliced green onions**
    4 **bacon strips, cooked and crumbled,** *divided*
    4 **cups torn romaine**
    1 **cup fresh snow peas, trimmed and halved**
    1 **cup fresh cauliflowerets**
    1 **cup fresh broccoli florets**
    1 **large sweet red pepper, chopped**
1/2 **cup shredded Swiss cheese**

1. Cook pasta according to package directions. Meanwhile, in a small bowl, combine the mayonnaise, lemon juice, sugar and garlic powder; set aside. Drain pasta and rinse in cold water; toss with onions and half of the bacon.

2. In a large salad bowl, layer half of the romaine, pasta mixture, peas, cauliflower, broccoli, red pepper, mayonnaise mixture and cheese. Repeat layers. Sprinkle with remaining bacon. Cover and refrigerate until serving. **Yield:** 16 servings.

Nutrition Facts: 3/4 cup equals 186 calories, 13 g fat (2 g saturated fat), 9 mg cholesterol, 115 mg sodium, 13 g carbohydrate, 2 g fiber, 4 g protein.

Spicy Chicken Salad With Mango Salsa

Prep/Total Time: 30 min.

Jan Warren-Rucker, Clemmons, North Carolina

When I'm craving something different, I pull out this recipe. To make it fast, I use fully cooked chicken strips, jarred mango, bottled vinaigrette and packaged shredded cheese.

2 cups chopped peeled mangoes
1 medium red onion, chopped
1/2 cup chopped sweet red pepper
1/4 cup minced fresh cilantro
1 jalapeno pepper, seeded and chopped
2 tablespoons lime juice
2 packages (9 ounces *each*) ready-to-use grilled chicken breast strips
2 teaspoons ground cumin
1 teaspoon onion powder
1 teaspoon chili powder
1/4 teaspoon cayenne pepper
Dash salt
2 tablespoons olive oil
2 garlic cloves, minced
2 packages (8 ounces *each*) ready-to-serve European blend salad greens
1/3 cup oil and vinegar salad dressing
2 cups (8 ounces) shredded pepper Jack cheese
Tortilla chips

1. For salsa, in a large bowl, combine the first six ingredients; chill until serving. In a large skillet, saute the chicken, cumin, onion powder, chili powder, cayenne and salt in oil until heated through. Add garlic; cook 1 minute longer.

2. Toss greens with dressing; divide among seven serving plates. Top with chicken mixture, mango salsa and cheese. Serve immediately with tortilla chips. **Yield:** 7 servings.

Editor's Note: Wear disposable gloves when cutting hot peppers; the oils can burn skin. Avoid touching your face.

Garden State Salad

Prep: 20 min. + chilling

Weda Mosellie, Phillipsburg, New Jersey

New Jersey is the Garden State, so I enjoy preparing this vegetable salad using some of my state's best products.

 This recipe includes Nutrition Facts.

3 tablespoons cranberry juice
3 tablespoons olive oil
1 tablespoon lemon juice
1 tablespoon honey
2 green onions, finely chopped
2 garlic cloves, minced
1 teaspoon dried oregano
1/4 teaspoon salt
1/8 teaspoon pepper
SALAD:
1 medium head iceberg lettuce, shredded
2 medium carrots, shredded
2 celery ribs, chopped
2 green onions, thinly sliced
2 medium tomatoes, seeded and diced
1 small cucumber, sliced

1. In a small bowl, whisk the first nine ingredients. Refrigerate for at least 1 hour.

2. In a large salad bowl, combine the lettuce, carrots, celery, onions, tomatoes and cucumber. Just before serving, whisk dressing and pour over salad; toss to coat. **Yield:** 6 servings.

Nutrition Facts: 1 serving (1 cup) equals 116 calories, 7 g fat (1 g saturated fat), 0 cholesterol, 132 mg sodium, 13 g carbohydrate, 3 g fiber, 2 g protein.

Holiday Gelatin Mold

Prep: 25 min. + chilling

Mareen Robinson, Spanish Fork, Utah

Because I care for a teenager with diabetes, I decided to change my annual Thanksgiving salad so she could have some.

✓ This recipe includes Nutrition Facts & Diabetic Exchanges.

- 1 **package (.3 ounce) sugar-free lemon gelatin**
- 1 **package (.3 ounce) sugar-free strawberry gelatin**
- 1 **package (.3 ounce) sugar-free cherry gelatin**
- 1-3/4 **cups boiling water**
- 1 **can (20 ounces) unsweetened crushed pineapple**
- 1 **can (14 ounces) whole-berry cranberry sauce**
- 1 **medium navel orange, peeled and sectioned**
- 3/4 **cup reduced-fat whipped topping**
- 1/4 **cup fat-free sour cream**

1. In a large bowl, dissolve the gelatins in boiling water. Drain pineapple, reserving juice in a 2-cup measuring cup; add enough cold water to measure 2 cups. Stir into gelatin mixture.

2. Place the pineapple, cranberry sauce and orange in a food processor; cover and pulse until blended. Stir into gelatin mixture. Transfer to an 8-cup ring mold coated with cooking spray. Refrigerate until firm.

3. In a small bowl, combine whipped topping and sour cream. Unmold gelatin; serve with topping. **Yield:** 12 servings (3/4 cup topping).

Nutrition Facts: 2/3 cup gelatin with 1 tablespoon topping equals 105 calories, 1 g fat (1 g saturated fat), 1 mg cholesterol, 62 mg sodium, 24 g carbohydrate, 1 g fiber, 1 g protein. **Diabetic Exchanges:** 1 fruit, 1/2 starch.

Dijon-Walnut Spinach Salad

Prep/Total Time: 10 min.

DeMontravel Chris, Mohegan Lake, New York

So much flavor for so few fixings! This family favorite of ours has a fabulous taste, lots of different textures and can be tossed together in a heartbeat. For variety, change up the dressing to honey mustard or any other favorite.

This recipe includes Nutrition Facts & Diabetic Exchanges.

- 1 package (9 ounces) fresh baby spinach
- 1 package (4 ounces) crumbled feta cheese
- 1 cup dried cranberries
- 1 cup walnut halves, toasted
- 1/2 cup honey Dijon vinaigrette

1. In a large salad bowl, combine the spinach, feta cheese, cranberries and walnuts. Drizzle with honey Dijon vinaigrette; toss to coat. Serve immediately. **Yield:** 13 servings.

Nutrition Facts: 3/4 cup equals 120 calories, 7 g fat (1 g saturated fat), 5 mg cholesterol, 177 mg sodium, 12 g carbohydrate, 2 g fiber, 3 g protein. **Diabetic Exchanges:** 1 vegetable, 1 fat, 1/2 starch.

Herbed Raspberry-Hazelnut Salad

Prep/Total Time: 20 min.

Wendy Matejek, Colorado Springs, Colorado

I receive great compliments whenever I serve this salad at parties. I especially appreciate how simple it is to prepare.

✓ This recipe includes Nutrition Facts.

- 9 cups torn iceberg lettuce
- 1 medium red onion, sliced and separated into rings
- 1 cup chopped fresh parsley
- 1/2 cup chopped fresh cilantro
- 1/4 cup chopped fresh tarragon
- 1 cup raspberry vinaigrette
- 1/2 cup fresh raspberries
- 1/2 cup chopped hazelnuts

1. In a large salad bowl, combine the lettuce, onion, parsley, cilantro and tarragon. Add vinaigrette and toss to coat. Top with raspberries and hazelnuts. **Yield:** 9 servings.

Nutrition Facts: 1 serving (1 cup) equals 183 calories, 17 g fat (2 g saturated fat), 0 cholesterol, 232 mg sodium, 6 g carbohydrate, 2 g fiber, 2 g protein.

Bowled Over

Bread bowls are a fun and tasty way to serve salads. Many bakeries carry small round loaves specifically for this purpose. If you can't find any, look for extra-large crusty buns or firm sourdough rolls instead.

Raspberry Poppy Seed Dressing

Prep/Total Time: 10 min.

Kendra Stoller, Kouts, Indiana

I love this creamy, fresh-tasting dressing! It's so quick to assemble and adds a summery gourmet touch to salads.

✓ This recipe includes Nutrition Facts.

6 tablespoons red wine vinegar
1/2 cup plus 2 tablespoons sugar
1 teaspoon salt
1 teaspoon ground mustard
1 cup canola oil
1 cup fresh *or* frozen raspberries, thawed
1 teaspoon poppy seeds

1. In a blender, combine the vinegar, sugar, salt and mustard. While processing, gradually add oil in a steady stream. Add raspberries; cover and process until blended. Stir in poppy seeds. Serve immediately. Refrigerate leftovers. **Yield:** 2 cups.

Nutrition Facts: 1 serving (2 tablespoons) equals 161 calories, 14 g fat (2 g saturated fat), 0 cholesterol, 148 mg sodium, 10 g carbohydrate, 1 g fiber, trace protein.

Selecting Perfect Raspberries

Buy brightly colored berries without the hulls attached. At home, discard any that are soft, shriveled or moldy. Rinse and place in a single layer in a paper towel-lined bowl. They'll stay fresh in the refrigerator for up to 3 days.

Special Summer Berry Medley

Prep/Total Time: 25 min.

✓ This recipe includes Nutrition Facts & Diabetic Exchanges.

1 cup sparkling wine *or* white grape juice
1/2 cup sugar
1 tablespoon lemon juice
1-1/2 teaspoons grated lemon peel
1/2 teaspoon vanilla extract
1/8 teaspoon salt
3 cups sliced fresh strawberries
2 cups fresh blueberries
1 cup fresh raspberries
1 cup fresh blackberries
1 tablespoon minced fresh mint

1. In a small heavy saucepan, bring wine and sugar to a boil. Cook, uncovered, for about 15 minutes or until reduced to 1/2 cup, stirring occasionally. Cool slightly. Stir in the lemon juice and peel, vanilla and salt.

2. In a large bowl, combine berries and mint. Add syrup and toss gently to coat. Cover and refrigerate until serving. **Yield:** 12 servings.

Nutrition Facts: 1/2 cup equals 85 calories, trace fat (trace saturated fat), 0 cholesterol, 26 mg sodium, 18 g carbohydrate, 3 g fiber, 1 g protein. **Diabetic Exchanges:** 1 fruit, 1/2 starch.

NANCY WHITFORD EDWARDS, NEW YORK

No matter how big the meal, folks always find room for this delightfully special treat.
With its hint of citrus and mint, this medley makes a light side dish at casual cookouts
or potlucks. Best of all, it's as fast and easy to make as it is to clean up!

GRAND PRIZE WINNER

Hot Fruit Compote

Prep: 15 min. **Bake:** 40 min.

Joyce Moynihan, Lakeville, Minnesota

This elegant and colorful fruit compote is perfect with an egg casserole at a special brunch. It can bake right alongside the eggs, so everything is conveniently done at the same time.

✓ This recipe includes Nutrition Facts.

2 cans (15-1/4 ounces *each*) sliced pears, drained
1 can (29 ounces) sliced peaches, drained
1 can (20 ounces) unsweetened pineapple chunks, drained
1 package (20 ounces) pitted dried plums
1 jar (16 ounces) unsweetened applesauce
1 can (21 ounces) cherry pie filling
1/4 cup packed brown sugar

1. In a large bowl, combine the first five ingredients. Pour into a 13-in. x 9-in. baking dish coated with cooking spray. Spread pie filling over fruit mixture; sprinkle with brown sugar.

2. Cover and bake at 350° for 40-45 minutes or until bubbly. Serve warm. **Yield:** 20 servings.

Nutrition Facts: 1/2 cup equals 193 calories, trace fat (trace saturated fat), 0 cholesterol, 16 mg sodium, 47 g carbohydrate, 3 g fiber, 1 g protein.

Orange Gelatin Pretzel Salad

Prep: 30 min. + chilling

Peggy Boyd, Northport, Alabama

Salty pretzels pair nicely with the sweet fruit in this lovely layered gelatin salad. It's the perfect potluck dish.

2 cups crushed pretzels
3 teaspoons plus 3/4 cup sugar, *divided*
3/4 cup butter, melted
2 packages (3 ounces *each*) orange gelatin
2 cups boiling water
2 cans (8 ounces *each*) crushed pineapple, drained
1 can (11 ounces) mandarin oranges, drained
1 package (8 ounces) cream cheese, softened
2 cups whipped topping
Additional whipped topping, optional

1. In a small bowl, combine pretzels and 3 teaspoons sugar; stir in butter. Press into an ungreased 13-in. x 9-in. baking dish. Bake at 350° for 10 minutes. Cool on a wire rack.

2. In a large bowl, dissolve gelatin in boiling water. Add pineapple and oranges. Chill until partially set, about 30 minutes.

3. In a small bowl, beat cream cheese and remaining sugar until smooth. Fold in whipped topping. Spread over crust.

4. Gently spoon gelatin mixture over cream cheese layer. Cover; refrigerate for 2-4 hours or until firm.

5. Cut into squares. Garnish with additional whipped topping if desired. **Yield:** 15 servings.

Red, White and Blue Slaw

Prep/Total Time: 10 min.

Bonnie Hawkins, Elkhorn, Wisconsin

Perfect for Fourth of July celebrations or any time you have a craving for picnic fare, this all-time favorite salad balances a wonderful blend of flavors!

> **6 cups angel hair coleslaw mix**
> **12 cherry tomatoes, halved**
> **3/4 cup coleslaw salad dressing**
> **3/4 cup crumbled blue cheese, *divided***
> **1/2 cup real bacon bits**

1. In a large bowl, combine the coleslaw mix, tomatoes, salad dressing and 1/2 cup blue cheese. Cover and refrigerate until serving. Just before serving, sprinkle with bacon bits and remaining cheese. **Yield:** 6 servings.

Roasted Beet and Potato Salad

Prep: 20 min. **Bake:** 35 min.

Jennifer Fisher, Austin, Texas

I guarantee you'll love the combination of beets and balsamic dressing in this lovely addition to just about any meal.

> ✓ This recipe includes Nutrition Facts & Diabetic Exchanges.

> **1-1/2 pounds small red potatoes, halved**
> **2 medium red onions, cut into wedges**
> **1/2 teaspoon salt, *divided***
> **2 tablespoons olive oil**
> **1-1/2 pounds fresh beets, peeled and cut into wedges**
> **2/3 cup reduced-sodium chicken broth *or* vegetable broth**
> **1/3 cup balsamic vinegar**
> **2 teaspoons brown sugar**
> **2 teaspoons minced fresh thyme *or* 1/2 teaspoon dried thyme**
> **1/2 teaspoon pepper**
> **2 tablespoons minced fresh parsley**

1. Place potatoes and onions in two 15-in. x 10-in. x 1-in. baking pans coated with cooking spray. Sprinkle with 1/4 teaspoon salt; drizzle with oil and toss to coat.

2. Place the beets in the pans (do not stir). Bake, uncovered, at 425° for 35-40 minutes or until the vegetables are tender.

3. For dressing, in a small saucepan, combine the broth, vinegar, brown sugar, thyme, pepper and remaining salt. Bring to a boil. Reduce heat; simmer, uncovered, until reduced to 1/3 cup.

4. Transfer vegetables to a large bowl. Drizzle with dressing and toss to coat. Sprinkle with parsley. **Yield:** 9 servings.

Nutrition Facts: 3/4 cup equals 135 calories, 3 g fat (trace saturated fat), 0 cholesterol, 244 mg sodium, 24 g carbohydrate, 3 g fiber, 3 g protein. **Diabetic Exchanges:** 1 starch, 1 vegetable, 1/2 fat.

Beet Basics

New to beets? Purchase beets with smooth, unblemished skin. The greens, if attached, should be brightly colored and not wilted. Before storing, remove the greens and place the beets in a plastic bag; refrigerate for up to 3 weeks.

Spring Greens with Berries

Prep/Total Time: 15 min.

Vikki Peck, Poland, Ohio

My busy sister-in-law gave me this refreshing salad recipe years ago, and it quickly became a frequent request at my house—just as it is at hers. It's crisp, colorful, goes together in a snap and complements a variety of entrees. Plus, the dressing can be refrigerated several days for make-ahead convenience.

> ✓ This recipe includes Nutrition Facts.

> 2 **packages (5 ounces *each*) spring mix salad greens**
> 1 **can (11 ounces) mandarin oranges, drained**
> 3/4 **cup sliced fresh strawberries**
> 3/4 **cup fresh raspberries**
> 1/2 **cup slivered almonds, toasted**
> **ORANGE VINAIGRETTE:**
> 1/4 **cup canola oil**
> 1 **tablespoon red wine vinegar**
> 1 **tablespoon orange juice**
> 1 **tablespoon honey**
> 1 **teaspoon grated orange peel**
> 1 **teaspoon Dijon mustard**
> 1/4 **teaspoon salt**
> 1/8 **teaspoon pepper**

1. In a large bowl, combine the greens, oranges, berries and almonds. In a jar with a tight-fitting lid, combine the vinaigrette ingredients; shake well. Drizzle over salad and toss to coat. **Yield:** 7 servings.

Nutrition Facts: 1 serving (1-1/2 cups) equals 157 calories, 12 g fat (1 g saturated fat), 0 cholesterol, 110 mg sodium, 12 g carbohydrate, 3 g fiber, 3 g protein.

Nuts for Salad Toppers

Nuts are naturally high in fat. Toasting them intensifies the flavor so much that you can often cut down on the amount of nuts used and still end up with a very tasty dish. Toasting nuts may also give them a prettier appearance, which can be especially desirable on salads.

Wild Rice Apple Salad

Prep/Total Time: 15 min.

Elaine Stichter, Milford, Indiana

We have an orchard in our family, so I'm always looking for ways to use the fruit. I turn to this crisp and crunchy dish often during apple season. Sometimes I double the batch so I have leftovers to enjoy the next day.

✓ This recipe includes Nutrition Facts & Diabetic Exchanges.

2/3 cup cooked wild rice, chilled
1/2 cup coarsely chopped apple
1/3 cup sliced celery
2 teaspoons dried currants
1 teaspoon sunflower kernels
2 teaspoons balsamic vinegar
1 teaspoon olive oil
1 small garlic clove, minced
3/4 teaspoon honey
3/4 teaspoon Dijon mustard
1/4 teaspoon grated orange peel
Dash salt

1. In a small bowl, combine the wild rice, apple, celery, currants and sunflower kernels. In another bowl, whisk the remaining ingredients. Drizzle over

rice mixture; toss to coat. Serve immediately. **Yield:** 2 servings.

Nutrition Facts: 3/4 cup equals 130 calories, 4 g fat (trace saturated fat), 0 cholesterol, 150 mg sodium, 23 g carbohydrate, 3 g fiber, 3 g protein. **Diabetic Exchanges:** 1-1/2 starch, 1/2 fat.

Albacore Tuna Salad

Prep/Total Time: 15 min.

Barbara Moravek, Jay, Florida

There are so many great things about this recipe, it's difficult to decide what I like best. Sweet apples, golden raisins, celery, nuts, tuna and a tropical taste of pineapple add up to a simply wonderful mix. It's delicious the next day, too!

2 cans (8 ounces *each*) unsweetened crushed pineapple, drained
2 cans (5 ounces *each*) white water-packed tuna, drained
1 large apple, chopped
1 cup sliced celery
1 cup golden raisins
1/2 cup sliced almonds, toasted
1 cup mayonnaise
1 tablespoon lemon juice
Bread slices or lettuce leaves

1. In a large bowl, combine the pineapple, tuna, apple, celery, raisins and almonds. Combine mayonnaise and lemon juice; stir into tuna mixture. Spread tuna salad on bread or serve on lettuce-lined plates. **Yield:** 5 servings.

Apple and Goat Cheese Salad

Prep/Total Time: 20 min.

Radelle Knappenberger, Oviedo, Florida

The medley of apples, raisins and grapes featured here goes well with the tart goat cheese and homemade dressing. It's a light and delicious side option for almost any meal.

✓ This recipe includes Nutrition Facts & Diabetic Exchanges.

> 6 cups torn mixed salad greens
> 2 medium apples, chopped
> 1/2 cup raisins
> 1/2 cup green grapes, halved
> 2 tablespoons olive oil
> 4-1/2 teaspoons balsamic vinegar
> 1 tablespoon honey
> 1-1/2 teaspoons lemon juice
> 1 garlic clove, minced
> 3 tablespoons chopped walnuts, toasted
> 2 tablespoons crumbled goat cheese

1. In a large bowl, combine the greens, apples, raisins and grapes. In a small bowl, whisk the oil, vinegar, honey, lemon juice and garlic. Pour over salad and toss to coat. Sprinkle with walnuts and goat cheese. **Yield:** 8 servings.

Nutrition Facts: 3/4 cup equals 133 calories, 6 g fat (1 g saturated fat), 3 mg cholesterol, 31 mg sodium, 19 g carbohydrate, 2 g fiber, 3 g protein. **Diabetic Exchanges:** 1 vegetable, 1 fruit, 1 fat.

Cashew-Pear Tossed Salad

Prep/Total Time: 15 min.

Arlene Muller, Kingwood, Texas

A friend who does a lot of catering fixed this salad for our staff Christmas party several years ago, and we all asked for the recipe. The unexpected sweet-salty mix and lovely dressing make it a hit with everyone.

✓ This recipe includes Nutrition Facts.

> 1 bunch romaine, torn
> 1 cup (4 ounces) shredded Swiss cheese
> 1 cup salted cashews
> 1 medium pear, thinly sliced
> 1/2 cup dried cranberries
> **POPPY SEED VINAIGRETTE:**
> 2/3 cup olive oil
> 1/2 cup sugar
> 1/3 cup lemon juice
> 2 to 3 teaspoons poppy seeds
> 2 teaspoons finely chopped red onion
> 1 teaspoon prepared mustard
> 1/2 teaspoon salt

1. In a large salad bowl, combine the romaine, cheese, cashews, pear and cranberries. In a small bowl, whisk the vinaigrette ingredients. Drizzle over salad and toss to coat. **Yield:** 15 servings.

Nutrition Facts: 1 serving (1 cup) equals 228 calories, 17 g fat (4 g saturated fat), 7 mg cholesterol, 171 mg sodium, 16 g carbohydrate, 1 g fiber, 4 g protein.

Winter Salad

Prep/Total Time: 20 min.

Lynn Ganser, Oakland, California

I make this salad for special dinners, especially around the holidays. Everyone loves the flavor combination and interesting textures of the pears, walnuts, greens and Gorgonzola cheese. It's nice for winter when other fruits aren't readily available.

> ✓ This recipe includes Nutrition Facts.

    1 garlic clove, peeled and halved
    2 tablespoons lemon juice
    2 tablespoons honey
1/8 teaspoon salt
    2 medium ripe pears, thinly sliced
    8 cups torn mixed salad greens
1/2 cup chopped walnuts, toasted
1/3 cup crumbled Gorgonzola cheese

1. Rub garlic clove over the bottom and sides of a large salad bowl; discard garlic. In the bowl, combine the lemon juice, honey and salt. Add pears; gently toss to coat. Add the greens, walnuts and cheese; toss to coat. **Yield:** 6 servings.

Nutrition Facts: 1 serving equals 154 calories, 8 g fat (2 g saturated fat), 6 mg cholesterol, 153 mg sodium, 18 g carbohydrate, 4 g fiber, 5 g protein.

Pear Pointer

To core a fresh pear, insert an apple corer into the bottom of the pear to within 1 in. of its top. Twist the corer to cut around the core, then slowly pull the corer out of the pear to remove the core. Then slice or chop as directed by your recipe.

PG. 43

PG. 57

PG. 42

SOUPS & SANDWICHES

Admit it! It's hard to find a more perfect pairing than a bowl of piping hot soup and a piled–high sandwich. Savor this dynamic duo with the classic steamy spoonfuls and new palate pleasers found here.

PG. 61

Prosciutto Provolone Panini

Prep/Total Time: 25 min.

Candy Summerhill, Alexander, Arkansas

For a quick lunch or supper, try this fancy, up-town take on grilled cheese sandwiches. They're fast and easy but sophisticated enough for entertaining. I sometimes replace the fresh sage with 1 tablespoon of Italian seasoning for a tasty variation without additional work.

- 8 slices white bread
- 8 slices provolone cheese
- 4 thin slices prosciutto
- 3 tablespoons olive oil
- 3 tablespoons minced fresh sage

1. On four slices of bread, layer a slice of cheese, a slice of prosciutto and a second slice of cheese. Top with remaining bread.

2. Brush both sides of sandwiches with oil; sprinkle with sage. Cook in a panini maker or indoor grill until toasted and the cheese is melted. **Yield:** 4 servings.

Cheddar Seafood Chowder

Prep: 25 min. **Cook:** 25 min.

Ami Paton, Waconia, Minnesota

Flavored with crab, shrimp and cheddar cheese, my chowder is so good that I make it weekly. Sometimes I substitute chicken or ham for the seafood and leave out the Clamato juice. Either way, this pretty soup is a winner!

- 1/2 cup finely chopped onion
- 1/4 cup butter, cubed
- 1 can (14-1/2 ounces) chicken broth
- 1 cup cubed peeled potato
- 2 celery ribs, chopped
- 2 medium carrots, chopped
- 1/4 cup Clamato juice
- 1/4 teaspoon lemon-pepper seasoning
- 1/4 cup all-purpose flour
- 2 cups 2% milk
- 2 cups (8 ounces) shredded sharp cheddar cheese
- 1 can (6 ounces) crabmeat, drained, flaked and cartilage removed
- 1 cup cooked medium shrimp, peeled and deveined

1. In a large saucepan, saute onion in butter until tender. Stir in the broth, potato, celery, carrots, Clamato juice and lemon-pepper. Bring to a boil. Reduce heat; cover and simmer for 15-20 minutes or until vegetables are tender.

2. In a small bowl, whisk flour and milk until smooth; add to soup. Bring to a boil; cook and stir for 2 minutes or until thickened. Reduce heat. Add sharp cheddar cheese, crab and shrimp; cook and stir until cheese is melted. **Yield:** 4 servings.

Simple Substitution

If you're on a tight grocery budget or real crab meat is unavailable, imitation crabmeat, most often made with Alaskan pollack, can be used in equal proportions in salads, appetizers and soups such as Cheddar Seafood Chowder.

Cinnamon-Apple Grilled Cheese

Prep/Total Time: 25 min.

Deborah Puette, Lilburn, Georgia

These sandwiches are great for breakfast or lunch—or even as a snack. To amp up the cinnamon flavor, try using cinnamon raisin bread instead of raisin bread.

   1 cup sliced peeled tart apple
   3 teaspoons butter, softened, *divided*
 1/3 cup chopped walnuts
   1 tablespoon honey
   3 tablespoons cheese, softened
   2 tablespoons confectioners' sugar
 1/4 teaspoon ground cinnamon
   4 slices raisin bread
   2 slices Muenster cheese (3/4 ounce *each*)

1. In a large skillet, saute apple slices in 1 teaspoon butter until tender. Meanwhile, in a small skillet, cook and stir the walnuts and honey over medium heat for 2-3 minutes or until lightly toasted.

2. In a small bowl, beat the cream cheese, confectioners' sugar and cinnamon until smooth. Stir in walnut mixture. Spread over two slices of bread; layer with Muenster cheese, apple slices and remaining bread. Spread remaining butter over the outsides of each sandwich.

3. In a large nonstick skillet coated with cooking spray, toast sandwiches for 1-2 minutes on each side or until golden brown and cheese is melted. **Yield:** 2 servings.

Tortilla Turkey Sandwiches

Prep/Total Time: 20 min.

Leslie Heath, Salt Lake City, Utah

As my kids learned how to cook, this was one of their favorite lunches to fix. We love these wraps' savory blend of flavors.

   4 ounces cream cheese, softened
   2 tablespoons mayonnaise
 1-1/2 teaspoons prepared pesto
   4 flour tortillas (8 inches), room temperature
   1 cup shredded lettuce
 1/2 pound sliced deli smoked turkey
 3/4 cup chopped tomato
   1 can (2-1/4 ounces) sliced ripe olives, drained
   1 cup (4 ounces) shredded Colby-Monterey Jack cheese

1. In a small bowl, beat the cream cheese, mayonnaise and pesto until blended. Spread about 2 tablespoons over each tortilla.

2. Layer with shredded lettuce, turkey, chopped tomato, olives and cheese; roll up. Secure with toothpicks. **Yield:** 4 servings.

Refried Bean Soup

Prep/Total Time: 25 min.

Darlene Brenden, Salem, Oregon

You'll love the way my recipe combines the ease of soup with the heartiness of chili. It's a perfect filler-upper on cold afternoons and a great last-minute lunch. If you like it spicier, use medium or hot green chilies instead of mild.

✓ This recipe includes Nutrition Facts.

- 1 can (16 ounces) spicy fat-free refried beans
- 1 can (15-1/4 ounces) whole kernel corn, drained
- 1 can (15 ounces) black beans, rinsed and drained
- 1 can (14-1/2 ounces) chicken broth
- 1 can (14-1/2 ounces) stewed tomatoes, cut up
- 1/2 cup water
- 1 can (4 ounces) chopped green chilies
- 1/4 cup salsa
- Tortilla chips

1. In a large saucepan, combine the first eight ingredients. Bring to a boil. Reduce heat; simmer, uncovered, for 8-10 minutes or until heated through. Serve with tortilla chips. **Yield:** 8 servings (2 quarts).

Nutrition Facts: 1 cup (calculated without chips) equals 117 calories, 1 g fat (trace saturated fat), 1 mg cholesterol, 720 mg sodium, 21 g carbohydrate, 4 g fiber, 5 g protein.

Zesty Turkey Burgers

Prep/Total Time: 25 min.

✓ This recipe includes Nutrition Facts & Diabetic Exchanges.

- 1/2 cup ketchup
- 1 tablespoon cider vinegar
- 1 tablespoon Worcestershire sauce
- 2 garlic cloves, minced
- 1/4 teaspoon pepper
- 1/4 teaspoon crushed red pepper flakes
- 1/4 teaspoon hot pepper sauce
- 1/3 cup quick-cooking oats
- 1 pound lean ground turkey
- 4 lettuce leaves
- 4 hamburger buns, split

1. In a small bowl, combine the first seven ingredients. Transfer half of the mixture to a large bowl; stir in oats. Set remaining ketchup mixture aside for basting. Crumble turkey over oat mixture and mix well. Shape into four patties.

2. Using long-handled tongs, moisten a paper towel with cooking oil and lightly coat the grill rack. Grill patties, covered, over medium heat or broil 4 in. from the heat for 5-7 minutes on each side or until a meat thermometer reads 165° and juices run clear, basting occasionally with ketchup mixture. Serve the burgers on lettuce-lined buns. **Yield:** 4 servings.

Nutrition Facts: 1 burger equals 355 calories, 12 g fat (3 g saturated fat), 90 mg cholesterol, 746 mg sodium, 36 g carbohydrate, 2 g fiber, 25 g protein.
Diabetic Exchanges: 3 lean meat, 2 starch.

LOUISE GILBERT QUESNEL, BRITISH COLUMBIA

When my husband and I were watching our weight one summer, this easy, healthier option became our favorite grilled fare. The moist, hearty patties were even a hit with company.

GRAND
PRIZE
WINNER

Soups & Sandwiches **45**

Roasted Pepper Chicken Sandwiches

Prep: 30 min. + marinating **Grill:** 10 min.

Laura Merkle, Dover, Delaware

Try this wonderful alternative for your next casual dinner or special lunch. The focaccia bread makes it deliciously different from a run-of-the-mill sandwich.

✓ This recipe includes Nutrition Facts & Diabetic Exchanges.

1 tablespoon lemon juice
1 tablespoon Dijon mustard
2 teaspoons olive oil
1 garlic clove, minced
1/4 teaspoon dried thyme
1/4 teaspoon dried marjoram
4 boneless skinless chicken breast halves
   (4 ounces *each*)
PEPPER MIXTURE:
1 large onion, thinly sliced
1 teaspoon sugar
3/4 teaspoon fennel seed, crushed
1/4 teaspoon crushed red pepper flakes
1/8 teaspoon salt
1/8 teaspoon pepper
4 garlic cloves, minced
1 jar (7 ounces) roasted sweet red peppers,
   drained and sliced
1 tablespoon red wine vinegar

SANDWICHES:
1 loaf (8 ounces) focaccia bread
4 teaspoons fat-free mayonnaise
4 slices reduced-fat Swiss cheese

1. In a large resealable plastic bag, combine the first six ingredients; add chicken. Seal bag and turn to coat; refrigerate for 1 hour.

2. In a large nonstick skillet coated with cooking spray, cook and stir the onion, sugar and seasonings over medium heat until tender. Add garlic; cook for 1 minute. Stir in roasted peppers and vinegar; cook 2 minutes longer. Remove from the heat; keep warm.

3. Drain chicken if necessary, discarding any excess marinade. Using long-handled tongs, moisten a paper towel with cooking oil and lightly coat the grill rack.

4. Grill chicken, covered, over medium heat or broil 4 in. from the heat for 4-7 minutes on each side or until a meat thermometer reads 170°. Cut chicken into 1/2-in. strips.

5. Cut focaccia bread in half lengthwise; spread mayonnaise over cut side of bread bottom. Layer with cheese, chicken strips and pepper mixture. Replace bread top; lightly press down. Grill, covered, for 2-3 minutes or until cheese is melted. Cut into four sandwiches. **Yield:** 4 servings.

Nutrition Facts: 1 sandwich equals 404 calories, 11 g fat (3 g saturated fat), 73 mg cholesterol, 795 mg sodium, 41 g carbohydrate, 2 g fiber, 35 g protein.
Diabetic Exchanges: 4 lean meat, 2 starch, 1 vegetable.

Mushroom Burgers

Prep/Total Time: 30 min.

Denise Hollebeke, Penhold, Alberta

Ready to turn over a new burger? I guarantee no one will be missing the beef after they've tasted these vegetarian patties. They're moist, tender and full of flavor.

> ✓ This recipe includes Nutrition Facts.

    2 eggs, lightly beaten
    2 cups finely chopped fresh mushrooms
1/2 cup dry bread crumbs
1/2 cup shredded cheddar cheese
1/2 cup finely chopped onion
1/4 cup all-purpose flour
1/2 teaspoon salt
1/4 teaspoon dried thyme
1/4 teaspoon pepper
    1 tablespoon canola oil
    4 whole wheat hamburger buns, split

1. In a large bowl, combine the first nine ingredients. Shape into four patties.

2. In a large skillet, cook patties in oil over medium heat for 3 minutes on each side or until crisp and lightly browned. Serve on buns. **Yield:** 4 servings.

Nutrition Facts: 1 serving (1 each) equals 330 calories, 13 g fat (5 g saturated fat), 121 mg cholesterol, 736 mg sodium, 42 g carbohydrate, 5 g fiber, 14 g protein.

Zesty Turkey Tomato Soup

Prep/Total Time: 30 min.

Katherine Preiss, Penfield, Pennsylvania

My chunky soup is full of zip and so versatile! If you don't want as much heat, just eliminate the jalapeno pepper. To make it vegetarian, I omit the turkey and add a small can of garbanzo beans in the last few minutes of cooking.

> ✓ This recipe includes Nutrition Facts & Diabetic Exchanges.

1/4 pound lean ground turkey
    1 small zucchini, diced
    1 small onion, chopped
    1 can (14-1/2 ounces) reduced-sodium chicken broth
    1 cup canned Mexican diced tomatoes
1/3 cup uncooked whole wheat spiral pasta
1/2 teaspoon minced fresh basil
1/4 teaspoon ground cumin
1/8 teaspoon pepper
    1 tablespoon chopped jalapeno pepper, optional
Shredded fat-free cheddar cheese, optional

1. In a large saucepan, cook the turkey, zucchini and onion over medium heat until the turkey is no longer pink; drain.

2. Stir in the chicken broth, tomatoes, pasta, basil, cumin, pepper and jalapeno if desired. Bring to a boil. Reduce heat; simmer, uncovered, for 13-15 minutes or until pasta is tender. Garnish with cheddar cheese if desired. **Yield:** 3 cups.

Editor's Note: Wear disposable gloves when cutting hot peppers; the oils can burn skin. Avoid touching your face.

Nutrition Facts: 1 cup (calculated without optional ingredients) equals 143 calories, 4 g fat (1 g saturated fat), 30 mg cholesterol, 719 mg sodium, 17 g carbohydrate, 3 g fiber, 11 g protein. **Diabetic Exchanges:** 1 starch, 1 lean meat.

Bavarian Meatballs

Prep: 15 min. **Cook:** 3-1/2 hours

Peggy Rios, Mechanicsville, Virginia

I use my slow cooker more than any other kitchen appliance, and these mouthwatering meatballs are just one reason why. They're a guaranteed crowd-pleaser when served as appetizers, or when I spoon them over crusty rolls topped with cheese.

- 1 package (32 ounces) frozen fully cooked Italian meatballs
- 1/2 cup chopped onion
- 1/4 cup packed brown sugar
- 1 envelope onion soup mix
- 1 can (12 ounces) beer or nonalcoholic beer
- 12 hoagie buns, split
- 3 cups (12 ounces) shredded Swiss cheese

1. In a 3-qt. slow cooker, combine the meatballs, onion, brown sugar, onion soup mix and beer. Cover and cook on low for 3 to 4 hours or until heated through.

2. Place six meatballs on each bun bottom. Sprinkle each sandwich with 1/4 cup Swiss cheese. Place sandwiches on baking sheets. Broil 4-6 in. from the heat for 2-3 minutes or until cheese is melted. Replace bun tops. **Yield:** 12 servings.

Double-Cheese Beef Panini

Prep/Total Time: 30 min.

Lisa Huff, Wilton, Connecticut

Nothing beats a piping hot panini when it comes to a speedy, satisfying lunch or supper. Blue cheese and horseradish add extra zing to my family-approved sandwich.

- 1/3 cup mayonnaise
- 1/4 cup crumbled blue cheese
- 2 teaspoons prepared horseradish
- 1/8 teaspoon pepper
- 1 large sweet onion, thinly sliced
- 1 tablespoon olive oil
- 8 slices white bread
- 8 slices provolone cheese
- 8 slices deli roast beef
- 2 tablespoons butter, softened

1. In a small bowl, combine the mayonnaise, blue cheese, horseradish and pepper; set aside. In a large skillet, saute onion in oil until tender.

2. Spread mayonnaise mixture over one side of each slice of bread. On four slices, layer one piece of cheese, two slices of roast beef, sauteed onion and another piece of cheese; top with remaining bread.

3. Spread butter over both sides of sandwiches. Cook on a panini maker or indoor grill for 2-3 minutes or until the bread is browned and the cheese is melted. **Yield:** 4 servings.

Grilled Veggie Tortilla Wraps

Prep: 20 min. + marinating **Grill:** 10 min.

Marta Northcutt, Lebanon, Tennessee

There is something so summery and delicious about this recipe. Soft whole wheat tortillas are stuffed with cream cheese and grilled marinated veggies.

> 3 tablespoons red wine vinegar
> 3 tablespoons olive oil
> 1 teaspoon lemon-pepper seasoning
> 1 garlic clove, minced
> 1/2 teaspoon dried oregano
> 1/2 teaspoon dried basil
> 2 medium zucchini, cut lengthwise into 1/4-inch slices
> 1 medium yellow summer squash, cut lengthwise into 1/4-inch slices
> 1 medium sweet red pepper, cut into strips
> 4 ounces cream cheese, softened
> 1 tablespoon prepared pesto
> 4 whole wheat tortillas (8 inches), warmed

1. In a large resealable plastic bag, combine the first six ingredients; add zucchini, yellow squash and red pepper. Seal bag and turn to coat; refrigerate overnight, turning once.

2. In a small bowl, combine cream cheese and pesto; set aside. Drain and discard marinade. Place vegetables in a grill basket or disposable foil pan with slits cut in the bottom. Grill, covered, over medium-high heat for 3-4 minutes on each side or until tender.

3. Spread reserved pesto cream cheese over tortillas; top with vegetables. Fold sides over filling. Serve immediately. **Yield:** 4 servings.

Ranch Turkey Burgers

Prep/Total Time: 30 min.

Sandy Umber, Springdale, Arkansas

Chopped jalapeno gives this interesting turkey burger a slight kick. Every bite is flavorful and cheesy. Top patties off with ranch dressing sauce, and it's the best thing under a bun!

> 5 ounces sharp cheddar cheese, diced
> 1 small sweet onion, diced
> 4 teaspoons chili powder
> 1 jalapeno pepper, seeded and finely chopped
> 2 teaspoons ground cumin
> 2 garlic cloves, minced
> 3/4 teaspoon salt
> 1/4 teaspoon pepper
> 1-1/4 pounds ground turkey
> 3 tablespoons olive oil
> 1/4 cup sour cream
> 4-1/2 teaspoons prepared ranch salad dressing
> 4 hamburger buns, split

1. In a large bowl, combine the first eight ingredients. Crumble turkey over mixture and mix well. Shape into four patties; brush with oil.

2. Grill on a greased indoor grill for 2-3 minutes on each side or until a meat thermometer reads 165° and juices run clear. Meanwhile, in a small bowl, combine sour cream and salad dressing. Serve burgers on buns with sauce. **Yield:** 4 servings.

Editor's Note: Wear disposable gloves when cutting hot peppers; the oils can burn skin. Avoid touching your face.

Vegetable Chili

Prep: 15 min. Cook: 45 min.

Charlene Martorana, Madison, Ohio

My family can't get enough of this chili. Packed with beans and vegetables, it has an appealing color and fabulous flavor.

2 large onions, chopped
1 medium green pepper, chopped
1 tablespoon canola oil
3 garlic cloves, minced
1/2 cup water
2 medium carrots, cut into chunks
2 medium potatoes, peeled and cubed
1 can (14-1/2 ounces) chicken broth
1 to 2 tablespoons chili powder
2 tablespoons sugar
1 teaspoon ground cumin
3/4 teaspoon dried oregano
1 small zucchini, sliced 1/4 inch thick
1 small yellow squash, sliced 1/4 inch thick
2 cans (28 ounces *each*) crushed tomatoes
1/3 cup ketchup
1 can (16 ounces) kidney beans, rinsed and drained
1 can (15 ounces) garbanzo beans *or* chickpeas, rinsed and drained
1 can (15 ounces) black beans, rinsed and drained
1 can (15-1/2 ounces) black-eyed peas, rinsed and drained

1. In a Dutch oven, saute onions and green pepper in oil until tender. Add garlic; cook 1 minute longer. Stir in water and carrots.

2. Cover; cook over medium-low heat for 5 minutes. Add the potatoes, broth, chili powder, sugar, cumin and oregano; cover and cook for 10 minutes.

3. Add zucchini, squash, tomatoes and ketchup; bring to a boil. Reduce heat. Cover; simmer for 15 minutes. Stir in beans and black-eyed peas; simmer for 10 minutes. **Yield:** 12-16 servings.

Strawberry Dessert Soup

Prep: 20 min. + chilling

Sharon Delaney-Chronis, South Milwaukee, Wisconsin

When I first prepared this change-of-pace soup for a party, everyone called it a hit. My husband always likes it warmed up, but I prefer my soup chilled.

1 cup water, *divided*
1 cup unsweetened apple juice
2/3 cup sugar
1/2 teaspoon ground cinnamon
1/8 teaspoon ground cloves
2 cups fresh strawberries, hulled
2 cups strawberry yogurt
2 to 3 drops red food coloring, optional
1/4 cup sour cream
2 tablespoons whole milk

1. In a large saucepan, combine 3/4 cup water, apple juice, sugar, cinnamon and cloves. Bring to a boil, stirring occasionally. Remove from the heat.

2. Place strawberries and remaining water in a blender; cover and process until smooth. Pour into apple juice mixture. Stir in yogurt and food coloring if desired. Cover; refrigerate 2 hours or until chilled.

3. Ladle soup into bowls. Combine sour cream and milk; spoon about 2-1/2 teaspoons into the center of each bowl. Using a toothpick, pull mixture out, forming a flower shape or design of your choice. **Yield:** 7 servings.

Cream of Crab Soup

Prep/Total Time: 25 min.

Wanda Weller, Westminster, Maryland

One of our Chesapeake Bay delicacies is the Maryland Blue Crab. It's abundant from May through October and used in a variety of dishes, like this rich, satisfying soup.

    1/2 cup butter
    1/2 cup all-purpose flour
      1 to 2 tablespoons seafood seasoning
      1 teaspoon salt
    1/2 teaspoon curry powder
      4 cups milk
      1 pound fresh crabmeat *or* 3 cans (6 ounces)
        crabmeat, drained, flaked and cartilage
        removed
      2 tablespoons minced fresh parsley
Additional milk and parsley, optional

1. Melt butter in a 3-qt. saucepan; stir in flour, seafood seasoning, salt and curry powder. Cook until thickened and bubbly. Gradually add milk; cook and stir until mixture is hot (do not boil).

2. Remove cartilage from crab if necessary. Add crab and parsley to soup; cook and stir just until crab is heated. If desired, thin soup with additional milk; garnish with parsley. **Yield:** 6-8 servings.

Black Bean Sausage Chili

Prep: 20 min. Cook: 30 min.

Nanci Keatley, Salem, Oregon

My entire family urged me to send in this recipe! I came up with it one day when I wasn't sure what to do with a can of black beans I had. I just threw a bunch of stuff together, and out came a new chili that's become our favorite.

 This recipe includes Nutrition Facts.

      1 pound bulk Italian sausage
      3 garlic cloves, minced
    1/2 cup chopped green pepper
    1/2 cup chopped onion
      1 can (15 ounces) black beans, rinsed and
        drained
      1 can (14-1/2 ounces) diced tomatoes,
        undrained
      1 can (11 ounces) whole kernel corn, drained
      1 can (8 ounces) tomato sauce
      1 can (6 ounces) tomato paste
    1/2 cup water
      1 tablespoon chili powder
      1 teaspoon dried oregano
    3/4 teaspoon salt
    1/2 teaspoon dried basil
    1/4 teaspoon pepper
Shredded cheddar cheese, optional

1. In a large saucepan, cook sausage and garlic over medium heat until the sausage is not longer pink.

2. Add green pepper and onion. Cook and stir until onion is tender; drain. Stir in the beans, tomatoes, corn, tomato sauce and paste, water, chili powder, oregano, salt, basil and pepper; bring to a boil. Reduce heat; cover and simmer for 30 minutes.

3. Garnish with cheese if desired. **Yield:** 6 servings (1-3/4 quarts).

Nutrition Facts: 1 serving (1 cup) equals 282 calories, 11 g fat (4 g saturated fat), 30 mg cholesterol, 1,222 mg sodium, 31 g carbohydrate, 8 g fiber, 15 g protein.

Roasted Yellow Pepper Soup

Prep: 25 min. **Cook:** 40 min.

Amy Spurrier, Wellsburg, West Virginia

We got this recipe from a good friend and Merchant Marine in New Hampshire. My husband and our two children liked it so much that I started growing yellow peppers! We enjoy it in the middle of summer or on cool fall days.

✓ This recipe includes Nutrition Facts.

6 **large sweet yellow peppers**
1 **large onion, chopped**
1 **cup chopped leeks (white portion only)**
1/4 **cup butter, cubed**
3 **small potatoes, peeled and cubed**
5 **cups chicken broth**
1/2 **teaspoon salt**
1/2 **teaspoon pepper**
Shredded Parmesan cheese, optional

1. Halve peppers; remove and discard tops and seeds. Broil peppers 4 in. from the heat until skins blister, about 4 minutes. Immediately place peppers in a bowl; cover and let stand for 15-20 minutes.

2. Meanwhile, in a large saucepan, saute onion and leeks in butter until tender. Add the potatoes, broth, salt and pepper. Bring to a boil. Reduce the heat; cover and simmer for 30 minutes or until the potatoes are tender.

3. Peel off and discard charred skin from the peppers. Finely chop the peppers; add to the potato mixture. Cool slightly.

4. In a blender, cover and process soup in batches until smooth. Return to the pan; heat through (do not boil). Serve with Parmesan cheese if desired. **Yield:** 8 cups (2 quarts).

Nutrition Facts: 1 cup equals 124 calories, 6 g fat (4 g saturated fat), 18 mg cholesterol, 807 mg sodium, 16 g carbohydrate, 2 g fiber, 3 g protein.

Creamy Bacon Mushroom Soup

Prep/Total Time: 30 min.

Toby Mercer, Inman, South Carolina

I enjoy cooking and recently created this fabulous soup. It's always a hit. You can also garnish it with chopped green onion tops or shredded Swiss cheese. For a creamier, smoother consistency, pour the soup through a strainer.

10 **bacon strips, diced**
1 **pound sliced fresh mushrooms**
1 **medium onion, chopped**
3 **garlic cloves, minced**
1 **quart heavy whipping cream**
1 **can (14-1/2 ounces) chicken broth**
1-1/4 **cups shredded Swiss cheese**
3 **tablespoons cornstarch**
1/2 **teaspoon salt**
1/2 **teaspoon pepper**
3 **tablespoons water**

1. In a large saucepan, cook bacon over medium heat until crisp. Using a slotted spoon, remove to paper towels; drain, reserving 2 tablespoons drippings. In the drippings, saute the mushrooms, onion and garlic. Stir in the cream and broth. Gradually stir in the cheese until melted.

2. In a small bowl, combine the cornstarch, salt, pepper and water until smooth. Stir into soup. Bring to a boil; cook and stir for 2 minutes or until thickened. Garnish with bacon. **Yield:** 8 servings (2 quarts).

Minestrone with Italian Sausage

Prep: 25 min. **Cook:** 1 hour

Linda Reis, Salem, Oregon

I make this zippy, homestyle soup all the time. The recipe is great when you need to serve a hungry crowd, but the soup also freezes well and tastes just as good reheated the next day.

- 1 **pound bulk Italian sausage**
- 1 **large onion, chopped**
- 2 **large carrots, chopped**
- 2 **celery ribs, chopped**
- 1 **medium leek (white portion only), chopped**
- 1 **medium zucchini, cut into 1/2-inch pieces**
- 1/4 **pound fresh green beans, trimmed and cut into 1/2-inch pieces**
- 3 **garlic cloves, minced**
- 6 **cups beef broth**
- 2 **cans (14-1/2 ounces *each*) diced tomatoes with basil, oregano and garlic**
- 3 **cups shredded cabbage**
- 1 **teaspoon dried basil**
- 1 **teaspoon dried oregano**
- 1/4 **teaspoon pepper**
- 1/2 **cup uncooked small pasta shells**
- 1 **can (15 ounces) garbanzo beans or chickpeas, rinsed and drained**
- 3 **tablespoons minced fresh parsley**
- 1/3 **cup grated Parmesan cheese**

1. In a Dutch oven, cook sausage and onion over medium heat until meat is no longer pink; drain. Stir in the carrots, celery and leek; cook for 3 minutes. Add the zucchini, green beans and garlic; cook 1 minute longer.

2. Stir in the broth, tomatoes, cabbage, basil, oregano and pepper. Bring to a boil. Reduce heat; cover and simmer for 45 minutes.

3. Return to a boil. Stir in the garbanzo beans, pasta and parsley. Cook for 6-9 minutes or until the pasta is tender. Serve with Parmesan cheese. **Yield:** 11 servings (about 3 quarts).

Gingered Butternut Squash Soup

Prep: 45 min. **Cook:** 40 min.

Kim Pettipas, Oromocto, New Brunswick

Roasting the squash really adds a wonderful flavor to this delightful pureed soup. If you want a true vegetarian dish, simply substitute vegetable stock for the chicken broth.

 This recipe includes Nutrition Facts.

4 pounds butternut squash, peeled and cubed (about 8 cups)
6 teaspoons olive oil, *divided*
1 large onion, chopped
2 tablespoons butter
1 tablespoon minced fresh gingerroot
2-1/2 teaspoons curry powder
3/4 teaspoon salt
1/4 teaspoon pepper
3 large potatoes, peeled and cubed
6 cups chicken broth
1-1/2 cups whole milk
Sour cream, optional

1. Place squash in a greased 15-in. x 10-in. x 1-in. baking pan. Drizzle with 4-1/2 teaspoons oil; toss to coat. Bake, uncovered, at 450° for 30 minutes, stirring every 15 minutes. Bake 5-10 minutes longer or until tender. Set aside.

2. In a soup kettle, saute onion in butter and remaining oil for 5 minutes or until tender. Stir in the ginger, curry, salt and pepper; cook for 2 minutes. Stir in potatoes; cook 2 minutes longer. Stir in broth. Bring to a boil. Reduce heat; cover and simmer for 15-20 minutes or until potatoes are tender. Cool slightly.

3. Stir in reserved squash. In a blender, puree soup in batches until smooth. Return to the pan. Stir in milk; heat through. Garnish soup with sour cream if desired. **Yield:** 9 servings (about 3 quarts).

Nutrition Facts: 1-1/4 cups equals 266 calories, 8 g fat (3 g saturated fat), 12 mg cholesterol, 877 mg sodium, 46 g carbohydrate, 8 g fiber, 7 g protein.

Colorful Chicken 'n' Squash Soup

Prep: 25 min. **Cook:** 1-1/2 hours

✓ This recipe includes Nutrition Facts & Diabetic Exchanges.

1 broiler/fryer chicken (4 pounds), cut up
13 cups water
5 pounds butternut squash, peeled and cubed (about 10 cups)
1 bunch kale, trimmed and chopped
6 medium carrots, chopped
2 large onions, chopped
3 teaspoons salt

1. Place chicken and water in a stockpot. Bring to a boil. Reduce heat; cover and simmer for 1 hour or until chicken is tender.

2. Remove chicken from broth. Strain broth and skim fat. Return broth to the pan; add the squash, kale, carrots and onions. Bring to a boil. Reduce heat; cover and simmer for 25-30 minutes or until vegetables are tender.

3. When the chicken is cool enough to handle, remove the meat from bones and cut into bite-size pieces. Discard the bones and skin. Add the chicken and salt to the soup; heat through. **Yield:** 14 servings (5-1/2 quarts).

Nutrition Facts: 1-1/2 cups equals 228 calories, 8 g fat (2 g saturated fat), 50 mg cholesterol, 579 mg sodium, 22 g carbohydrate, 6 g fiber, 18 g protein.
Diabetic Exchanges: 2 lean meat, 1 starch, 1 vegetable, 1/2 fat.

TRINA BIGHAM FAIRHAVEN, MASSACHUSETTS

When I turned 40, I decided to live a healthier lifestyle, which included cooking smarter for my family. My gang requests this soup every week.

Cheeseburger Paradise Soup

Prep: 30 min. **Cook:** 25 min.

Nadina Iadimarco, Burton, Ohio

I've never met a person who didn't enjoy this creamy, hearty soup. Pair it with your choice of bread or rolls and it can stand as the main course.

- 6 medium potatoes, peeled and cubed
- 1 small carrot, grated
- 1 small onion, chopped
- 1/2 cup chopped green pepper
- 2 tablespoons chopped seeded jalapeno pepper
- 3 cups water
- 2 tablespoons plus 2 teaspoons beef bouillon granules
- 2 garlic cloves, minced
- 1/8 teaspoon pepper
- 2 pounds ground beef
- 1/2 pound sliced fresh mushrooms
- 2 tablespoons butter
- 5 cups 2% milk, *divided*
- 6 tablespoons all-purpose flour
- 1 package (16 ounces) process cheese (Velveeta), cubed

Crumbled cooked bacon

1. In a Dutch oven, combine the first nine ingredients; bring to a boil. Reduce heat; cover and simmer for 10-15 minutes or until potatoes are tender.

2. Meanwhile, in a large skillet, cook beef and mushrooms in butter over medium heat until meat is no longer pink; drain. Add to soup. Stir in 4 cups milk; heat through.

3. In a small bowl, combine flour and remaining milk until smooth; gradually stir into soup. Bring to a boil; cook and stir for 2 minutes or until thickened. Reduce heat; stir in cheese until melted. Garnish with bacon. **Yield:** 14 servings (about 3-1/2 quarts).

Editor's Note: Wear disposable gloves when cutting hot peppers; the oils can burn skin. Avoid touching your face.

Chicken Soup with Potato Dumplings

Prep: 25 min. **Cook:** 40 min.

Marie McConnell, Shelbyville, Illinois

Our family calls this comforting, old-fashioned soup our "Sunday dinner soup" because it's almost a complete dinner in a bowl. You'll love the flavor!

- 1/4 cup chopped onion
- 1 tablespoon canola oil
- 2 garlic cloves, minced
- 6 cups chicken broth
- 2 cups cubed cooked chicken
- 2 celery ribs, chopped
- 2 medium carrots, sliced
- 1/4 teaspoon dried sage leaves

DUMPLINGS:
- 1-1/2 cups biscuit/baking mix
- 1 cup cold mashed potatoes (with added milk)
- 1/4 cup milk
- 1 tablespoon chopped green onion
- 1/8 teaspoon pepper

1. In a large saucepan, saute onion in oil for 3-4 minutes or until tender. Add garlic; cook 1 minute longer. Stir in the broth, chicken, celery, carrots and

sage. Bring to a boil. Reduce heat; cover and simmer for 10-15 minutes or until vegetables are tender.

2. In a small bowl, combine the dumpling ingredients. Drop heaping tablespoonfuls of batter onto simmering soup. Cover and simmer for 20 minutes or until a toothpick inserted in a dumpling comes out clean (do not lift cover while simmering). **Yield:** 5 servings.

Mushroom Tomato Bisque

Prep: 30 min. **Cook:** 10 min.

Connie Stevens, Schaefferstown, Pennsylvania

After tasting a similar soup in a restaurant, I tinkered around with a few recipes at home and this was the result. The dish might seem complicated, but it's really not. People love the blend of flavors.

- 1-1/2 pounds plum tomatoes, halved lengthwise
- 5 tablespoons olive oil, *divided*
- 2 garlic cloves, minced
- 1/2 teaspoon salt
- 1/2 teaspoon dried basil
- 1/2 teaspoon dried oregano
- 1/2 teaspoon pepper
- 1/2 pound sliced fresh mushrooms
- 1/2 cup finely chopped sweet onion
- 1-1/4 cups chicken broth
- 1/3 to 1/2 cup tomato paste

Pinch sugar, optional
- 3/4 cup heavy whipping cream
- 2 tablespoons grated Parmesan cheese

1. Place tomatoes cut side down in a greased 15-in. x 10-in. x 1-in. baking pan. Brush with 3 tablespoons oil. Combine garlic, salt, basil, oregano and pepper; sprinkle over tomatoes. Bake, uncovered, at 450° for 20-25 minutes or until edges are well browned.

2. Cool slightly. Place tomatoes and pan drippings in a blender. Cover and process until blended; process 1 minute longer.

3. In a large saucepan, saute mushrooms and onion in remaining oil for 5-8 minutes or until tender. Stir in broth, tomato paste, sugar if desired and tomato puree. Bring to a boil. Remove from the heat; stir in cream. Garnish with Parmesan cheese. **Yield:** 4 servings.

Hearty Beef Vegetable Soup

Prep: 20 min. **Cook:** 2 hours

Sherman Snowball, Salt Lake City, Utah

My stew-like soup is loaded with nutritious ingredients and is incredibly easy to prepare. We like to soak up the rich broth with homemade bread or breadsticks.

✓ This recipe includes Nutrition Facts.

   3 tablespoons all-purpose flour
1/2 teaspoon salt
1/4 teaspoon pepper
   1 pound beef stew meat, cut into 1/2-inch cubes
   2 tablespoons olive oil
   1 can (14-1/2 ounces) Italian diced tomatoes
   1 can (8 ounces) tomato sauce

   2 tablespoons red wine vinegar
   2 tablespoons Worcestershire sauce
   3 garlic cloves, minced
   1 teaspoon dried oregano
   3 cups hot water
   4 medium potatoes, peeled and cubed
   6 medium carrots, sliced
   2 medium turnips, peeled and cubed
   1 medium zucchini, halved lengthwise and sliced
   1 medium green pepper, julienned
   1 cup sliced fresh mushrooms
   1 medium onion, chopped
   1 can (4 ounces) chopped green chilies
   2 tablespoons sugar

1. In a large resealable plastic bag, combine the flour, salt and pepper. Add beef, a few pieces at a time, and shake to coat.

2. In a Dutch oven, brown beef in oil. Stir in the tomatoes, tomato sauce, vinegar, Worcestershire sauce, garlic and oregano. Bring to a boil. Reduce heat; cover and simmer for 1 hour.

3. Stir in the remaining ingredients. Bring to a boil. Reduce heat; cover and simmer for 1 hour or until meat and vegetables are tender. **Yield:** 8 servings (about 2-1/2 quarts).

Nutrition Facts: 1-1/2 cups equals 276 calories, 8 g fat (2 g saturated fat), 35 mg cholesterol, 638 mg sodium, 38 g carbohydrate, 5 g fiber, 15 g protein.

Lemony Chicken Soup

Prep/Total Time: 25 min.

Brenda Tollett, San Antonio, Texas

While living in California, I enjoyed a delicious chicken-lemon soup at a local restaurant. When I returned to Texas, I longed for it but never came across a recipe. I experimented with many versions before creating this one.

1/3 cup butter, cubed
3/4 cup all-purpose flour
   6 cups chicken broth
   1 cup milk
   1 cup half-and-half cream
1-1/2 cups cubed cooked chicken
   1 tablespoon lemon juice
1/2 teaspoon salt
1/8 teaspoon pepper
Dash ground nutmeg
   8 lemon slices

1. In a soup kettle or large saucepan, melt butter. Stir in flour until smooth; gradually add the broth, milk and cream. Bring to a boil; cook and stir for 2 minutes or until thickened.

2. Stir in the chicken, lemon juice, salt, pepper and nutmeg. Cook over medium heat until heated through, stirring occasionally. Garnish each serving with a lemon slice. **Yield:** 8 servings (2 quarts).

Turkey & Cornmeal Dumpling Soup

Prep: 35 min. **Cook:** 3 hours

Karen Sue Garback-Pristera, Albany, New York

Nothing satisfies on a chilly evening like homemade soup—especially if it stars chewy, from-scratch dumplings! I got this recipe from my grandmother, who was a caterer.

✓ This recipe includes Nutrition Facts.

1 leftover turkey carcass (from a 12- to
    14-pound turkey)
9 cups water
3 teaspoons chicken bouillon granules
1 bay leaf
1 can (14-1/2 ounces) stewed tomatoes, cut up
1 medium turnip, peeled and diced
2 celery ribs, chopped
1 medium onion, chopped
1 medium carrot, chopped
1/4 cup minced fresh parsley
1 teaspoon salt
DUMPLINGS:
1/2 cup water
1/4 cup butter, cubed
1/2 cup all-purpose flour
1 teaspoon baking powder
1/8 teaspoon salt
2 eggs
1 tablespoon minced fresh parsley

1. Place carcass, water, bouillon and bay leaf in a stockpot. Bring to a boil. Reduce heat; cover and simmer for 1-1/2 hours.

2. Remove carcass. Strain broth and skim fat; discard bay leaf. Return broth to pan. Add the tomatoes, vegetables, parsley and salt. Remove turkey from bones and cut into bite-size pieces; add to soup. Discard bones. Bring to a boil. Reduce heat; cover and simmer for 25-30 minutes or until vegetables are crisp-tender.

3. For dumplings, in a large saucepan, bring water and butter to a boil. Combine the flour, baking powder and salt; add all at once to pan and stir until a smooth ball forms. Remove from heat; let stand for 5 minutes. Add eggs, one at a time, beating well after each addition. Continue beating until mixture is smooth and shiny. Stir in parsley.

4. Drop batter in 12 mounds into simmering soup. Cover; simmer for 20 minutes or until a toothpick inserted in a dumpling comes out clean (do not lift cover while simmering). **Yield:** 6 servings (about 2 quarts).

Nutrition Facts: 1-1/2 cups equals 202 calories, 10 g fat (5 g saturated fat), 92 mg cholesterol, 1,238 mg sodium, 24 g carbohydrate, 3 g fiber, 6 g protein.

Chipotle Butternut Squash Soup

Prep: 25 min. **Cook:** 30 min.

Roxanne Chan, Albany, California

Using herbs and vegetables from the garden along with convenient pantry items makes this hearty soup easy and fast to fix. Your family will devour it.

✓ This recipe includes Nutrition Facts.

- 2 cups diced peeled butternut squash
- 1 small carrot, finely chopped
- 1 green onion, sliced
- 1/2 teaspoon ground cumin
- 1 tablespoon olive oil
- 2 garlic cloves, minced
- 2 cups vegetable broth, *divided*
- 1 can (14-1/2 ounces) diced tomatoes, undrained
- 1 package (3 ounces) cream cheese, cubed
- 1/4 cup minced fresh basil
- 1 chipotle pepper in adobo sauce, chopped
- 1 can (15 ounces) black beans, rinsed and drained
- 1 can (11 ounces) Mexicorn, drained
- 2 cups fresh baby spinach

1. In a large saucepan, saute the squash, carrot, onion and cumin in oil for 10 minutes. Add garlic; cook 1 minute longer. Add 1-1/2 cups broth; bring to a boil. Reduce heat. Cover and simmer for 10-12 minutes or until vegetables are tender; cool slightly.

2. Transfer mixture to a blender; add the tomatoes, cream cheese, basil, chipotle pepper and remaining broth. Cover; process mixture for 1-2 minutes or until smooth.

3. Return to the saucepan; stir in the beans, corn and spinach. Cook and stir until spinach is wilted and soup is heated through. **Yield:** 5 servings.

Editor's Note: If garnish is desired, sprinkle butternut squash seeds with 1/8 teaspoon salt. Place on a baking sheet. Bake at 350° for 10-13 minutes or until seeds are golden brown.

Nutrition Facts: 1-1/3 cups equals 279 calories, 9 g fat (4 g saturated fat), 19 mg cholesterol, 1,097 mg sodium, 43 g carbohydrate, 10 g fiber, 10 g protein.

Roast Beef Roll-Ups

Prep/Total Time: 15 min.

Clarissa Jo Seeger, Columbiana, Ohio

Quick to make, these party sandwiches are great for tailgating and other events. Serve them in thin slices for an appetizer or "Reubenize" them by substituting corned beef, sauerkraut, caraway seeds and Thousand Island dressing.

- 1 package (14 ounces) coleslaw mix
- 3/4 cup coleslaw salad dressing
- 1/2 cup mayonnaise
- 1/4 cup Dijon mustard
- 2 tablespoons cider vinegar
- 2 teaspoons sugar
- 1/2 teaspoon celery seed
- 1 pound thinly sliced deli roast beef
- 4 Italian herb flatbread wraps
- 1/2 pound Swiss cheese, thinly sliced

1. In a small bowl, combine the first seven ingredients. Divide roast beef among flatbread wraps. Top with cheese and coleslaw mixture; roll up tightly. **Yield:** 4 servings.

Land of Enchantment Posole

Prep: 30 min. **Cook:** 1 hour

Suzanne Caldwell, Artesia, New Mexico

We make this spicy soup over the holidays, when we have lots of family over. Even with a group, there are never leftovers.

1-1/2 pounds pork stew meat, cut into 3/4-inch cubes
  1 large onion, chopped
  2 tablespoons canola oil
  2 garlic cloves, minced
  3 cups beef broth
  2 cans (15-1/2 ounces *each*) hominy, rinsed and drained
  2 cans (4 ounces *each*) chopped green chilies
  1 to 2 jalapeno peppers, seeded and chopped, optional
1/2 teaspoon salt
1/2 teaspoon ground cumin
1/2 teaspoon dried oregano
1/4 teaspoon pepper
1/4 teaspoon cayenne pepper
1/2 cup minced fresh cilantro
Tortilla strips, optional

1. In a Dutch oven, cook pork and onion in oil over medium heat until meat is no longer pink. Add garlic; cook 1 minute longer. Drain. Stir in the broth, hominy,

chilies, jalapeno if desired, salt, cumin, oregano, pepper and cayenne.

2. Bring to a boil. Reduce heat; cover and simmer for 45-60 minutes or until meat is tender. Stir in cilantro. Serve with tortilla strips if desired. **Yield:** 5 servings.

Editor's Note: Wear disposable gloves when cutting hot peppers; the oils can burn skin. Avoid touching your face.

Tomato-Basil Orzo Soup

Prep/Total Time: 30 min.

Mary Lu Wasniewski, Orland Park, Illinois

Tender pasta, sauteed vegetables and lots of flavor! This tasty soup comes really close to the tomato rosa marina soup they serve in the best Greek restaurants in Chicago.

1/2 cup *each* chopped carrot, celery and onion
1/8 teaspoon *each* dried basil, oregano and thyme
  2 tablespoons olive oil
  1 can (19 ounces) ready-to-serve tomato basil *or* hearty tomato soup
  1 cup chicken broth
1/3 cup uncooked orzo pasta

1. In a small saucepan, saute the carrot, celery, onion, basil, oregano and thyme in oil for 8-10 minutes or until vegetables are crisp-tender.

2. Add soup and chicken broth. Bring to a boil. Stir in orzo. Reduce heat; simmer, uncovered, for 10-12 minutes or until the orzo and vegetables are tender. **Yield:** 2 servings.

Editor's Note: This recipe was tested with ready-to-serve Progresso Tomato Basil soup.

PG. 79

PG. 76

PG. 65

BREAKFAST & BRUNCH

Now here's a reason—or 33 reasons—to jump out of bed in the morning. Delight in this assortment of daybreak specialties including ooey-gooey cinnamon rolls, fluffy eggs, tender muffins and everything in between.

PG. 75

Vanilla Cinnamon Rolls

Prep: 30 min. + rising **Bake:** 20 min.

Linda Martin, Warsaw, Indiana

I dare you to find a better recipe for cinnamon rolls! These bake up incredibly tender and have an irresistible frosting.

- 2 cups cold milk
- 1 package (3.4 ounces) instant vanilla pudding mix
- 2 packages (1/4 ounce *each*) active dry yeast
- 1/2 cup warm water (110° to 115°)
- 1/2 cup plus 2 tablespoons butter, melted, *divided*
- 2 eggs
- 2 tablespoons sugar
- 1 teaspoon salt
- 6 cups all-purpose flour
- 1/2 cup packed brown sugar
- 1 teaspoon ground cinnamon

FROSTING:
- 1 cup packed brown sugar
- 1/2 cup heavy whipping cream
- 1/2 cup butter, cubed
- 2 cups confectioners' sugar

1. In a large bowl, whisk the milk and vanilla pudding mix for 2 minutes. Let stand for 2 minutes or until soft set; set aside.

2. In a large bowl, dissolve yeast in warm water. Add 1/2 cup butter, eggs, sugar, salt and 2 cups flour. Beat on medium speed for 3 minutes. Add pudding; beat until smooth. Stir in enough remaining flour to form a soft dough (dough will be sticky).

3. Turn onto a floured surface; knead until smooth and elastic, about 6-8 minutes. Place in a greased bowl, turning once to grease top. Cover and let rise in a warm place until doubled, about 1 hour.

4. Punch dough down. Turn onto a floured surface; divide in half. Roll each portion into an 18-in. x 11-in. rectangle; brush with remaining butter. Combine brown sugar and cinnamon; sprinkle over dough to within 1/2 in. of edges.

5. Roll up jelly-roll style, starting with a long side; pinch seams to seal. Cut each into 16 slices. Place cut side down in two greased 13-in. x 9-in. baking dishes. Cover; let rise until doubled, about 30 minutes. Bake at 350° for 20-25 minutes or until golden brown.

6. Meanwhile, in a large saucepan, combine the brown sugar, cream and butter. Bring to a boil; cook and stir for 2 minutes. Remove from the heat. Beat in confectioners' sugar with a hand mixer until creamy. Frost warm rolls. Serve warm. **Yield:** 32 rolls.

Orange-Mascarpone Breakfast Rolls

Prep: 25 min. **Bake:** 20 min.

Pamela Shank, Parkersburg, West Virginia

These special rolls are melt-in-your-mouth good and smell wonderful while baking. I came up with the recipe while teaching my grandchildren how to make monkey bread.

- 1/4 **cup chopped pecans**
- 1/4 **cup sugar**
- 1 **teaspoon ground cinnamon**
- 2 **tablespoons plus 1-1/2 teaspoons Mascarpone cheese,** *divided*
- 1 **teaspoon grated orange peel**
- 1 **tube (6 ounces) refrigerated flaky buttermilk biscuits**
- 2 **tablespoons butter, melted**
- 1/2 **cup confectioners' sugar**
- 2 **teaspoons orange juice**

1. Sprinkle pecans into a 6-in. round baking pan coated with cooking spray; set aside. In a small bowl, combine sugar and cinnamon. In another bowl, combine 2 tablespoons Mascarpone cheese and orange peel; set aside.

2. On a lightly floured surface, roll out biscuits into 4-in. circles. Spread 1/2 teaspoon cheese mixture

down center of each circle. Bring dough from opposite sides over filling just until edges meet; pinch to seal.

3. Brush with some of the butter; roll in sugar mixture. Place seam side down over pecans. Sprinkle with remaining sugar mixture; drizzle with remaining butter.

4. Bake at 350° for 20-25 minutes or until golden brown. Immediately invert onto a serving plate. In a small bowl, combine the confectioners' sugar, orange juice and remaining Mascarpone cheese. Drizzle over rolls. Serve warm. **Yield:** 5 rolls.

Savory Apple-Chicken Sausage

Prep/Total Time: 25 min.

Angela Buchanan, Longmont, Colorado

These easy-to-make sausages taste great and make an elegant brunch dish. The recipe is also very versatile as it can be doubled or tripled for a crowd, and the sausage freezes well either cooked or raw.

✓ This recipe includes Nutrition Facts & Diabetic Exchange.

- 1 **large tart apple, peeled and diced**
- 2 **teaspoons poultry seasoning**
- 1 **teaspoon salt**
- 1/4 **teaspoon pepper**
- 1 **pound ground chicken**

1. In a large bowl, combine the apple, poultry seasoning, salt and pepper. Crumble chicken over mixture and mix well. Shape into eight 3-in. patties.

2. In a large skillet coated with cooking spray, cook patties over medium heat for 5-6 minutes on each side or until a meat thermometer reads 165° and juices run clear. **Yield:** 8 patties.

Nutrition Facts: 1 sausage patty equals 92 calories, 5 g fat (1 g saturated fat), 38 mg cholesterol, 328 mg sodium, 4 g carbohydrate, 1 g fiber, 9 g protein. **Diabetic Exchange:** 1 medium-fat meat.

Spinach Omelet Brunch Roll

Prep: 20 min. **Bake:** 15 min.

Laine Beal, Topeka, Kansas

Veggies from one favorite recipe and the rolling technique of another resulted in this stunning brunch offering.

 This recipe includes Nutrition Facts & Diabetic Exchanges.

> 2 cups egg substitute
> 4 eggs
> 1/2 teaspoon salt

1/8 teaspoon hot pepper sauce
1 package (10 ounces) frozen chopped spinach, thawed and squeezed dry
1/4 cup chopped red onion
1 teaspoon Italian seasoning
5 turkey bacon strips, diced and cooked, *divided*
1 pound sliced fresh mushrooms
2 teaspoons canola oil
1 cup (4 ounces) shredded part-skim mozzarella cheese, *divided*

1. Line a 15-in. x 10-in. x 1-in. baking pan with parchment paper; coat paper with cooking spray and set aside. In a large bowl, whisk the egg substitute, eggs, salt and pepper sauce. Stir in the spinach, onion, Italian seasoning and 1/4 cup bacon.

2. Pour into prepared pan. Bake at 375° for 15-20 minutes or until set. Meanwhile, in a large nonstick skillet, saute mushrooms in oil for 6-8 minutes or until tender. Drain on paper towels; blot to remove excess moisture. Keep warm.

3. Turn omelet onto a work surface; peel off parchment paper. Sprinkle omelet with mushrooms and 3/4 cup cheese; roll up jelly-roll style, starting with a short side. Place on a serving platter. Sprinkle with remaining cheese and bacon. **Yield:** 8 servings.

Nutrition Facts: 1 slice equals 160 calories, 8 g fat (3 g saturated fat), 122 mg cholesterol, 505 mg sodium, 6 g carbohydrate, 2 g fiber, 17 g protein. **Diabetic Exchanges:** 2 lean meat, 1 vegetable, 1/2 fat.

Asparagus Strata

Prep: 20 min. + chilling **Bake:** 55 min. + standing

Ethel Pressel, New Oxford, Pennsylvania

You can easily prepare this mouthwatering strata starring ham, eggs, cheese and asparagus the night before a luncheon or during the morning for a change-of-pace dinner.

> 12 slices white bread
> 12 ounces process cheese (Velveeta), diced
> 1-1/2 pounds fresh asparagus, trimmed
> 2 cups diced cooked ham
> 6 eggs
> 3 cups milk
> 2 tablespoons finely chopped onion
> 1/2 teaspoon salt
> 1/4 teaspoon ground mustard

1. Using a doughnut cutter, cut 12 circles and holes from bread; set aside. Tear remaining bread in pieces and place in a greased 13-in. x 9-in. baking dish.

2. Layer with cheese, asparagus and ham; arrange bread circles and holes on top. Lightly beat eggs with milk. Add onion, salt and mustard; mix well. Pour egg

mixture over bread circles and holes. Cover and refrigerate at least 6 hours or overnight.

3. Bake, uncovered, at 325° for 55 minutes or until top is light golden brown. Let stand for 10 minutes before serving. **Yield:** 6-8 servings.

Festive Poppy Seed Scones

Prep: 20 min. **Bake:** 15 min.

Lisa Varner, El Paso, Texas

With their eye-opening citrus burst, these scones are perfect for holiday brunches. They're best served warm from the oven.

✓ This recipe includes Nutrition Facts & Diabetic Exchanges.

> 2 cups all-purpose flour
> 1/2 cup sugar
> 1/2 cup quick-cooking oats
> 1 tablespoon poppy seeds
> 2 teaspoons baking powder
> 1/2 teaspoon salt
> 1/4 teaspoon baking soda
> 1/3 cup cold butter
> 1 egg
> 1/2 cup orange juice
> 3 tablespoons buttermilk
> 1/2 cup dried cranberries
> 1 teaspoon grated orange peel

1. In a large bowl, combine the first seven ingredients. Cut in butter until mixture resembles coarse crumbs. In a small bowl, whisk the egg, orange juice and buttermilk; add to crumb mixture just until moistened. Stir in cranberries and orange peel.

2. Turn onto a lightly floured surface; gently knead 6-8 times. Divide dough in half. Pat each portion into a 6-in. circle. Place on a baking sheet coated with cooking spray. Cut each circle into six wedges, but do not separate.

3. Bake at 375° for 15-20 minutes or until golden brown. Cool for 5 minutes before removing to a wire rack. Serve warm. **Yield:** 1 dozen.

Nutrition Facts: 1 scone equals 197 calories, 6 g fat (3 g saturated fat), 31 mg cholesterol, 253 mg sodium, 32 g carbohydrate, 1 g fiber, 4 g protein. **Diabetic Exchanges:** 2 starch, 1 fat.

Coffee Lover's Coffee Cake

Prep: 25 min. **Bake:** 25 min.

Gale Lalmond, Deering, New Hampshire

I first tried this wonderful cake at a friend's brunch. She shared the recipe with me, and now it's my turn to pass it along!

> 1/3 cup sugar
> 4-1/2 teaspoons instant coffee granules
> 1-1/2 teaspoons ground cinnamon
> BATTER:
> 3 tablespoons butter, softened
> 1/2 cup sugar
> 1 egg
> 1 teaspoon vanilla extract
> 1-1/2 cups all-purpose flour
> 1 teaspoon baking powder
> 1/2 teaspoon baking soda
> 1/8 teaspoon salt
> 1 cup (8 ounces) plain yogurt
> 2 tablespoons chopped walnuts *or* pecans

1. In a small bowl, combine the sugar, coffee granules and cinnamon; set aside. In a large bowl, beat butter and sugar until crumbly, about 2 minutes. Beat in egg and vanilla. Combine the flour, baking powder, baking soda and salt; add to butter mixture alternately with yogurt, beating just until combined.

2. Spread half of the batter evenly into a 9-in. square baking pan coated with cooking spray; sprinkle with half the reserved sugar mixture. Repeat layers; cut through batter with a knife to swirl. Sprinkle with nuts.

3. Bake at 350° for 25-30 minutes or until a toothpick inserted near the center comes out clean. Cool for 5 minutes on a wire rack. Serve warm. **Yield:** 9 servings.

Crustless Four-Cheese Quiche

Prep: 30 min. **Bake:** 35 min.

Susan Anderson, Park City, Utah

My husband is a real meat fan—but this luscious quiche is one meatless recipe he loves. He'll even go to the store and bring home Jarlsberg cheese just to hint that it's time for me to make it!

- 1/4 cup butter, cubed
- 1/4 cup all-purpose flour
- 3/4 cup milk
- 1-1/4 cups 4% cottage cheese
- 1/2 teaspoon baking powder
- 1/2 teaspoon ground mustard
- 1/4 teaspoon salt
- 5 eggs
- 2 packages (3 ounces *each*) cream cheese, cubed
- 1/2 pound Jarlsberg or Swiss cheese, shredded
- 1/4 cup grated Parmesan cheese

1. In a small saucepan, melt butter. Stir in flour until smooth; gradually add milk. Bring to a boil; cook and stir for 2 minutes or until thickened and bubbly. Remove from the heat; cool for 15 minutes.

2. Meanwhile, in a small bowl, combine the cottage cheese, baking powder, mustard and salt. In a large bowl, beat eggs. Slowly beat in the cream cheese, cottage cheese mixture and white sauce until smooth. Fold in the Jarlsberg and Parmesan cheeses.

3. Pour into a greased 9-in. pie plate. Bake at 350° for 35-40 minutes or until a knife inserted near the center comes out clean. Let stand for 5 minutes before cutting. Serve quiche warm. Refrigerate any leftovers. **Yield:** 6 servings.

Puff Pancake with Blueberry Sauce

Prep/Total Time: 30 min.

Barbara Mohr, Millington, Michigan

I collect cookbooks and discovered this recipe while I was in Texas on vacation. The light and puffy pancake really does melt in your mouth! It's a definite family-pleaser.

- 2 tablespoons butter
- 2 eggs
- 1/2 cup milk
- 1/2 cup all-purpose flour
- 2 tablespoons sugar
- 1/8 teaspoon ground cinnamon

BLUEBERRY SAUCE:
- 1/4 cup packed brown sugar
- 1 tablespoon cornstarch
- 1/4 cup orange juice
- 1 cup fresh or frozen blueberries
- 1/4 teaspoon vanilla extract

1. Place butter in a 9-in. pie plate; place in a 425° oven for 4-5 minutes or until melted.

2. Meanwhile, in a small bowl, whisk eggs and milk. In another small bowl, combine the flour, sugar and cinnamon; whisk in egg mixture until smooth. Pour into prepared pie plate. Bake for 18-22 minutes or until sides are crisp and golden brown.

3. Meanwhile, in a small saucepan, combine brown sugar and cornstarch. Gradually whisk in orange juice until smooth. Stir in blueberries. Bring to a boil over medium heat, stirring constantly. Cook and stir 1-2 minutes longer or until thickened. Remove from the heat; stir in vanilla. Serve the blueberry sauce with pancake. **Yield:** 4 servings.

So-Healthy Smoothies

Prep/Total Time: 15 min.

Jessica Gerschitz, Jericho, New York

This tastes like a milk shake but comes without all the guilt or fat. My husband and I look forward to it every morning. It's so good for you and keeps you energized for hours.

    1 cup fat-free milk
  1/4 cup orange juice
    2 tablespoons vanilla yogurt
    1 tablespoon honey
    1 small banana, sliced and frozen
  2/3 cup frozen blueberries
  1/2 cup chopped peeled mango, frozen
1-1/4 cups frozen unsweetened sliced peaches

1. In a blender, combine all ingredients; cover and process until smooth. Pour into chilled glasses; serve immediately. **Yield:** 4 servings.

    1 can (11 ounces) mandarin oranges, drained
    1 teaspoon vanilla extract
    1 carton (8 ounces) frozen whipped topping, thawed
Confectioners' sugar

1. In a large bowl, beat the milk, eggs and oil. Combine the flour, sugar and salt; add to milk mixture and mix well. Cover and refrigerate for 1 hour.

2. Coat an 8-in. nonstick skillet with cooking spray; heat over medium heat. Stir crepe batter; pour 2 tablespoons into center of skillet. Lift and tilt pan to coat bottom evenly. Cook until top appears dry; turn and cook 15-20 seconds longer. Remove to a wire rack. Repeat with remaining batter, coating skillet as needed. When cool, stack crepes with waxed paper or paper towels in between.

3. For filling, in a large bowl, combine the pineapple, oranges and vanilla; fold in whipped topping. Spoon 1/3 cup down the center of each crepe; roll up. Dust with confectioners' sugar. **Yield:** 6 servings.

Sunshine Crepes

Prep: 15 min. + chilling **Cook:** 15 min.

Mary Hobbs, Campbell, Missouri

My family wanted something light and original for a family breakfast, so I whipped up these sweet and fruity crepes.

  2/3 cup milk
    2 eggs
    1 tablespoon canola oil
  1/2 cup all-purpose flour
    1 teaspoon sugar
  1/4 teaspoon salt
FILLING:
    1 can (20 ounces) crushed pineapple, drained

Busy Morning Solution

The next time you make Sunshine Crepes, make a few extra crepes for a speedy breakfast on busy mornings. Stack unfilled crepes between layers of waxed paper or white paper towel. Cool; place in an airtight container. Freeze for up to 4 months. When ready to use, simply thaw the frozen crepes overnight in the refrigerator.

Cherry Chocolate Chip Muffins

Prep: 15 min. **Bake:** 20 min.

Joanne Minke, St Petersburg, Florida

I made these yummy muffins for my husband, who considers himself a muffin expert, and he polished off four of them in one sitting. It's a good thing the recipe only makes six!

> 1 cup all-purpose flour
> 1/3 cup sugar
> 1 teaspoon baking powder
> 1/4 teaspoon salt
> 1 egg
> 1/3 cup 2% milk
> 1/4 cup canola oil
> 1 teaspoon almond extract
> 1/2 cup halved maraschino cherries
> 1/2 cup semisweet chocolate chips

1. In a small bowl, combine the flour, sugar, baking powder and salt. In another bowl, whisk the egg, milk, oil and extract. Stir into dry ingredients just until moistened. Fold in cherries and chocolate chips.

2. Fill paper-lined muffin cups three-fourths full. Bake at 350° for 20-25 minutes or until a toothpick inserted near the center comes out clean. Cool for 5 minutes before removing from pan to a wire rack. Serve warm. **Yield:** 6 muffins.

Swedish Tea Ring

Prep: 30 min. + rising **Bake:** 20 min. + cooling

 This recipe includes Nutrition Facts & Diabetic Exchanges.

> 1 tablespoon active dry yeast
> 1-1/2 cups warm water (110° to 115°)
> 1/4 cup sugar
> 1/4 cup canola oil
> 2 egg whites, lightly beaten
> 1-1/4 teaspoons salt
> 5-1/2 to 6 cups all-purpose flour
> 1/2 cup chopped walnuts
> 1/2 cup chopped maraschino cherries, patted dry
> 1/4 cup packed brown sugar
> 1 teaspoon ground cinnamon
> 2 tablespoons butter, melted
> **ICING:**
> 1 cup confectioners' sugar
> 1 to 2 tablespoons fat-free milk

1. In a large bowl, dissolve yeast in warm water. Add the sugar, oil, egg whites, salt and 1 cup flour; beat until smooth. Stir in enough remaining flour to form a soft dough.

2. Turn onto a lightly floured surface; knead until smooth, about 6-8 minutes. Place in a bowl coated with cooking spray, turning once to coat the top. Cover and let rise until doubled, about 1 hour.

3. Combine the walnuts, cherries, brown sugar and cinnamon; set aside. Punch dough down; roll into an 18-in. x 12-in. rectangle. Brush with butter; sprinkle with nut mixture to within 1/2 in. of edges. Roll up jelly-roll style, starting with a long side; pinch seam to seal.

4. Place seam side down on a 14-in. pizza pan coated with cooking spray; pinch ends together to form a ring. With scissors, cut from outside edge two-thirds of the way toward center of ring at scant 1-in. intervals. Separate strips slightly; twist to allow filling to show. Cover and let rise until doubled, about 40 minutes.

5. Bake at 400° for 20-25 minutes or until golden brown. Remove from pan to a wire rack to cool.

6. In a small bowl, combine confectioners' sugar and enough milk to achieve desired consistency; drizzle over warm tea ring. **Yield:** 1 ring (24 slices).

Nutrition Facts: 1 slice equals 196 calories, 5 g fat (1 g saturated fat), 3 mg cholesterol, 142 mg sodium, 34 g carbohydrate, 1 g fiber, 4 g protein. **Diabetic Exchanges:** 2 starch, 1 fat.

ELSIE EPP NEWTON, KANSAS

A longtime family favorite, this traditional Swedish tea ring complements any special brunch.

Egg and Sausage Strata

Prep: 15 min. + chilling Bake: 1-1/2 hours

Gail Carney, Arlington, Texas

I especially like to make this breakfast dish when we have weekend guests. I fix it the night before, and the next morning I can sit, eat and enjoy their company. People often think I spent hours preparing it.

12 slices white bread, crusts removed, cubed
1-1/2 pounds bulk pork sausage
1/3 cup chopped onion
1/4 cup chopped green pepper
1 jar (2 ounces) chopped pimientos, drained
6 eggs
3 cups milk
2 teaspoons Worcestershire sauce
1 teaspoon ground mustard
1/2 teaspoon salt
1/4 teaspoon pepper
1/4 teaspoon dried oregano

1. Line a greased 13-in. x 9-in. baking dish with bread cubes; set aside.

2. In a skillet, cook sausage with the onion and green pepper over medium heat until meat is no longer pink; drain. Stir in pimientos; sprinkle over bread.

3. In a bowl, beat eggs, milk, Worcestershire sauce, mustard, salt, pepper and oregano. Pour over sausage mixture. Cover and refrigerate overnight.

4. Cover and bake at 325° for 1 hour 20 minutes. Uncover; bake 10 minutes longer or until a knife inserted near the center comes out clean. Let stand for 10 minutes before serving. **Yield:** 12-15 servings.

Cinnamon Doughnut Muffins

Prep: 15 min. Bake: 20 min.

Sharon Pullen, Alvinston, Ontario

When my children were young, they loved these jelly-filled muffins as after-school treats. Luckily for me, it was relatively quick and easy to whip up a batch.

1-3/4 cups all-purpose flour
1-1/2 teaspoons baking powder
1/2 teaspoon salt
1/2 teaspoon ground nutmeg
1/4 teaspoon ground cinnamon
3/4 cups sugar
1/3 cup canola oil
1 egg, lightly beaten
3/4 cup milk
Jam
TOPPING:
1/4 cup butter, melted
1/3 cup sugar
1 teaspoon ground cinnamon

1. In a large bowl, combine flour, baking powder, salt, nutmeg and cinnamon. In a small bowl, combine sugar, oil, egg and milk; stir into dry ingredients just until moistened.

2. Fill greased or paper-lined muffin cups half full; place 1 teaspoon jam on top. Cover jam with enough batter to fill muffin cups three-fourths full. Bake at 350° for 20-25 minutes or until a toothpick inserted near the center of a muffin comes out clean.

3. Place melted butter in a small bowl; combine sugar and cinnamon in another bowl. Immediately after removing muffins from the oven, dip tops in butter, then in cinnamon-sugar. Serve warm. **Yield:** 10 standard-size muffins.

Delicious Potato Doughnuts

Prep: 20 min. **Cook:** 40 min.

Pat Davis, Beulah, Michigan

I first tried these tasty treats at my sister's house and thought they were better than any bakery variety. They're easy to make, and the fudge frosting tops them off well.

> 2 cups hot mashed potatoes (with added milk and butter)
> 2-1/2 cups sugar
> 2 cups buttermilk
> 2 eggs, lightly beaten
> 2 tablespoons butter, melted
> 2 teaspoons baking soda
> 2 teaspoons baking powder
> 1 teaspoon salt
> 1 teaspoon ground nutmeg
> 6-1/2 to 7 cups all-purpose flour
> Oil for deep-fat frying
> FAST FUDGE FROSTING:
> 3-3/4 cups confectioners' sugar
> 1/2 cup baking cocoa
> 1/4 teaspoon salt
> 1/3 cup boiling water
> 1/3 cup butter, melted
> 1 teaspoon vanilla extract

1. In a large bowl, combine the potatoes, sugar, buttermilk and eggs. Stir in the butter, baking soda, baking powder, salt, nutmeg and enough of the flour to form a soft dough. Turn onto a lightly floured surface; pat out to 3/4-in. thickness. Cut with a 2-1/2-in. floured doughnut cutter.

2. In an electric skillet, heat 1 in. of oil to 375°. Fry the doughnuts for 2 minutes on each side or until browned. Place on paper towels.

3. For frosting, combine the confectioners' sugar, cocoa and salt in a large bowl. Stir in the water, butter and vanilla. Dip tops of warm doughnuts in frosting. **Yield:** 4 dozen.

Ham and Potato Frittata

Prep: 10 min. **Cook:** 30 min.

Katie Dreibelbis, State College, Pennsylvania

Simple and delicious, this hearty dish is appreciated whenever I serve it…for breakfast, lunch or dinner. We love the leftovers, too, whether reheated or enjoyed cold.

> 1 pound red potatoes, cooked and sliced
> 3 tablespoons butter, *divided*
> 1-1/2 cups thinly sliced fresh mushrooms
> 1 cup thinly sliced onion
> 1 sweet red pepper, cut into thin strips
> 2 cups diced fully cooked ham
> 2 teaspoons minced fresh garlic
> 1/2 cup minced fresh parsley *or* basil
> 1 tablespoon olive oil
> 8 eggs
> Salt and pepper to taste
> 1-1/2 cups (6 ounces) shredded cheddar *or* Swiss cheese

1. In a 10-in. cast-iron or other ovenproof skillet, brown potatoes in 2 tablespoons butter over medium-high heat; remove and set aside.

2. In the same skillet, saute the mushrooms, onion, red pepper and ham in remaining butter until vegetables are tender. Add garlic; cook 1 minute longer; drain. Remove and set aside.

3. In the same skillet, cook the potatoes, ham mixture and parsley in oil over medium-high heat. In a large bowl, beat the eggs, salt and pepper. Pour into skillet; cover and cook for 10-15 minutes or until eggs are nearly set.

4. Broil 5-6 in. from the heat for 2-3 minutes or until eggs are set. Sprinkle with the cheese and broil until melted. Cut into wedges. **Yield:** 6 servings.

Fruit 'n' Nut Stollen

Prep: 40 min. + rising **Bake:** 15 min.

Rebekah Radewahn, Wauwatosa, Wisconsin

Making this stollen has become a tradition. My family, friends and neighbors look forward to it every Christmas. We like it because it doesn't contain the usual candied fruits and citron.

> 4 to 4-1/2 cups all-purpose flour
> 1/4 cup sugar
> 3 teaspoons active dry yeast
> 1 teaspoon ground cardamom
> 1/2 teaspoon salt
> 1-1/4 cups 2% milk
> 1/2 cup plus 3 tablespoons butter, softened, *divided*
> 1 egg
> 1/4 cup *each* raisins and dried cranberries
> 1/4 cup *each* chopped dried pineapple and apricots
> 1/4 cup *each* chopped pecans, almonds, Brazil nuts and walnuts
> 1/2 teaspoon lemon extract

LEMON GLAZE:
> 1 cup confectioners' sugar
> 4-1/2 teaspoons lemon juice

1. In a large bowl, combine 2 cups flour, sugar, yeast, cardamom and salt. In a small saucepan, heat milk and 1/2 cup butter to 120°-130°. Add to dry ingredients; beat just until moistened. Add egg; beat until smooth. Stir in enough remaining flour to form a soft dough (dough will be sticky).

2. Turn onto a floured surface; knead until smooth and elastic, about 6-8 minutes. Place in a bowl coated with cooking spray, turning once to coat top. Cover and let rise in a warm place until doubled, about 1 hour. In a small bowl, combine the dried fruits, nuts and extract; set aside.

3. Punch dough down. Turn onto a lightly floured surface; knead fruit mixture into dough. Divide into thirds. Roll each portion into a 10-in. x 8-in. oval. Melt remaining butter; brush over dough. Fold a long side over to within 1 in. of opposite side; press edges lightly to seal. Place on baking sheets coated with cooking spray. Cover and let rise until doubled, about 45 minutes.

4. Bake at 375° for 14-16 minutes or until golden brown. Remove to wire racks. Combine glaze ingredients; drizzle over warm loaves. **Yield:** 3 loaves (12 slices each).

Apple Pancakes with Cider Syrup

Prep/Total Time: 30 min.

April Harmon, Greeneville, Tennessee

These tender pancakes are filled with minced apple and raisin and drizzled with apple cider syrup. They're an especially wonderful way to start a new day.

- 1/2 cup all-purpose flour
- 1/4 cup whole wheat flour
- 2 teaspoons sugar
- 1/4 teaspoon baking soda
- 1/4 teaspoon salt
- 1/4 teaspoon ground cinnamon
- 2/3 cup finely chopped peeled apple
- 1/4 cup raisins
- 2/3 cup buttermilk
- 1 egg, *separated*
- 2 teaspoons butter, melted
- 1/4 teaspoon vanilla extract

SYRUP:
- 1/4 cup sugar
- 2 teaspoons cornstarch
- 2/3 cup apple cider *or* juice
- 1 cinnamon stick (1-1/2 inches)

Dash ground nutmeg
Additional butter, optional

1. In a small bowl, combine the first six ingredients; stir in apple and raisins. Combine the buttermilk, egg yolk, butter and vanilla; stir into dry ingredients. In a small bowl, beat egg white until soft peaks form; fold into batter.

2. Pour batter by heaping 1/4 cupfuls onto a hot griddle coated with cooking spray; turn when bubbles form on top. Cook until the second side is lightly browned.

3. Meanwhile, in a small saucepan, combine the sugar, cornstarch and cider until smooth; add cinnamon stick. Bring to a boil over medium heat; cook and stir for 2 minutes or until thickened. Discard cinnamon stick. Stir nutmeg into syrup. Serve pancakes with warm syrup and additional butter if desired. **Yield:** 6 pancakes (2/3 cup syrup).

Stuffed Apricot French Toast

Prep/Total Time: 25 min.

Deb Leland, Three Rivers, Michigan

While we usually enjoy this special recipe for our holiday brunch, it's welcomed any time of the year. I'm always looking for something unique to serve, and this rich, colorful dish certainly meets all requirements.

- 1 package (8 ounces) cream cheese, softened
- 1-1/2 teaspoons vanilla extract, *divided*
- 1/2 cup finely chopped walnuts
- 1 loaf (1-1/2 pounds) French bread
- 4 eggs
- 1 cup heavy whipping cream
- 1/2 teaspoon ground nutmeg
- 1 jar (12 ounces) apricot preserves
- 1/2 cup orange juice

1. In a bowl, beat cream cheese and 1 teaspoon vanilla until fluffy. Stir in nuts; set aside.

2. Cut bread into 1-1/2-in. slices; cut a pocket in the top of each slice. Fill each pocket with about 2 tablespoons cream cheese mixture. In another bowl, beat eggs, cream, nutmeg and remaining vanilla. Dip both sides of bread into egg mixture, being careful not to squeeze out the filling.

3. Cook on a lightly greased griddle until lightly browned on both sides. Place on an ungreased baking sheet; bake at 325° for 15-20 minutes or until a knife inserted near the middle comes out clean.

4. Meanwhile, combine preserves and orange juice in a small saucepan; heat through. Drizzle over hot French toast. **Yield:** 8 servings.

Mini Ham 'n' Cheese Frittatas

Prep: 15 min. **Bake:** 25 min.

Susan Watt, Basking Ridge, New Jersey

Looking for breakfast in just a few bites? Portion control is easy with these satisfying mini frittatas.

 This recipe includes Nutrition Facts & Diabetic Exchange.

> 1/4 **pound cubed fully cooked ham**
> 1 **cup (4 ounces) shredded fat-free cheddar cheese**
> 6 **eggs**
> 4 **egg whites**
> 3 **tablespoons minced chives**
> 2 **tablespoons fat-free milk**
> 1/4 **teaspoon salt**
> 1/4 **teaspoon pepper**

1. Divide ham among eight muffin cups coated with cooking spray; top with cheese. In a large bowl, beat eggs and whites. Beat in the chives, milk, salt and pepper. Pour over cheese, filling each muffin cup three-fourths full.

2. Bake at 375° for 22-25 minutes or until a knife inserted near the center comes out clean. Carefully run a knife around edges to loosen; remove from pan. Serve warm. **Yield:** 8 frittatas.

Nutrition Facts: 1 frittata equals 106 calories, 4 g fat (1 g saturated fat), 167 mg cholesterol, 428 mg sodium, 2 g carbohydrate, trace fiber, 14 g protein. **Diabetic Exchange:** 2 medium-fat meat.

Florence-Inspired Soufflé

Prep: 35 min. **Bake:** 35 min.

This recipe includes Nutrition Facts & Diabetic Exchanges.

> 6 **egg whites**
> 3/4 **cup onion and garlic salad croutons**
> 1 **small onion, finely chopped**
> 1/4 **cup finely chopped sweet red pepper**
> 2 **ounces thinly sliced prosciutto, chopped**
> 2 **teaspoons olive oil**
> 1 **garlic clove, minced**
> 2 **cups fresh baby spinach**
> 1/3 **cup all-purpose flour**
> 1/2 **teaspoon salt**
> 1/4 **teaspoon pepper**
> 1-1/4 **cups fat-free milk**
> 1 **egg yolk, lightly beaten**
> 1/4 **teaspoon cream of tartar**
> 1/4 **cup shredded Italian cheese blend**

1. Place egg whites in a large bowl; let stand at room temperature for 30 minutes.

2. In a food processor, process croutons until ground. Sprinkle the croutons evenly onto the bottom and 1 in. up the sides of a greased 2-qt. baking dish; set aside.

3. In a large saucepan, saute the onion, red pepper and prosciutto in oil for 3-5 minutes or until vegetables are crisp-tender. Add garlic; cook 1 minute longer. Add spinach; cook just until wilted. Stir in flour, salt and pepper until blended. Gradually add milk. Bring to a boil; cook and stir for 2 minutes or until thickened.

4. Transfer to a large bowl. Stir a small amount of hot mixture into egg yolk; return all to the bowl, stirring constantly. Cool slightly.

5. Add cream of tartar to egg whites; beat until stiff peaks form. Fold into vegetable mixture. Transfer to prepared dish; sprinkle with cheese.

6. Bake at 350° for 35-40 minutes or until top is puffed and center appears set. Serve immediately. **Yield:** 4 servings.

Nutrition Facts: 1 serving equals 223 calories, 9 g fat (3 g saturated fat), 73 mg cholesterol, 843 mg sodium, 20 g carbohydrate, 2 g fiber, 16 g protein. **Diabetic Exchanges:** 2 lean meat, 1-1/2 starch.

JENNY FLAKE NEWPORT BEACH, CALIFORNIA

This soufflé is not only absolutely delicious, but also light and beautiful. Your guests will be impressed every time, so grab your fork and dig into this little taste of Florence!

GRAND
PRIZE
WINNER

Waffles with Peach-Berry Compote

Prep: 25 min. **Cook:** 5 min./batch

Brandi Waters, Fayetteville, Arkansas

I created this recipe one summer Sunday morning when I was looking for a more healthful alternative to butter and maple syrup to top my waffles. I was amazed at the results!

✓ This recipe includes Nutrition Facts & Diabetic Exchanges.

1 cup chopped peeled fresh peaches *or* frozen unsweetened sliced peaches, thawed and chopped
1/2 cup orange juice
2 tablespoons brown sugar
1/4 teaspoon ground cinnamon
1 cup fresh *or* frozen blueberries
1/2 cup sliced fresh *or* frozen strawberries
BATTER:
1-1/4 cups all-purpose flour
1/2 cup whole wheat flour
2 tablespoons flaxseed
1 teaspoon baking powder
1 teaspoon baking soda
1/2 teaspoon ground cinnamon
1 cup buttermilk
3/4 cup orange juice
1 tablespoon canola oil
1 teaspoon vanilla extract

1. In a small saucepan, combine the peaches, orange juice, brown sugar and cinnamon; bring to a boil over medium heat. Add berries; cook and stir for 8-10 minutes or until thickened.

2. In a large bowl, combine the flours, flaxseed, baking powder, baking soda and cinnamon. Combine the buttermilk, orange juice, oil and vanilla; stir into dry ingredients just until moistened.

3. Bake waffles in a preheated waffle iron according to the manufacturer's directions until golden brown. Serve the waffles with peach-berry compote. **Yield:** 12 waffles (1-1/2 cups compote).

Nutrition Facts: 2 waffles with 1/4 cup compote equals 251 calories, 4 g fat (1 g saturated fat), 2 mg cholesterol, 324 mg sodium, 47 g carbohydrate, 4 g fiber, 7 g protein. **Diabetic Exchanges:** 2-1/2 starch, 1/2 fruit, 1/2 fat.

Hash Brown Quiche

Prep: 15 min. **Bake:** 50 min. + standing

Jan Peters, Chandler, Minnesota

We love to have overnight guests. When we do, it's a safe bet this dish will make an appearance the next morning. To save time, I sometimes make the hash brown crust and chop the ham, cheese and peppers the night before.

3 cups frozen loose-pack shredded hash browns, thawed
1/3 cup butter, melted
1 cup diced fully cooked ham
1 cup (4 ounces) shredded cheddar cheese
1/4 cup diced green pepper
2 eggs
1/2 cup milk
1/2 teaspoon salt
1/4 teaspoon pepper

1. Press hash browns between paper towel to remove excess moisture. Press onto the bottom and up the sides of an ungreased 9-in. pie plate. Drizzle with butter. Bake at 425° for 25 minutes.

2. Combine the ham, cheese and green pepper; spoon over crust. In a small bowl, beat eggs, milk, salt and pepper. Pour over all.

3. Reduce heat to 350°; bake for 25-30 minutes or until a knife inserted near the center comes out clean. Let the quiche stand for 10 minutes before cutting. **Yield:** 6 servings.

Christmas Morning Croissants

Prep: 50 min. + chilling **Bake:** 20 min.

Tish Stevenson, Grand Rapids, Michigan

Growing up in France, we often enjoyed buttery croissants for breakfast with steaming cups of hot chocolate. I've tried to re-create the experience for my family with this recipe, and now, it's a Christmas tradition.

- 2 packages (1/4 ounce *each*) active dry yeast
- 1 cup warm water (110° to 115°)
- 1-1/4 cups cold butter, *divided*
- 5 cups all-purpose flour
- 1/3 cup sugar
- 1-1/2 teaspoons salt
- 3/4 cup evaporated milk
- 2 eggs
- 1 tablespoon water

1. In a large bowl, dissolve yeast in warm water; let stand for 5 minutes. Melt 1/4 cup butter; set aside. Combine 1 cup flour, sugar and salt; add to yeast mixture. Add the milk, 1 egg and melted butter; beat until smooth.

2. Place remaining flour in a large bowl; cut in remaining butter until crumbly. Add the yeast mixture; mix well. Do not knead the dough. Cover dough and refrigerate overnight.

3. Punch dough down. Turn onto a lightly floured surface; knead about six times. Divide dough into four pieces. Roll each piece into a 16-in. circle; cut each circle into eight wedges.

4. Roll up wedges from the wide ends and place point side down 3 in. apart on ungreased baking sheets. Curve ends to form crescents. Cover and let rise in a warm place for 1 hour.

5. Beat water and remaining egg; brush over rolls. Bake at 325° for 20-25 minutes or until lightly browned. Serve warm. **Yield:** 32 rolls.

Breakfast Crepes with Berries

Prep/Total Time: 20 min.

Jennifer Weisbrodt, Oconomowoc, Wisconsin

After a long day of blackberry picking, I made a sauce to dress up some crepes I had on hand. This speedy dish really hit the spot and tied everything together beautifully! The crepes make an elegant addition to any brunch, and the sauce is delectable over warm waffles, too.

☑ This recipe includes Nutrition Facts & Diabetic Exchanges.

- 1-1/2 cups fresh raspberries
- 1-1/2 cups fresh blackberries
- 1 cup (8 ounces) sour cream
- 1/2 cup confectioners' sugar
- 1 carton (6 ounces) orange creme yogurt
- 1 tablespoon lime juice
- 1-1/2 teaspoons grated lime peel
- 1/2 teaspoon vanilla extract
- 1/8 teaspoon salt
- 8 prepared crepes (9 inches)

1. In a large bowl, combine raspberries and blackberries; set aside. In a small bowl, combine sour cream and confectioners' sugar until smooth. Stir in the yogurt, lime juice, lime peel, vanilla and salt.

2. Spread 2 tablespoons sour cream mixture over each crepe; top with about 1/3 cup berries. Roll up; drizzle with remaining sour cream mixture. Serve immediately. **Yield:** 8 servings.

Nutrition Facts: 1 crepe equals 182 calories, 7 g fat (4 g saturated fat), 27 mg cholesterol, 144 mg sodium, 27 g carbohydrate, 3 g fiber, 3 g protein. **Diabetic Exchanges:** 1-1/2 starch, 1-1/2 fat.

Cranberry Doughnuts

Prep/Total Time: 20 min.

Roberta Archer, Passadumkeag, Maine

During cranberry season, I always get this recipe out and make these tasty doughnuts. When my children were small, I'd usually double the recipe, and sometimes the doughnuts would all be gone before they could even cool!

        1 egg
    1/2 cup sugar
        1 tablespoon butter, melted
    1-1/2 cups all-purpose flour
        2 teaspoons baking powder
    1/2 teaspoon ground cinnamon
    1/2 teaspoon ground nutmeg
    1/4 teaspoon salt
    1/2 cup milk
    1/2 cup chopped fresh *or* frozen cranberries
Oil for deep-fat frying
Additional sugar

1. In a bowl, beat egg; add sugar and butter. Combine flour, baking powder, cinnamon, nutmeg and salt; add to sugar mixture alternately with milk. Stir in the cranberries.

2. Heat oil in an electric skillet or deep-fat fryer to 375°. Drop tablespoonfuls of batter into oil. Fry doughnuts a few at a time, turning with a slotted spoon until golden, about 2 minutes per side. Drain doughnuts on paper towels; roll in sugar while still warm. **Yield:** 1-1/2 dozen.

Garden Vegetable Quiche

Prep: 20 min. **Bake:** 40 min. + standing

Kristina Ledford, Indianapolis, Indiana

Make your next brunch special with a fluffy, deep-dish quiche. Fresh rosemary enhances this delightful egg entree that's chock-full of savory garden ingredients. It cuts nicely, too.

        1 frozen pie shell (9 inches)
        1 small red onion, sliced
    1/2 cup sliced fresh mushrooms
    1/4 cup diced yellow summer squash
        1 tablespoon butter
    1/2 cup fresh baby spinach
        3 garlic cloves, minced
        1 cup (4 ounces) shredded Swiss cheese
        4 eggs, lightly beaten
    1-2/3 cups heavy whipping cream
    1/2 teaspoon salt
    1/2 teaspoon minced fresh rosemary
    1/4 teaspoon pepper

1. Let pastry shell stand at room temperature for 10 minutes. Line unpricked pastry shell with a double thickness of heavy-duty foil. Bake at 400° for 4 minutes. Remove foil; bake 4 minutes longer. Cool on a wire rack. Reduce heat to 350°.

2. In a large skillet, saute the onion, mushrooms and squash in butter until tender. Add spinach and garlic; cook 1 minute longer. Spoon into crust; top with shredded Swiss cheese.

3. In a large bowl, whisk the eggs, cream, salt, rosemary and pepper until blended; pour over cheese.

4. Cover edges of crust loosely with foil. Bake for 40-45 minutes or until a knife inserted near the center comes out clean. Let stand for 10 minutes before cutting. **Yield:** 6-8 servings.

Check the Temperature

To avoid water on the bottom of the dish when making Garden Vegetable Quiche, use an oven thermometer to check your oven temperature before baking the pie.

Black Raspberry Bubble Ring

Prep: 35 min. + rising **Bake:** 25 min.

Kila Frank, Reedsville, Ohio

I first made this pretty bread years ago for a 4-H project. It helped me win Grand Champion for my county and took me to the Ohio State Fair. It takes some time to make, but I promise one bite is worth all the effort.

        1 package (1/4 ounce) active dry yeast
    1/4 cup warm water (110° to 115°)
        1 cup warm milk (110° to 115°)
    1/4 cup plus 2 tablespoons sugar, *divided*
    1/2 cup butter, melted, *divided*
        1 egg
        1 teaspoon salt
        4 cups all-purpose flour
        1 jar (10 ounces) seedless black raspberry
          preserves
    SYRUP:
    1/3 cup corn syrup
        2 tablespoons butter, melted
    1/2 teaspoon vanilla extract

1. In a large bowl, dissolve yeast in warm water. Add the milk, 1/4 cup sugar, 1/4 cup butter, egg, salt and 3-1/2 cups flour. Beat until smooth. Stir in enough remaining flour to form a soft dough.

2. Turn onto a floured surface; knead until smooth and elastic, about 6-8 minutes. Place in a greased bowl, turning once to grease top. Cover and let rise in a warm place until doubled, about 1-1/4 hours.

3. Punch dough down. Turn onto a lightly floured surface; divide into 32 pieces. Flatten each into a 3-in. disk. Place about 1 teaspoon of preserves on the center of each piece; bring edges together and seal.

4. Place 16 dough balls in a greased 10-in. fluted tube pan. Brush with half of the remaining butter; sprinkle with 1 tablespoon sugar. Top with remaining balls, butter and sugar. Cover and let rise until doubled, about 35 minutes.

5. Bake at 350° for 25-30 minutes or until golden brown. Combine syrup ingredients; pour over warm bread. Cool for 5 minutes before inverting onto a serving plate. **Yield:** 1 loaf.

Cranberry Surprise Muffins

Prep/Total Time: 30 min.

Helen Howley, Mount Laurel, New Jersey

This recipe has been in my family since 1943, so these muffins have been enjoyed for many years. The "surprise" is a dollop of cranberry sauce in the center of each one. My family likes to eat them warm, fresh from the oven.

        2 cups all-purpose flour
        2 tablespoons sugar
        3 teaspoons baking powder
    1/2 teaspoon salt
        2 eggs
        1 cup milk
    1/4 cup butter, melted
        1 cup jellied cranberry sauce

1. In a large bowl, combine the flour, sugar, baking powder and salt. In another bowl, whisk the eggs, milk and butter. Stir into dry ingredients just until moistened.

2. Fill 12 greased muffin cups one-fourth full. Drop a rounded tablespoonful of cranberry sauce into each cup. Top with remaining batter.

3. Bake at 400° for 12-15 minutes or until muffin tops spring back when lightly touched. Cool for 5 minutes before removing from pan to a wire rack. Serve warm. **Yield:** 1 dozen.

Editor's Note: These muffins are best served the day they're made.

Maple Walnut Rolls

Prep: 45 min. + rising **Bake:** 20 min. + cooling

Elleen Oberreuter, Danbury, Iowa

For old-fashioned flavor, you can't beat this attractive nut roll. The recipe makes four rolls, so you'll have enough to serve your family and even share some with friends!

>   6 to 7 cups all-purpose flour
>   3 tablespoons sugar
>   2 packages (1/4 ounce *each*) active dry yeast
>   1 teaspoon salt
>   1 cup (8 ounces) sour cream
>   1 cup butter, softened
>   1/2 cup water
>   3 eggs, lightly beaten
> FILLING:
>   3/4 cup butter, melted
>   1/2 cup sugar
>   3 tablespoons maple syrup
>   5 cups ground walnuts
> ICING:
>   2 cups confectioners' sugar
>   2 to 3 tablespoons milk

1. In a large bowl, combine 2 cups flour, sugar, yeast and salt. In a small saucepan, heat sour cream, butter and water to 120°-130°; add to dry ingredients. Beat on medium speed for 2 minutes. Add eggs and 1/2 cup flour; beat 2 minutes longer. Stir in enough remaining flour to form a soft dough.

2. Turn onto a floured surface; knead until smooth and elastic, about 6-8 minutes. Place in a greased bowl; turn once to grease top. Cover and let rise in a warm place until doubled, about 1-1/4 hours. Punch dough down; divide into four portions. Roll each portion into a 14-in. x 12-in. rectangle.

3. In a large bowl, combine the butter, sugar and syrup; stir in walnuts. Sprinkle 1 cup over each rectangle. Roll up, jelly-roll style, starting with a long side; pinch seam to seal. Place seam side down on greased baking sheets. Cover and let rise in a warm place until doubled, about 45 minutes.

4. Bake at 350° for 20-25 minutes or until lightly browned. Remove from pans to wire racks to cool. In a small bowl, combine confectioners' sugar and enough milk to achieve desired consistency; drizzle over rolls. **Yield:** 4 rolls (14 slices each).

Oat Pancakes

Prep/Total Time: 20 min.

Linda Hicks, Pinconning, Michigan

My daughter brought this recipe home from school one day, and we loved it. Since then, these pancakes have been a regular part of Sunday morning breakfast, served with maple syrup, flavored syrup or applesauce and a big helping of grits.

✓ This recipe includes Nutrition Facts & Diabetic Exchanges.

1 cup quick-cooking oats
1 cup all-purpose flour
2 tablespoons sugar
2 teaspoons baking powder
1 teaspoon salt
2 eggs, lightly beaten
1-1/2 cups milk
1/4 cup canola oil
1 teaspoon lemon juice

1. In a large bowl, combine the first five ingredients. Combine the eggs, milk, oil and lemon juice; add to dry ingredients and stir just until moistened.

2. Pour batter by 1/4 cupfuls onto a lightly greased hot griddle; turn when bubbles form on top of pancakes. Cook until second side is golden brown. **Yield:** 6 servings.

Nutrition Facts: 2 pancakes (prepared with skim milk) equals 241 calories, 12 g fat (0 saturated fat), 71 mg cholesterol, 581 mg sodium, 25 g carbohydrate, 0 fiber, 8 g protein. **Diabetic Exchanges:** 1-1/2 starch, 1 fat, 1/2 fat-free milk.

Raspberry-Chocolate Mini Muffins

Prep: 40 min. Bake: 10 min.

Wendy Nickel, Kiester, Minnesota

These delicious little bites have a scrumptious surprise inside: a sweet raspberry jam filling. They're easy to make, fast to bake…and oh, so good! My husband ate almost an entire pan of these tasty morsels one time.

2 tablespoons baking cocoa
1/4 cup boiling water
1/4 cup butter, softened

1/3 cup sugar
1 egg
2/3 cup all-purpose flour
1/2 teaspoon baking powder
4 teaspoons seedless raspberry jam
2 tablespoons chopped sliced almonds
1 teaspoon coarse sugar

1. Dissolve cocoa in water; let stand until cool. Meanwhile, in a small bowl, cream butter and sugar until light and fluffy. Beat in egg. Combine flour and baking powder; add to the creamed mixture alternately with cocoa mixture.

2. Fill paper-lined miniature muffin cups half full. Drop 1/4 teaspoon of jam into the center of each; cover with 2 teaspoons batter. Sprinkle with the almonds and sugar.

3. Bake at 350° for 10-12 minutes or until a toothpick inserted in the chocolate portion comes out clean. Cool for 5 minutes before removing from pans to a wire rack. Serve warm. **Yield:** 16 muffins.

Mix It Up…But Not Too Much

Be careful not to overmix muffin ingredients. Overmixing can cause muffins to "peak" or form pointy tops and become tough. Leaving a few lumps in the batter is just fine.

PG. 93

PG. 86

PG. 104

BEEF & POULTRY ENTREES

Dinner is ready! And thanks to winners of our Southwestern, slow cooker and lasagna contests, there are plenty of meal-in-one sensations to tempt your entire family—any night of the week!

PG. 103

1 tablespoon minced fresh parsley
6 lasagna noodles, cooked and drained
2 cups (8 ounces) shredded white cheddar cheese
3 teaspoons Italian seasoning, *divided*
2 cups (8 ounces) shredded part-skim mozzarella cheese

1. In a large skillet, cook the beef, sausage, green pepper and onion over medium heat until meat is no longer pink; drain. Set aside 1 cup spaghetti sauce; stir the remaining sauce into the meat mixture. Simmer, uncovered, for 10 minutes or until thickened.

2. In a small saucepan, melt cream cheese over medium heat. Remove from the heat. Stir in cottage cheese, eggs and parsley.

3. Spread the meat sauce in a greased 13-in. x 9-in. baking dish. Top with three noodles, cheddar cheese, 1-1/2 teaspoons Italian seasoning and cream cheese mixture. Layer with remaining noodles and reserved spaghetti sauce; sprinkle with mozzarella and remaining Italian seasoning.

4. Cover and bake at 350° for 35 minutes. Uncover; bake 10-15 minutes more or until bubbly. Let stand 15 minutes before serving. **Yield:** 12 servings.

Beef 'n' Sausage Lasagna

Prep: 45 min. **Bake:** 45 min. + standing

Eydee Bernier, Louisville, Kentucky

Here's a traditional lasagna with a dash of imagination. I make it unique by using cream cheese and white cheddar. The layering is a little unusual, too, with meat on the bottom and the cheese on top.

1 pound ground beef
1 pound bulk Italian sausage
1 medium green pepper, chopped
1 medium onion, chopped
1 jar (26 ounces) spaghetti sauce
1 package (8 ounces) cream cheese, cubed
1 cup (8 ounces) 4% cottage cheese
2 eggs, lightly beaten

Pastry Blender: Not Just for Pies

When browning ground beef or other ground meat, try using a pastry blender to break up larger pieces of meat shortly before it is completely cooked. This handy trick makes the meat much more suitable for chili, stews, soups and casseroles.

Easy Chicken Potpie

Prep/Total Time: 30 min.

1 medium onion, chopped
2 tablespoons canola oil
1/2 cup all-purpose flour
1 teaspoon poultry seasoning
1 can (14-1/2 ounces) chicken broth
3/4 cup 2% milk
3 cups cubed cooked chicken
2 cups frozen mixed vegetables, thawed
1 sheet refrigerated pie pastry

1. In a large saucepan, saute onion in oil until tender. Stir in flour and poultry seasoning until blended; gradually add broth and milk. Bring to a boil; cook and stir for 2 minutes or until thickened. Add chicken and vegetables.

2. Transfer to a greased 9-in. deep-dish pie plate. Top with pastry. Trim, seal and flute edges. Cut slits in pastry. Bake potpie at 450° for 15-20 minutes or until the crust is golden brown and the filling is bubbly. **Yield:** 6 servings.

AMY BRIGGS GOVE, KANSAS

Why look for potpies in the frozen food aisle when this easy, homemade version tastes much better? Under its golden-brown crust, you'll find the ultimate comfort food for kids and adults.

GRAND PRIZE WINNER

Biscuit-Topped Lemon Chicken

Prep: 40 min. **Bake:** 35 min.

Pattie Ishee, Stringer, Mississippi

This homestyle recipe combines two of my favorite things—hot, tender biscuits and a flavorful lemon-pepper sauce.

     2 large onions, finely chopped
     4 celery ribs, finely chopped
     1 cup butter, cubed
     2 garlic cloves, minced
     8 green onions, thinly sliced
  2/3 cup all-purpose flour
     8 cups 2% milk
    12 cups cubed cooked chicken
     2 cans (10-3/4 ounces *each*) condensed cream
        of chicken soup, undiluted
  1/2 cup lemon juice
     2 tablespoons grated lemon peel
     2 teaspoons pepper
     1 teaspoon salt
CHEDDAR BISCUITS:
     5 cups self-rising flour
     2 cups 2% milk
     2 cups (8 ounces) shredded cheddar cheese
  1/4 cup butter, melted

1. In a Dutch oven, saute onions and celery in butter. Add garlic; cook 1 minute longer. Add green onions. Stir in flour until blended; gradually add milk. Bring to a boil. Cook; stir for 2 minutes or until thickened.

2. Stir in the chicken, soup, lemon juice and peel, pepper and salt; heat through. Pour into two greased 13-in. x 9-in. baking dishes; set aside.

3. In a large bowl, combine biscuit ingredients just until moistened. Turn onto a lightly floured surface; knead 8-10 times. Roll out to 3/4-in. thickness. With a floured 2-1/2-in. biscuit cutter, cut out 30 biscuits.

4. Place over chicken mixture. Bake, uncovered, at 350° for 35-40 minutes or until golden brown. **Yield:** 15 servings (30 biscuits).

Editor's Note: As a substitute for each cup of self-rising flour, place 1-1/2 teaspoons baking powder and 1/2 teaspoon salt in a measuring cup. Add all-purpose flour to measure 1 cup.

Zippy Spaghetti Sauce

Prep: 20 min. **Cook:** 6 hours

Elaine Priest, Dover, Pennsylvania

This thick and hearty sauce goes a long way to fill a hungry family! Any leftovers they can enjoy another day ladled over grilled slices of garlic bread. To make sure I have the ingredients on hand, I keep a bag of chopped green pepper in my freezer and minced garlic in my fridge.

✓ | This recipe includes Nutrition Facts.

2 pounds ground beef
1 cup chopped onion
1/2 cup chopped green pepper
2 cans (15 ounces *each*) tomato sauce
1 can (28 ounces) diced tomatoes, undrained
1 can (12 ounces) tomato paste
1/2 pound sliced fresh mushrooms
1 cup grated Parmesan cheese
1/2 to 3/4 cup dry red wine *or* beef broth
1/2 cup sliced pimiento-stuffed olives
1/4 cup dried parsley flakes
1 to 2 tablespoons dried oregano
2 teaspoons Italian seasoning
2 teaspoons minced garlic
1 teaspoon salt
1 teaspoon pepper
Hot cooked spaghetti

1. In a large skillet, cook the ground beef, onion and green pepper over medium heat until meat is no longer pink; drain.

2. Transfer to a 5-qt. slow cooker. Stir in the tomato sauce, tomatoes, tomato paste, mushrooms, cheese, wine, olives, parsley, oregano, Italian seasoning, garlic, salt and pepper. Cover and cook on low for 6-8 hours. Serve with spaghetti. **Yield:** about 3 quarts.

Nutrition Facts: 1 cup equals 212 calories, 9 g fat (4 g saturated fat), 39 mg cholesterol, 704 mg sodium, 14 g carbohydrate, 4 g fiber, 18 g protein.

Brisket in a Bag

Prep: 15 min. **Bake:** 2-1/2 hours

Peggy Stigers, Fort Worth, Texas

A savory cranberry gravy is the perfect complement to this tender brisket that's made right in the bag. You'll want to serve the slices with mashed potatoes just so you can drizzle some of that gravy over them!

3 tablespoons all-purpose flour, *divided*
1 large oven roasting bag
1 fresh beef brisket (5 pounds), trimmed
1 can (14 ounces) whole-berry cranberry sauce
1 can (10-3/4 ounces) condensed cream of mushroom soup, undiluted
1 can (8 ounces) tomato sauce
1 envelope onion soup mix

1. Place 1 tablespoon flour in oven bag; shake to coat. Place bag in an ungreased 13-in. x 9-in. baking pan; place brisket in bag.

2. Combine the cranberry sauce, soup, tomato sauce, soup mix and remaining flour; pour over beef. Seal bag. Cut slits in top of bag according to package directions.

3. Bake at 325° for 2-1/2 to 3 hours or until meat is tender. Carefully remove brisket from bag. Let stand 5 minutes before slicing. Thinly slice meat across the grain; serve with gravy. **Yield:** 12 servings.

Editor's Note: This recipe calls for a fresh beef brisket, not corned beef.

Chicken & Corn Bread Bake

Prep: 25 min. Bake: 25 min.

Ann Hillmeyer, Sandia Park, New Mexico

Southern comfort food at its best! That's how I'd describe this creamy casserole. It's often on the menu when I cook for my husband, our four children, their spouses and our 10 grandkids. Be sure to check out the two handy variations, too.

2-1/2 cups reduced-sodium chicken broth
1 small onion, chopped
1 celery rib, chopped
1/8 teaspoon pepper
4-1/2 cups corn bread stuffing mix, *divided*
4 cups cubed cooked chicken
1-1/2 cups (12 ounces) sour cream
1 can (10-3/4 ounces) condensed cream of chicken soup, undiluted
3 green onions, thinly sliced
1/4 cup butter, cubed

1. In a large saucepan, combine the broth, onion, celery and pepper. Bring to a boil. Reduce heat; cover and simmer for 5-6 minutes or until vegetables are tender. Stir in 4 cups stuffing mix.

2. Transfer to a greased 13-in. x 9-in. baking dish. Top with chicken. In a small bowl, combine the sour cream, soup and green onions. Spread over the chicken. Sprinkle with the remaining stuffing mix and dot with butter.

3. Bake, uncovered, for 325° for 25-30 minutes or until heated through. **Yield:** 8 servings.

Chicken Broccoli Stuffing Bake: Top chicken with 1-1/4 cups thawed frozen broccoli florets before covering with soup mixture. Proceed as directed.

Double Corn Chicken Stuffing Bake: Top chicken with 2 cups thawed frozen corn before covering it with the soup mixture. Proceed as directed.

Onion-Beef Muffin Cups

Prep: 25 min. Bake: 15 min.

3 medium onions, thinly sliced
1/4 cup butter, cubed
1 beef top sirloin steak (1-inch thick and 6 ounces), cut into 1/8-inch slices
1 teaspoon all-purpose flour
1 teaspoon brown sugar
1/4 teaspoon salt
1/2 cup beef broth
1 tube (16.3 ounces) large refrigerated flaky biscuits
3/4 cup shredded part-skim mozzarella cheese
1/3 cup grated Parmesan cheese, *divided*

1. In a large skillet, cook onions in butter over medium heat for 10-12 minutes or until very tender. Remove and keep warm. In the same skillet, cook steak for 2-3 minutes or until no longer pink.

2. Return onions to pan. Stir in the flour, brown sugar and salt until blended; gradually add broth. Bring to a boil; cook and stir for 4-6 minutes or until thickened.

3. Separate biscuits; split each horizontally into three portions. Press onto the bottom and up the sides of eight ungreased muffin cups, overlapping the sides and tops. Fill each with about 2 tablespoons beef mixture.

4. Combine mozzarella cheese and 1/4 cup Parmesan cheese; sprinkle over filling. Fold dough over completely to enclose filling. Sprinkle with remaining Parmesan cheese.

5. Bake at 375° for 12-15 minutes or until golden brown. Let stand for 2 minutes before removing from pan. Serve warm. **Yield:** 4 servings.

BARBARA CARLUCCI ORANGE PARK, FLORIDA

A tube of refrigerated biscuits makes these delicious bites so quick and easy! They're one of my tried-and-true lunch favorites. I usually double the recipe just to be sure I have leftovers.

GRAND
PRIZE
WINNER

Beef Potpie

Prep: 30 min. **Bake:** 45 min. + standing

Lucile Cline, Wichita, Kansas

I discovered this deliciously different way to put leftover roast beef to use. Grated onion adds a nice flavor to the pie crust.

1/4 cup *each* chopped onion, green pepper and
    sweet red pepper
1 tablespoon canola oil
2 garlic cloves, minced
3 cups cubed cooked roast beef
2 cups frozen cubed hash brown potatoes
1 can (10-3/4 ounces) condensed cream of
    mushroom soup, undiluted
1 package (10 ounces) frozen corn
1 jar (4-1/2 ounces) sliced mushrooms, drained
1 teaspoon Worcestershire sauce
1/8 teaspoon salt
Dash pepper
ONION PASTRY:
2-1/2 cups all-purpose flour
1-1/4 teaspoons salt
1 cup butter-flavored shortening
4 teaspoons grated onion
4 to 5 tablespoons cold water

1. In a large skillet, saute onion and peppers in oil for 3 minutes. Add garlic; cook 1 minute longer. Stir in the roast beef, hash brown potatoes, soup, corn, mushrooms, Worcestershire sauce, salt and pepper. Bring to a boil. Reduce the heat; cover and simmer for 10 minutes.

2. For pastry, combine flour and salt in a large bowl. Cut in shortening until crumbly; sprinkle with onion. Gradually add water, tossing with a fork until dough forms a ball.

3. Divide dough in half so that one ball is slightly larger than the other. On a lightly floured surface, roll out larger ball to fit a 9-in. deep-dish pie plate.

4. Transfer the pastry to the pie plate; trim even with edge. Add filling. Roll out remaining pastry to fit top of pie; place over filling. Trim, seal and flute edges. Cut slits in top.

5. Bake at 375° for 45-50 minutes or until filling is bubbly and crust is golden brown. Let stand for 15 minutes before cutting. **Yield:** 8 servings.

Spiral Pepperoni Pizza Bake

Prep: 30 min. **Bake:** 40 min.

Kimberly Howland, Fremont, Michigan

My grandmother used to fix this yummy dish for my Girl Scout troop when I was growing up. Now, I make it for my stepdaughters' scout troop. It's easy to prepare, and the girls always beg me to make it.

- 1 package (16 ounces) spiral pasta
- 2 pounds ground beef
- 1 large onion, chopped
- 1 teaspoon salt
- 1/2 teaspoon pepper
- 2 cans (15 ounces *each*) pizza sauce
- 1/2 teaspoon garlic salt
- 1/2 teaspoon Italian seasoning
- 2 eggs
- 2 cups milk
- 1/2 cup shredded Parmesan cheese
- 4 cups (16 ounces) shredded part-skim mozzarella cheese
- 1 package (3-1/2 ounces) sliced pepperoni

1. Cook pasta according to package directions. Meanwhile, in a Dutch oven, cook ground beef, onion,

salt and pepper over medium heat until meat is no longer pink; drain. Stir in pizza sauce, garlic salt and Italian seasoning; remove from the heat and set aside.

2. In a small bowl, combine the eggs, milk and Parmesan cheese. Drain pasta; toss with egg mixture. Transfer to a greased 3-qt. baking dish. Top with beef mixture, mozzarella cheese and pepperoni.

3. Cover and bake at 350° for 20 minutes. Uncover and bake 20-25 minutes longer or until golden brown. **Yield:** 12 servings.

Tex-Mex Lasagna

Prep: 20 min. **Bake:** 45 min. + standing

Athena Russell, Florence, South Carolina

This recipe satisfies both my love of lasagna and my love of Mexican food. I tried to make the recipe healthier by using extra-lean ground beef, and I increased the fiber by adding two varieties of beans.

- 1 pound lean ground beef (90% lean)
- 1 can (16 ounces) refried black beans
- 1 can (15 ounces) black beans, rinsed and drained
- 1/2 cup frozen corn, thawed
- 1 jalapeno pepper, seeded and chopped
- 1 envelope taco seasoning
- 1 can (15 ounces) tomato sauce, *divided*
- 2-1/2 cups salsa
- 12 no-cook lasagna noodles
- 1-1/2 cups (6 ounces) shredded reduced-fat Monterey Jack cheese *or* Mexican cheese blend, *divided*
- 1-1/2 cups (6 ounces) shredded reduced-fat cheddar cheese, *divided*
- 1 cup (8 ounces) fat-free sour cream
- 1 medium ripe avocado, peeled and cubed
- 4 green onions, thinly sliced

1. In a large nonstick skillet, cook beef over medium heat until no longer pink; drain. Stir in beans, corn, jalapeno, taco seasoning and 3/4 cup tomato sauce.

2. Combine salsa and remaining tomato sauce. Spread 1/4 cup into a 13-in. x 9-in. baking dish coated with cooking spray. Layer with four noodles (noodles will overlap slightly), half of the meat sauce, 1 cup salsa mixture, 1/2 cup Monterey Jack cheese and 1/2 cup cheddar cheese. Repeat layers. Top with the remaining noodles, salsa mixture and cheeses.

3. Cover and bake at 350° for 45-50 minutes or until edges are bubbly and cheese is melted. Let stand for 10 minutes before cutting. Serve with sour cream, avocado and onions. **Yield:** 12 servings.

Editor's Note: Wear disposable gloves when cutting hot peppers; the oils can burn skin. Avoid touching your face.

Chicken with Mushroom Gravy

Prep: 10 min. **Cook:** 4-1/4 hours

Darolyn Jones, Fishers, Indiana

Looking for a comforting dish to serve family and friends? Look no further. A friend shared the recipe for this homey chicken main dish, which I adapted by adding a few new ingredients. I like to pour it over mashed potatoes or rice.

- 4 boneless skinless chicken breast halves (6 ounces *each*)
- 1 can (12 ounces) mushroom gravy
- 1 cup 2% milk
- 1 can (8 ounces) mushroom stems and pieces, drained
- 1 can (4 ounces) chopped green chilies
- 1 envelope Italian salad dressing mix
- 1 package (8 ounces) cream cheese, cubed

1. In a 3-qt. slow cooker, combine the chicken, gravy, milk, mushrooms, chilies and dressing mix. Cover and cook on low for 4-5 hours or until chicken is tender.

2. Stir in cream cheese; cover and cook 15 minutes longer or until cheese is melted. **Yield:** 4 servings.

Mexican Lasagna

Prep: 25 min. **Bake:** 40 min. + standing

Tina Newhauser, Peterborough, New Hampshire

Tortillas replace lasagna noodles in this beefy casserole with a south-of-the-border twist. With salsa, enchilada sauce, chilies, cheese and refried beans, it's a fiesta of flavors!

- 1-1/4 pounds ground beef
- 1 medium onion, chopped
- 4 garlic cloves, minced
- 2 cups salsa
- 1 can (16 ounces) refried beans
- 1 can (15 ounces) black beans, rinsed and drained
- 1 can (10 ounces) enchilada sauce
- 1 can (4 ounces) chopped green chilies
- 1 envelope taco seasoning
- 1/4 teaspoon pepper
- 6 flour tortillas (10 inches)
- 3 cups (12 ounces) shredded Mexican cheese blend, *divided*
- 2 cups crushed tortilla chips

Sliced ripe olives, guacamole, chopped tomatoes and sour cream, optional

1. In a large skillet, cook beef and onion over medium heat until meat is no longer pink. Add garlic; cook 1 minute longer. Drain. Stir in the salsa, beans, enchilada sauce, chilies, taco seasoning and pepper; heat through.

2. Spread 1 cup meat mixture in a greased 13-in. x 9-in. baking dish. Layer with two tortillas, a third of the remaining meat mixture and 1 cup cheese. Repeat layers. Top with remaining tortillas and meat mixture.

3. Cover and bake at 375° for 30 minutes. Uncover and sprinkle with remaining cheese and top with tortilla chips.

4. Bake 10-15 minutes longer or until cheese is melted. Let stand for 10 minutes before serving. Garnish with olives, guacamole, tomatoes and sour cream if desired. **Yield:** 12 servings.

Beef Burgundy

Prep: 10 min. **Cook:** 5-1/2 hours

Mary Jo Miller, Mansfield, Ohio

When I plan to make this dish, I trim the meat, cut up the vegetables and store them in separate containers the night before. The next day, I toss all of the ingredients into the slow cooker. Shortly before dinnertime, I cook the noodles and bake some cheesy garlic toast to complete the meal.

 This recipe includes Nutrition Facts.

1-1/2 pounds beef stew meat, cut into 1-inch cubes
  1/2 pound whole fresh mushrooms, halved
    4 medium carrots, chopped
    1 can (10-3/4 ounces) condensed golden mushroom soup, undiluted
    1 large onion, cut into thin wedges
  1/2 cup Burgundy wine *or* beef broth
  1/4 cup quick-cooking tapioca
  1/2 teaspoon salt
  1/4 teaspoon dried thyme
  1/4 teaspoon pepper
Hot cooked egg noodles

1. In a 5-qt. slow cooker, combine the first 10 ingredients.

2. Cover and cook on low for 5-6 hours or until meat is tender. Serve with noodles. **Yield:** 6 servings.

Nutrition Facts: 1 cup equals 273 calories, 9 g fat (3 g saturated fat), 73 mg cholesterol, 642 mg sodium, 19 g carbohydrate, 3 g fiber, 24 g protein.

Chipotle-Apple Chicken Breasts

Prep: 25 min. **Bake:** 15 min.

Shannon Abdollmohammadi, Woodinville, Washington

The sweetness of the apple, the smokiness of the bacon and the heat from the chipotle pepper blends so well together in this delicious entree. It's my husband's favorite.

 This recipe includes Nutrition Facts & Diabetic Exchanges.

  2 bacon strips, diced
  1 small tart apple, peeled and coarsely chopped
  2 tablespoons dried minced onion
  2 tablespoons unsweetened applesauce
1/2 to 1 teaspoon chipotle peppers in adobo sauce, chopped
  2 boneless skinless chicken breast halves (6 ounces *each*)
  2 teaspoons olive oil
  1 teaspoon all-purpose flour
1/2 cup unsweetened apple juice
1/4 teaspoon salt
1/8 teaspoon pepper

1. In a small skillet, cook bacon over medium heat until crisp. Using a slotted spoon, remove to paper towels; drain, reserving 1 teaspoon drippings. Saute apple in drippings until tender. Add onion, applesauce, chipotle peppers and bacon; saute 2 minutes longer.

2. Cut a pocket in each chicken breast half; stuff with apple mixture. In a small skillet, brown chicken in oil on both sides.

3. Transfer to an ungreased 8-in. square baking dish. Bake, uncovered, at 425° for 12-15 minutes or until a meat thermometer reads 170°.

4. Meanwhile, add flour, juice, salt and pepper to skillet; stir to loosen browned bits. Bring to a boil. Cook and stir for 2 minutes or until thickened. Serve with chicken. **Yield:** 2 servings.

Nutrition Facts: 1 stuffed chicken breast half with 3 tablespoons sauce equals 335 calories, 12 g fat (3 g saturated fat), 99 mg cholesterol, 489 mg sodium, 19 g carbohydrate, 1 g fiber, 37 g protein. **Diabetic Exchanges:** 5 lean meat, 1-1/2 fat, 1 fruit.

Spiced Chicken With Melon Salsa

Prep: 20 min. **Grill:** 15 min.

Roxanne Chan, Albany, California

Both sweet and spicy, this summery chicken entree can be grilled or broiled. Not only is it delicious, but it packs a punch of nutrition, too. To speed up preparation, I buy a container of mixed melon pieces at the supermarket.

1/4 teaspoon salt
1/4 teaspoon ground ginger
1/4 teaspoon ground nutmeg
1/8 to 1/4 teaspoon crushed red pepper flakes
2 boneless skinless chicken breast halves
(5 ounces *each*)
SALSA:
1/3 cup *each* diced cantaloupe, honeydew and watermelon
2 tablespoons diced celery
1 green onion, finely chopped
2 teaspoons minced fresh mint *or* 1/4 teaspoon dried mint
2 teaspoons chopped crystallized ginger
2 teaspoons lime juice
2 teaspoons honey
1/4 teaspoon grated lime peel

1. In a small bowl, combine the salt, ginger, nutmeg and pepper flakes; rub over chicken. Grill, covered, over medium heat or broil 6 in. from the heat for 6 minutes on each side or until a meat thermometer reads 170°.

2. Meanwhile, in a small bowl, combine the salsa ingredients. Serve with chicken. **Yield:** 2 servings.

Pecan Chicken with Chutney

Prep: 15 min. **Cook:** 20 min.

Carisa Bravoco, Furlong, Pennsylvania

Easy-fix peach chutney adds a delightful sweet-sour flavor to these zippy and tender pecan-crusted chicken breasts. I usually serve them with a side of hot, fluffy rice.

3/4 cup all-purpose flour
1/8 teaspoon salt
1/8 teaspoon pepper
2 eggs
1/3 cup buttermilk
1/8 teaspoon hot pepper sauce
1 cup finely chopped pecans
3/4 cup dry bread crumbs
6 boneless skinless chicken breast halves
(6 ounces *each*)
2 tablespoons butter
2 tablespoons canola oil
PEACH MANGO CHUTNEY:
2 cups sliced peeled fresh *or* frozen peaches, thawed
1 cup mango chutney

1. In a shallow bowl, combine the flour, salt and pepper. In another shallow bowl, whisk the eggs, buttermilk and hot pepper sauce. In a third bowl, combine pecans and bread crumbs.

2. Flatten chicken to 1/4-in. thickness. Coat chicken with flour mixture, then dip in egg mixture and coat with pecan mixture.

3. In a large skillet over medium heat, cook chicken in butter and oil for 8-10 minutes on each side or until a meat thermometer reads 170°.

4. Meanwhile, in a small saucepan, combine the peaches and chutney. Bring to a boil. Reduce heat; simmer, uncovered, for 15-20 minutes or until heated through. Serve chutney with chicken. **Yield:** 6 servings (1-3/4 cups chutney).

Chicken Chorizo Lasagna

Prep: 40 min. **Bake:** 55 min. + standing

Kari Wheaton, South Beloit, Illinois

The combination of roasted chicken and chorizo is so good, you just have to try this lasagna at your next Mexican-themed meal. The avocado-lime cream adds a refreshing touch of coolness to offset the recipe's heat.

    1 **package (15 ounces) chorizo**
1/4 **cup chopped seeded jalapeno peppers**
    1 **rotisserie chicken**
    2 **eggs, lightly beaten**
    1 **carton (15 ounces) ricotta cheese**
    4 **cans (10 ounces *each*) enchilada sauce**
  12 **no-cook lasagna noodles**
    4 **cups (16 ounces) shredded Monterey Jack cheese**
1/2 **cup minced fresh cilantro**
AVOCADO CREAM SAUCE:
    2 **medium ripe avocados, peeled, pitted and halved**
1/4 **cup sour cream**

    2 **tablespoons lime juice**
1/4 **teaspoon salt**

1. Crumble chorizo into a large skillet; add jalapenos. Cook over medium heat for 6-8 minutes or until meat is fully cooked; drain. Shred chicken; add to skillet. In a bowl, combine eggs and ricotta.

2. Spread 1 cup enchilada sauce in a greased 13-in. x 9-in. baking dish. Top with four noodles, a third of the ricotta mixture, half of the meat mixture, 1 cup Monterey Jack and 1 cup enchilada sauce. Repeat layers. Top with remaining noodles, ricotta mixture, enchilada sauce and Monterey Jack.

3. Cover and bake at 375° for 45-50 minutes. Uncover; bake 10 minutes longer or until bubbly. Sprinkle with cilantro. Let stand 15 minutes before serving.

4. Meanwhile, place sauce ingredients in a food processor; cover and process until smooth. Serve with lasagna. **Yield:** 12 servings.

Editor's Note: Wear disposable gloves when cutting hot peppers; the oils can burn skin. Avoid touching your face.

Skillet Tacos

Prep/Total Time: 30 min.

Maria Gobel, Greenfield, Wisconsin

If you like Mexican food and no-fuss meal preparation, you'll be whipping up these fast, healthy skillet tacos often.

 This recipe includes Nutrition Facts & Diabetic Exchanges.

1/4 pound lean ground turkey
2 tablespoons chopped onion
2 tablespoons chopped green pepper
1 can (8 ounces) tomato sauce
1/2 cup uncooked elbow macaroni
1/2 cup water
1/4 cup picante sauce
2 tablespoons shredded fat-free cheddar cheese
1/4 cup crushed baked tortilla chip scoops
1/4 cup chopped avocado
Iceberg lettuce wedges and fat-free sour cream, optional

1. In a large nonstick skillet coated with cooking spray, cook the turkey, onion and green pepper over medium heat until turkey is no longer pink.

2. Stir in the tomato sauce, elbow macaroni, water and picante sauce. Bring to a boil. Reduce heat; cover and simmer for 10-15 minutes or until the macaroni is tender.

3. Divide between two plates; top with cheese, tortilla chips and avocado. Serve with lettuce and sour cream if desired. **Yield:** 2 servings.

Nutrition Facts: 1 serving (calculated without lettuce and sour cream) equals 267 calories, 9 g fat (2 g saturated fat), 46 mg cholesterol, 795 mg sodium, 30 g carbohydrate, 3 g fiber, 18 g protein. **Diabetic Exchanges:** 2 lean meat, 1-1/2 starch, 1 vegetable, 1/2 fat.

Italian Sausage And Vegetables

Prep: 20 min. **Cook:** 5-1/2 hours

Ginny Stuby, Altoona, Pennsylvania

This easy and complete meal-in-a-pot is both healthful and delicious. It's wonderful served with a slice of Italian bread.

1-1/4 pounds sweet or hot Italian turkey sausage links
1 can (28 ounces) diced tomatoes, undrained
2 medium potatoes, cut into 1-inch pieces
4 small zucchini, cut into 1-inch slices
1 medium onion, cut into wedges
1/2 teaspoon garlic powder
1/4 teaspoon crushed red pepper flakes
1/4 teaspoon dried oregano
1/4 teaspoon dried basil
1 tablespoon dry bread crumbs
3/4 cup shredded pepper Jack cheese

1. In a nonstick skillet, cook sausages over medium heat until no longer pink; drain. Place in a 5-qt. slow cooker. Add vegetables and seasonings. Cover; cook on low for 5-1/2 to 6-1/2 hours.

2. Remove sausages and cut into 1-in. pieces; return to slow cooker. Stir in bread crumbs. Serve in bowls; sprinkle with cheese. **Yield:** 6 servings.

Roasted Pepper Chicken Penne

Prep/Total Time: 30 min.

Regina Cowles, Boulder, Colorado

My husband calls me an "aerobic cook" because I make this Italian dish in just 30 minutes. But no one will accuse you of cutting corners. It tastes like it's been simmering for hours.

- 1 pound boneless skinless chicken breasts, cut into 1-inch strips
- 1/4 cup balsamic vinegar
- 1 package (16 ounces) penne pasta
- 1 medium onion, sliced
- 3 garlic cloves, sliced
- 1/4 cup olive oil
- 1 can (28 ounces) crushed tomatoes
- 1 cup julienned roasted sweet red peppers
- 1 cup chicken broth
- 3 teaspoons Italian seasoning
- 1/4 teaspoon salt
- 1 cup shredded Parmesan cheese

1. Place chicken in a large resealable plastic bag; add balsamic vinegar. Seal the bag and turn to coat; refrigerate for 15 minutes.

2. Cook pasta according to package directions. Meanwhile, in a large skillet, saute onion and garlic in oil for 1 minute. Drain and discard vinegar. Add chicken to skillet; cook for 4-5 minutes or until the meat is no longer pink.

3. Stir in the tomatoes, red peppers, broth, Italian seasoning and salt. Bring to a boil over medium heat; cook and stir for 4-5 minutes or until heated through. Drain pasta; toss with chicken mixture. Sprinkle with cheese. **Yield:** 8 servings.

Fontina-Fruit Chicken Breasts

Prep: 30 min. + marinating **Grill:** 10 min.

Lily Julow, Gainesville, Florida

This is one of my favorite chicken dishes, festive enough for a special occasion but not loaded with fat and sugar.

> ✓ This recipe includes Nutrition Facts.

- 1/3 cup olive oil
- 3 tablespoons cider vinegar
- 2 tablespoons red wine vinegar
- 2 teaspoons honey
- 1 teaspoon Dijon mustard
- 1/2 teaspoon ground mustard

- 8 boneless skinless chicken breast halves (4 ounces *each*)
- 1 large tart apple, peeled and chopped
- 1 teaspoon butter
- 1/2 cup shredded fontina cheese
- 1/2 cup dried cherries, coarsely chopped
- 1/2 teaspoon salt
- 1/2 teaspoon pepper

1. In a large resealable plastic bag, combine the first six ingredients. Carefully cut a pocket in each chicken breast half; place in bag. Seal; turn to coat. Refrigerate for 1 hour.

2. In a small nonstick skillet, saute apple in butter until tender. Transfer to a small bowl. Stir in the cheese, cherries, salt and pepper. Drain chicken, discarding marinade; stuff with apple mixture. Secure with soaked toothpicks.

3. Using long-handled tongs, moisten a paper towel with cooking oil and lightly coat the grill rack. Grill the chicken, covered, over medium heat or broil 4 in. from the heat for 5-8 minutes on each side or until a meat thermometer reads 170°. Discard toothpicks. **Yield:** 8 servings.

Nutrition Facts: 1 stuffed chicken breast half equals 247 calories, 11 g fat (3 g saturated fat), 72 mg cholesterol, 274 mg sodium, 11 g carbohydrate, 1 g fiber, 25 g protein.

Melt-in-Your-Mouth Pot Roast

Prep: 10 min. **Cook:** 6 hours

Jeannie Klugh, Lancaster, Pennsylvania

Slow-simmered and seasoned with rosemary, mustard and thyme, this tender and tasty pot roast is so easy to make and always well received. Substitute burgundy or brandy plus a half cup of water for the broth—the aroma is heavenly!

> 1 pound medium red potatoes, quartered
> 1 cup fresh baby carrots
> 1 boneless beef chuck roast (3 to 4 pounds)
> 1/4 cup Dijon mustard
> 2 teaspoons dried rosemary, crushed
> 1 teaspoon garlic salt
> 1/2 teaspoon dried thyme
> 1/2 teaspoon pepper
> 1/3 cup chopped onion
> 1-1/2 cups beef broth

1. Place potatoes and carrots in a 5-qt. slow cooker. Cut roast in half. In a small bowl, combine the mustard, rosemary, garlic salt, thyme and pepper; rub over roast.

2. Place in slow cooker; top with onion and broth. Cover and cook on low for 6-8 hours or until meat and vegetables are tender. **Yield:** 6-8 servings.

Worth It Lasagna

Prep: 1 hour **Bake:** 55 min. + standing

> 2 jars (24 ounces *each*) meatless spaghetti sauce
> 1 can (14-1/2 ounces) diced tomatoes, drained
> 1/2 cup Burgundy wine
> 2 tablespoons brown sugar
> 3 garlic cloves, minced
> 2 pounds Italian turkey sausage links, casings removed
> 3/4 cup raisins
> 2 teaspoons Italian seasoning
> 1-1/2 pounds sliced fresh mushrooms
> 1 medium onion, chopped
> 2 eggs, lightly beaten
> 2 cartons (15 ounces *each*) ricotta cheese
> 1 package (10 ounces) frozen chopped spinach, thawed and squeezed dry
> 1 cup grated Parmesan cheese
> 2 packages (24 ounces *each*) frozen cheese ravioli, thawed
> 1 cup shredded Parmesan cheese
> 18 slices provolone cheese, cut in half
> 6 cups (24 ounces) shredded Monterey Jack cheese
> 5 large tomatoes, sliced

1. In a Dutch oven, bring first five ingredients to a boil. Reduce heat; simmer, uncovered, for 20 minutes or until the desired thickness is achieved, stirring often.

2. In a large skillet, cook sausage over medium heat until no longer pink; drain. Stir in raisins and Italian seasoning; add to sauce. In the same skillet, saute mushrooms and onion until moisture has evaporated. Stir into sauce. In a large bowl, combine the eggs, ricotta, spinach and grated Parmesan cheese; set aside.

3. In each of two greased 13-in. x 9-in. baking dishes, layer with 1-1/3 cups sauce, half of a package of ravioli, 1-1/3 cups sauce, 1/4 cup shredded Parmesan cheese, six half slices of provolone cheese, 1 cup Monterey Jack cheese and 2-1/2 cups spinach mixture.

4. Top each with six half slices of provolone cheese, 1 cup Monterey Jack cheese, 1-1/3 cups sauce, remaining ravioli and sauce, 1/4 cup shredded Parmesan cheese, six half slices of provolone cheese, sliced tomatoes and remaining Monterey Jack cheese (dishes will be full).

5. Cover and bake at 375° for 45 minutes. Uncover; bake 10-15 minutes longer or until a thermometer reads 160°. Let lasagna stand 15 minutes before serving. **Yield:** 2 casseroles (12 servings each).

JOAN BROXHOLME BOULDER CITY, NEVADA

I break out this scrumptious lasagna recipe whenever I need to feed a crowd. Often, I'll serve one pan to my guests and freeze the other one for a family meal later.

Chicken Tostadas With Mango Salsa

Prep: 30 min. + marinating **Cook:** 20 min.

Erin Renouf Mylroie, Santa Clara, Utah

The ginger adds a pleasant zing to this tasty twist on a traditional tostada. The fresh salsa really makes this dish.

> ✓ This recipe includes Nutrition Facts & Diabetic Exchanges.

1/3 cup orange juice
  5 tablespoons lime juice, *divided*
  1 teaspoon garlic powder
  1 teaspoon ground cumin
  1 pound boneless skinless chicken breast halves
  2 medium mangoes, peeled and diced
  1 small red onion, chopped
1/2 cup minced fresh cilantro
  1 serrano pepper, seeded and minced
  2 tablespoons finely chopped crystallized ginger
  1 tablespoon brown sugar
1/4 teaspoon salt
  6 corn tortillas (6 inches)
  3 cups coleslaw mix
  6 tablespoons fat-free sour cream

1. In a large resealable plastic bag, combine the orange juice, 3 tablespoons lime juice, garlic powder and cumin; add chicken. Seal bag and turn to coat; refrigerate for at least 20 minutes.

2. For salsa, in a small bowl, combine the mangoes, onion, cilantro, serrano pepper, ginger, brown sugar, salt and remaining lime juice. Cover and chill until serving.

3. Drain and discard marinade. Place chicken on a broiler pan coated with cooking spray. Broil 4-6 in. from the heat for 5-7 minutes on each side or until a meat thermometer reads 170°. Cut into thin strips.

4. In a nonstick skillet, cook tortillas over medium heat for 1-2 minutes on each side or until lightly browned. Top each with coleslaw mix, chicken, mango salsa and sour cream. **Yield:** 6 servings.

Editor's Note: Wear disposable gloves when cutting hot peppers; the oils can burn skin. Avoid touching your face.

Nutrition Facts: 1 chicken breast half equals 238 calories, 3 g fat (1 g saturated fat), 44 mg cholesterol, 203 mg sodium, 35 g carbohydrate, 3 g fiber, 19 g protein. **Diabetic Exchanges:** 2 lean meat, 1-1/2 starch.

Turkey Enchilada Casserole

Prep: 30 min. **Bake:** 25 min.

Debra Martin, Belleville, Michigan

Every time I make these hearty and tasty enchiladas for guests, I end up sharing my recipe! I bet you will, too.

✓ | This recipe includes Nutrition Facts.

- 1 **pound lean ground turkey**
- 1 **medium green pepper, chopped**
- 1 **medium onion, chopped**
- 3 **garlic cloves, minced**
- 2 **cans (15 ounces *each*) black beans, rinsed and drained**
- 1 **jar (16 ounces) salsa**
- 1 **can (15 ounces) tomato sauce**
- 1 **can (14-1/2 ounces) Mexican stewed tomatoes**
- 1 **teaspoon *each* onion powder, garlic powder and ground cumin**
- 12 **corn tortillas (6 inches)**
- 2 **cups (8 ounces) shredded reduced-fat cheddar cheese, *divided***

1. In a large nonstick saucepan coated with cooking spray, cook the turkey, green pepper and onion over medium heat until meat is no longer pink. Add garlic; cook 1 minute longer. Drain. Stir in the beans, salsa, tomato sauce, tomatoes, onion powder, garlic powder and cumin. Bring to a boil. Reduce heat; simmer, uncovered, for 10 minutes.

2. Spread 1 cup meat sauce into a 13-in. x 9-in. baking dish coated with cooking spray. Top with six tortillas. Spread with half of the remaining meat sauce; sprinkle with 1 cup cheese. Layer with the remaining tortillas and meat sauce.

3. Cover and bake at 350° for 20 minutes. Uncover; sprinkle with remaining cheese. Bake 5-10 minutes longer or until bubbly and the cheese is melted. **Yield:** 10 servings.

Nutrition Facts: 1 serving enchilada casserole equals 318 calories, 9 g fat (4 g saturated fat), 52 mg cholesterol, 936 mg sodium, 37 g carbohydrate, 7 g fiber, 21 g protein.

Broccoli Chicken Casserole

Prep: 15 min. **Bake:** 30 min.

Jennifer Schlachter, Big Rock, Illinois

All ages love this cheesy, scrumptious meal-in-one. It takes only a few ingredients and mere minutes to put together.

- 1-1/2 **cups water**
- 1 **package (6 ounces) chicken stuffing mix**
- 2 **cups cubed cooked chicken**
- 1 **cup frozen broccoli florets, thawed**
- 1 **can (10-3/4 ounces) condensed broccoli cheese soup, undiluted**
- 1 **cup (4 ounces) shredded cheddar cheese**

1. In a small saucepan, bring water to a boil. Stir in stuffing mix. Remove from the heat; cover and let stand for 5 minutes.

2. Meanwhile, layer chicken and broccoli in a greased 11-in. x 7-in. baking dish. Top with soup. Fluff stuffing with a fork; spoon over soup. Sprinkle with cheese.

3. Bake, uncovered, at 350° for 30-35 minutes or until heated through. **Yield:** 6 servings.

Rosemary Chicken With White Beans

Prep: 15 min. Cook: 3 hours

Sharon Johannes, Ashley, Illinois

With a full-time job and active children, I'm known as the "Slow Cooker Queen" in my family. I use my slow cookers at least twice a week and sometimes have two or three going at once with different dishes. I've made this recipe for years and, after a few tweaks, it's become a treasured favorite.

> 6 boneless skinless chicken breast halves (6 ounces *each*)
> 1 tablespoon canola oil
> 2 cans (15-1/2 ounces *each*) great northern beans, rinsed and drained
> 1 cup sliced fresh carrots
> 1/2 cup sliced celery
> 2/3 cup Italian salad dressing
> 2 teaspoons dried rosemary, crushed
> 1/2 teaspoon salt
> 1 teaspoon pepper

1. In a large skillet, brown chicken in oil in batches on both sides. Place the beans, carrots and celery in a 5-qt. slow cooker; top with chicken.

2. In a small bowl, combine the salad dressing, rosemary, salt and pepper; pour over chicken. Cover and cook on low for 3-4 hours or until a meat thermometer reads 170°. **Yield:** 6 servings.

Marvelous Chicken Enchiladas

Prep: 30 min. Bake: 25 min.

✓ This recipe includes Nutrition Facts & Diabetic Exchanges.

> 1 pound boneless skinless chicken breasts, cut into thin strips
> 4 teaspoons chili powder
> 2 teaspoons olive oil
> 2 tablespoons all-purpose flour
> 1-1/2 teaspoons ground coriander
> 1 teaspoon baking cocoa
> 1 cup fat-free milk
> 1 cup frozen corn, thawed
> 4 green onions, chopped
> 1 can (4 ounces) chopped green chilies, drained
> 1/2 teaspoon salt
> 1/2 cup minced fresh cilantro, *divided*
> 6 whole wheat tortillas (8 inches)
> 1/2 cup salsa
> 1/2 cup tomato sauce
> 1/2 cup shredded reduced-fat cheddar cheese

1. Sprinkle chicken with chili powder. In a large nonstick skillet coated with cooking spray, cook chicken in oil over medium heat until no longer pink. Sprinkle with flour, coriander and cocoa; stir until blended.

2. Gradually stir in milk. Bring to a boil; cook and stir for 2 minutes or until thickened. Add the corn, onions, chilies and salt; cook and stir 2 minutes longer or until heated through. Remove from the heat. Stir in 1/4 cup cilantro.

3. Spread 2/3 cup filling down the center of each tortilla. Roll up; place seam side down in a 13-in. x 9-in. baking dish coated with cooking spray.

4. In a small bowl, combine the salsa, tomato sauce and remaining cilantro; pour over the enchiladas. Sprinkle with cheddar cheese. Cover; bake at 375° for 25 minutes or until enchiladas are heated through. **Yield:** 6 enchiladas.

Nutrition Facts: 1 enchilada equals 336 calories, 9 g fat (2 g saturated fat), 49 mg cholesterol, 749 mg sodium, 37 g carbohydrate, 4 g fiber, 25 g protein. **Diabetic Exchanges:** 3 lean meat, 2-1/2 starch, 1/2 fat.

REBEKAH SABO ROCHESTER, NEW YORK

I love food with a Southwestern flair, and this dish tops my list of favorite recipes. Try using Monterey Jack cheese in place of the cheddar for a slightly milder flavor.

GRAND
PRIZE
WINNER

Pesto Chicken Lasagna

Prep: 30 min. **Bake:** 55 min. + standing

Michelle Larson, Eveleth, Minnesota

Pesto really perks up this mouthwatering chicken lasagna, while the marinara sauce adds a touch of sweetness. Serve it with warm bread for a meal that will wow!

       1 large sweet red pepper, diced
    1/4 cup finely chopped onion
       1 tablespoon butter
       4 garlic cloves, minced
    1/4 cup all-purpose flour
       2 cups milk
    1/4 cup chicken broth
  1-1/2 teaspoons dried basil
       1 teaspoon dried oregano
       2 cups cubed cooked chicken
    1/2 cup prepared pesto
       1 can (3.8 ounces) sliced ripe olives, drained
       1 egg, lightly beaten
       1 carton (15 ounces) ricotta cheese
       1 package (4 ounces) crumbled feta cheese
       2 cups marinara sauce
      12 no-cook lasagna noodles
       1 package (6 ounces) fresh baby spinach, chopped
       2 cups (8 ounces) shredded part-skim mozzarella cheese

1. In a large saucepan, saute red pepper and onion in butter until tender. Add garlic; cook 1 minute longer. Stir in flour until blended; gradually stir in milk, broth, basil and oregano. Bring to a boil over medium heat; cook and stir for 2 minutes or until thickened.

2. Stir in the chicken, pesto and olives. Remove from the heat. In a large bowl, combine the egg, ricotta cheese and feta cheese.

3. Spread 1 cup marinara sauce in a greased 13-in. x 9-in. baking dish. Layer with four noodles, half of the ricotta mixture, half of the spinach, half of the pesto mixture and 2/3 cup mozzarella cheese. Repeat layers. Top with remaining noodles, sauce and mozzarella.

4. Cover; bake at 375° for 45 minutes. Uncover; bake 10 minutes more or until a thermometer reads 160°. Let the lasagna stand 15 minutes before serving. **Yield:** 12 servings.

Slow 'n' Easy Barbecued Chicken

Prep: 20 min. **Cook:** 3 hours

Dreama Hughes, London, Kentucky

I rely on this yummy recipe often during the summer and fall when I know I'm going to be out working in the yard all day. Pair it with a side vegetable or salad and supper is served!

- 1/4 cup water
- 3 tablespoons brown sugar
- 3 tablespoons white vinegar
- 3 tablespoons ketchup
- 2 tablespoons butter
- 2 tablespoons Worcestershire sauce
- 1 tablespoon lemon juice
- 1 teaspoon salt
- 1 teaspoon paprika
- 1 teaspoon ground mustard
- 1/2 teaspoon cayenne pepper
- 1 broiler/fryer chicken (2-1/2 to 3 pounds), cut up and skin removed
- 4 teaspoons cornstarch
- 1 tablespoon cold water

1. In a small saucepan, combine the first 11 ingredients. Bring to a boil. Reduce heat; simmer, uncovered, for 5 minutes. Remove from the heat.

2. Place chicken in a 3-qt. slow cooker. Top with sauce. Cover; cook on low for 3-4 hours or until chicken juices run clear.

3. Remove chicken to a serving platter; keep warm. Skim fat from cooking juices; transfer to a small saucepan. Bring to a boil.

4. Combine cornstarch and water until smooth; gradually stir into pan. Bring to a boil; cook and stir until thickened. Spoon some of the sauce over chicken; serve remaining sauce on the side. **Yield:** 4 servings.

Spicy Nacho Bake

Prep: 1 hour **Bake:** 20 min.

Anita Wilson, Mansfield, Ohio

After making this layered Southwestern casserole for a dinner one time, I'm asked to bring it to every potluck. The ground beef and bean filling and crunchy, cheesy topping are a hit!

- 2 pounds ground beef
- 2 large onions, chopped
- 2 large green peppers, chopped
- 2 cans (28 ounces *each*) diced tomatoes, undrained
- 2 cans (16 ounces *each*) hot chili beans, undrained
- 2 cans (15 ounces *each*) black beans, rinsed and drained
- 2 cans (11 ounces *each*) whole kernel corn, drained
- 2 cans (8 ounces *each*) tomato sauce
- 2 envelopes taco seasoning
- 2 packages (13 ounces *each*) spicy nacho tortilla chips
- 4 cups (16 ounces) shredded cheddar cheese

1. In a Dutch oven, cook the beef, onions and green peppers over medium heat until meat is no longer pink; drain. Stir in the tomatoes, beans, corn, tomato sauce and taco seasoning. Bring to a boil. Reduce heat; simmer, uncovered, for 30 minutes (mixture will be thin).

2. In each of two greased 13-in. x 9-in. baking dishes, layer 5 cups of chips and 4-2/3 cups of meat mixture. Repeat layers. Top each with 4 cups of chips and 2 cups of cheese.

3. Bake, uncovered, at 350° for 20-25 minutes or until golden brown. **Yield:** 2 casseroles (15 servings each).

PG. 116

PG. 115

PG. 128

PORK & MORE ENTREES

Whether you want a special pork roast, a seafood sensation or a vegetarian delight, take your pick! Mouths will water over Smoked Chops with Cherry Sauce, Macadamia-Crusted Tilapia, Veggie Lasagna and more.

PG. 126

Smoked Chops With Cherry Sauce

Prep/Total Time: 20 min.

Betty Kleberger, Florissant, Missouri

The next time you fire up the grill, try these moist chops that feature a sweet-but-spicy sauce. With just a light touch of heat, they'll turn up the flavor on any summer night.

✓ This recipe includes Nutrition Facts.

6 fully cooked smoked pork chops (1-inch thick and 6 ounces *each*)
1 can (15 ounces) pitted dark sweet cherries, undrained
1 cup mild jalapeno pepper jelly
1/2 teaspoon ground coriander, optional

1. Grill pork chops, covered, over medium heat for 4-6 minutes on each side or until a thermometer reads 145°. Let meat stand 5 minutes before serving.

2. Meanwhile, in a small saucepan, combine cherries, jelly and coriander if desired. Bring to a boil, stirring constantly. Serve with chops. **Yield:** 6 servings.

Nutrition Facts: 1 pork chop equals 239 calories, 2 g fat (1 g saturated fat), 14 mg cholesterol, 365 mg sodium, 48 g carbohydrate, 2 g fiber, 8 g protein.

Easy Homemade Cherry Pitter

If using fresh cherries in this recipe, try this trick to remove the pits. Wash a metal paper clip and unfold one end, leaving the other end folded. Insert the U-shaped end into the cherry. Loosen the pit and pull it out. So easy!

Greek Spinach Pizza

Prep/Total Time: 20 min.

Kay Young, Port Clinton, Ohio

Round out this quick pizza with a salad or vegetable relish tray. Sometimes, I serve a side of low-fat ranch dressing to dip the veggies and pizza crust into.

2 cups fresh baby spinach
3 tablespoons olive oil
3 teaspoons Italian seasoning
1 prebaked 12-inch thin pizza crust
2 plum tomatoes, thinly sliced
1 cup (4 ounces) crumbled feta cheese
1/4 cup shredded part-skim mozzarella cheese
1/4 cup chopped pitted Greek olives
2 tablespoons chopped sweet onion

1. In a small bowl, toss the spinach, oil and Italian seasoning. Place crust on an ungreased 12-in. pizza pan. Arrange spinach mixture over crust to within 1/2 in. of edge. Place tomatoes on top; sprinkle with the cheeses, olives and onion.

2. Bake at 450° for 10-15 minutes or until cheese is melted and edges are lightly browned. **Yield:** 6-8 slices.

Honey-Dijon Pork Tenderloin

Prep/Total Time: 25 min.

Trisha Kruse, Eagle, Idaho

It's hard to believe such an elegant dish is table-ready in half an hour. To cut prep time, use a food processor to slice onions and mushrooms. Mixed vegetables make a quick side dish.

- 1 pound pork tenderloin, cut into 1-inch slices
- 1/4 teaspoon salt
- 1/4 teaspoon pepper
- 1 tablespoon olive oil
- 1 small onion, chopped
- 1/2 cup sliced fresh mushrooms
- 1 tablespoon butter
- 2 garlic cloves, minced
- 1/2 cup evaporated milk
- 2 tablespoons Dijon mustard
- 1 tablespoon soy sauce
- 1 tablespoon honey
- **Hot cooked pasta**

1. Flatten pork slices to 1/2-in. thickness; sprinkle with salt and pepper. In a large skillet over medium heat, cook pork in oil in batches until meat is no longer pink. Remove and keep warm.

2. In the same skillet, saute onion and mushrooms in butter until tender. Add garlic; saute 1 minute longer. Stir in the milk, mustard, soy sauce and honey. Return pork to the pan; heat through. Serve pork with hot cooked pasta. **Yield:** 4 servings.

French Canadian Meat Pie

Prep: 40 min. + cooling **Bake:** 45 min.

Angie Moline, Calgary, Alberta

I'm a seventh-generation French Canadian, and my ancestors started the tradition of serving this meat pie on Christmas Eve. One year I didn't make it, and my daughter and I both felt that something special was missing.

- 1-1/4 pounds ground pork
- 1/2 pound ground beef
- 1/4 pound ground veal
- 1 cup grated peeled potatoes
- 1/2 cup grated onion
- 3 garlic cloves, minced
- 1-1/2 teaspoons salt
- 1/2 teaspoon pepper
- 1/4 teaspoon dried savory
- 1/4 teaspoon rubbed sage
- 1/8 teaspoon ground cloves
- 1/4 cup plus 2 tablespoons water, *divided*
- 1/4 cup dry bread crumbs
- 1 egg
- **Pastry for double-crust pie (9 inches)**

1. In a large skillet over medium heat, cook the pork, beef, veal, potatoes and onion until meat is no longer pink; drain. Stir in the garlic, seasonings and 1/4 cup water. Bring to a boil. Reduce heat; cover and simmer for 15 minutes, stirring frequently.

2. Remove from the heat; cool to room temperature. Stir in bread crumbs. Combine egg and remaining water; stir into meat mixture.

3. Line a 9-in. pie plate with bottom pastry; trim even with edge. Fill with the meat mixture. Roll out remaining pastry to fit top of pie; place over filling. Trim, seal and flute the edges. Cut slits in pastry. Cover the edges loosely with foil.

4. Bake at 400° for 15 minutes. Remove foil. Reduce heat to 375°; bake 30-35 minutes longer or until crust is golden brown and a meat thermometer reads 160°. **Yield:** 6-8 servings.

1/2 pound boneless skinless chicken breasts, cut into 1-inch cubes
1 can (8 ounces) tomato sauce
1 cup diced onion
1 small sweet red pepper, diced
1 small green pepper, diced
1 cup chicken broth
1 celery rib with leaves, chopped
2 tablespoons tomato paste
2 teaspoons dried oregano
2 teaspoons Cajun seasoning
1-1/2 teaspoons minced garlic
2 bay leaves
1 teaspoon Louisiana-style hot sauce
1/2 teaspoon dried thyme
1 pound cooked medium shrimp, peeled and deveined
Hot cooked rice

1. In a 5-qt. slow cooker, combine the first 16 ingredients. Cover and cook on low for 6-7 hours or until chicken is no longer pink.

2. Stir in shrimp. Cover and cook 15 minutes longer or until heated through. Discard bay leaves. Serve with rice. **Yield:** 8 servings.

Hearty Jambalaya

Prep: 15 min. Cook: 6-1/4 hours

Jennifer Fulk, Moreno Valley, California

I love anything with Cajun spices, so I came up with this slow cooker jambalaya that's just as good as the kind served in New Orleans-style restaurants.

1 can (28 ounces) diced tomatoes, undrained
1 pound fully cooked andouille sausage links, cubed

Slow Cooker Success

When using a slow cooker, it's best not to lift the lid while the food is cooking unless the recipe instructs you to stir in additional ingredients. Every time you lift the slow cooker's lid, steam is lost and you add 15 to 30 minutes of cooking time!

Teriyaki Pork Roast

Prep: 10 min. Cook: 6 hours + standing

1 boneless pork shoulder butt roast (3 to 4 pounds)
1 cup packed brown sugar
1/3 cup unsweetened apple juice
1/3 cup reduced-sodium soy sauce
1/2 teaspoon salt
1/4 teaspoon pepper
2 tablespoons cornstarch
3 tablespoons cold water

1. Cut roast in half; rub with brown sugar. Place in a 5-qt. slow cooker. Pour apple juice and soy sauce over roast. Sprinkle with salt and pepper. Cover and cook on low for 6 to 8 hours or until meat is tender.

2. Remove roast; cover and let stand for 15 minutes before slicing. Meanwhile, strain cooking juices and return to slow cooker. Mix cornstarch and water until smooth; stir into juices. Cover and cook on high for 15 minutes or until thickened. Slice pork; serve with gravy. **Yield:** 6-8 servings.

DEBBIE DUNAWAY KETTERING, OHIO

How good is this dish? Well, it's the only kind of meat my young kids will eat and enjoy other than hot dogs! It's also incredibly easy to make and simply delicious!

GRAND
PRIZE
WINNER

Grilled Chiles Rellenos

Prep: 45 min. **Grill:** 10 min.

Lori Nelson, Austin, Texas

Here's a healthy version of one of my favorite Mexican dishes. The grilled peppers go great with Spanish rice, gazpacho or a refreshing salad with jicama and citrus.

- 1 cup (8 ounces) sour cream
- 2 tablespoons lime juice
- 1/2 cup minced fresh cilantro, *divided*
- 1 small onion, finely chopped
- 1 tablespoon butter
- 1 large portobello mushroom cap, finely chopped
- 1 small yellow summer squash, finely chopped
- 1 small zucchini, finely chopped
- 1 jalapeno pepper, seeded and finely chopped
- 1 garlic clove, minced
- 1 can (15 ounces) black beans, rinsed and drained
- 2 cups (8 ounces) shredded Mexican cheese blend, *divided*

- 1 cup frozen corn, thawed
- 1 teaspoon ground cumin
- 1/2 teaspoon salt
- 1/4 teaspoon pepper
- 4 large poblano peppers, halved and seeded

1. In a small bowl, combine the sour cream, lime juice and 1/4 cup cilantro. Cover mixture and refrigerate until serving.

2. In a large skillet, saute onion in butter until tender. Add the mushroom, yellow squash, zucchini, jalapeno and garlic; saute 3-5 minutes longer or until vegetables are crisp-tender.

3. Stir in the beans, 1-1/2 cups cheese, corn, cumin, salt, pepper and remaining cilantro. Remove from the heat. Spoon into poblano halves; sprinkle with remaining cheese.

4. Grill peppers, covered, over indirect medium heat for 10-14 minutes or until tender. Serve with sour cream sauce. **Yield:** 4 servings.

Editor's Note: Wear disposable gloves when cutting hot peppers; the oils can burn skin. Avoid touching your face.

Confetti Pasta

Prep/Total Time: 25 min.

Ellen Fiore, Ridgewood, New Jersey

This fabulous, easy pasta has become a holiday tradition at my house. All the prep is done before we attend Christmas Eve service. On returning, I just boil water and saute the veggies. It's so colorful with a tossed salad and garlic bread!

- 1 package (16 ounces) linguine
- 1 cup chopped sweet red pepper
- 1 cup chopped green pepper
- 1/3 cup chopped onion
- 3 garlic cloves, peeled and thinly sliced
- 1/4 teaspoon salt
- 1/4 teaspoon dried oregano
- 1/8 teaspoon crushed red pepper flakes
- 1/8 teaspoon pepper
- 1/4 cup olive oil
- 2 pounds cooked small shrimp, peeled and deveined
- 1/2 cup shredded Parmesan cheese

1. Cook linguine according to package directions. Meanwhile, in a Dutch oven, saute the peppers, onion, garlic and seasonings in oil until vegetables are tender.

2. Add the shrimp; cook and stir 2-3 minutes longer or until heated through. Drain linguine; toss with shrimp mixture. Sprinkle pasta and shrimp with Parmesan cheese. **Yield:** 8 servings.

Slow-Cooked Pork Tacos

Prep: 20 min. Cook: 4 hours

Kathleen Wolf, Naperville, Illinois

Sometimes I'll substitute Bibb lettuce leaves for the flour tortillas to make cool, crispy lettuce wraps. I also find that the filling can be used to make a tasty burrito.

> ✓ This recipe includes Nutrition Facts & Diabetic Exchanges.

- 1 boneless pork sirloin roast (2 pounds), cut into 1-inch pieces
- 1-1/2 cups salsa verde
- 1 medium sweet red pepper, chopped
- 1 medium onion, chopped
- 1/4 cup chopped dried apricots

- 2 tablespoons lime juice
- 2 garlic cloves, minced
- 1 teaspoon ground cumin
- 1/2 teaspoon salt
- 1/4 teaspoon white pepper
- Dash hot pepper sauce
- 10 flour tortillas (8 inches), warmed
- Reduced-fat sour cream, thinly sliced green onions, cubed avocado, shredded reduced-fat cheddar cheese and chopped tomato, optional

1. In a 3-qt. slow cooker, combine the first 11 ingredients. Cover and cook on high for 4-5 hours or until meat is tender.

2. Shred pork with two forks. Place about 1/2 cup pork mixture down the center of each tortilla. Serve with toppings if desired. **Yield:** 10 tacos.

Nutrition Facts: 1 taco (calculated without optional toppings) equals 301 calories, 8 g fat (2 g saturated fat), 54 mg cholesterol, 616 mg sodium, 32 g carbohydrate, 1 g fiber, 24 g protein. **Diabetic Exchanges:** 3 lean meat, 2 starch.

No-Tear Tortillas

To prevent tortillas from tearing while rolling them up, simply warm them slightly in a non-stick skillet before filling. The warm tortillas are more pliable.

Over-the-Top Mac 'n' Cheese

Prep: 15 min. **Bake:** 40 min.

Connie McDowell, Greenwood, Delaware

This fantastic bake is the ultimate comfort food! A blend of five cheeses, it makes a meatless entree or a special side.

- 1 package (16 ounces) elbow macaroni
- 2 ounces Muenster cheese, shredded
- 1/2 cup *each* shredded mild cheddar, sharp cheddar and Monterey Jack cheese
- 1/2 cup plus 1 tablespoon butter, *divided*
- 2 cups half-and-half cream
- 2 eggs, lightly beaten
- 1 cup cubed process cheese (Velveeta)
- 1/4 teaspoon seasoned salt
- 1/8 teaspoon pepper

1. Cook macaroni according to package directions. Meanwhile, in a large bowl, combine the Muenster, cheddar and Monterey Jack cheeses; set aside.

2. In a large saucepan, melt 1/2 cup butter over medium heat. Stir in the cream, eggs, process cheese, seasoned salt, pepper and 1-1/2 cups of the cheese mixture. Drain pasta; add to the cheese sauce and stir to coat.

3. Transfer to a greased 2-1/2-qt. baking dish. Sprinkle with remaining cheese mixture and dot with remaining butter. Bake, uncovered, at 350° for 40-45 minutes or until a thermometer reads 160°. **Yield:** 7 servings.

Lazy Man's Ribs

Prep: 20 min. **Cook:** 5 hours

Allan Stackhouse Jr., Jennings, Louisiana

Not only are these slow-cooker ribs finger-lickin' good, they're also fall-off-the-bone tender!

- 2-1/2 pounds pork baby back ribs, cut into eight pieces
- 2 teaspoons Cajun seasoning
- 1 medium onion, sliced
- 1 cup ketchup
- 1/2 cup packed brown sugar
- 1/3 cup orange juice
- 1/3 cup cider vinegar
- 1/4 cup molasses
- 2 tablespoons Worcestershire sauce
- 1 tablespoon barbecue sauce
- 1 teaspoon stone-ground mustard
- 1 teaspoon paprika
- 1/2 teaspoon garlic powder
- 1/2 teaspoon Liquid Smoke, optional
Dash salt
- 5 teaspoons cornstarch
- 1 tablespoon cold water

1. Rub ribs with Cajun seasoning. Layer ribs and onion in a 5-qt. slow cooker. In a small bowl, combine the ketchup, brown sugar, orange juice, vinegar, molasses, Worcestershire sauce, barbecue sauce, mustard, paprika, garlic powder, Liquid Smoke if desired and salt. Pour over ribs. Cover and cook on low for 5-6 hours or until meat is tender.

2. Remove ribs and keep warm. Strain cooking juices and skim fat; transfer to a small saucepan. Combine cornstarch and water until smooth; stir into juices. Bring to a boil; cook and stir for 2 minutes or until thickened. Serve with ribs. **Yield:** 4 servings.

Macadamia-Crusted Tilapia

Prep: 20 min. **Bake:** 15 min.

Jennifer Fisher, Austin, Texas

A refreshing pineapple salsa complements these crispy golden fillets. I like to garnish each one with whole macadamia nuts. The colorful entree always makes an impression with guests.

    2 eggs
1/8 teaspoon cayenne pepper

    1 cup all-purpose flour
1-3/4 cups macadamia nuts, finely chopped
    4 tilapia fillets (6 ounces *each*)
    1 tablespoon butter, melted
PINEAPPLE SALSA:
    1 cup cubed fresh pineapple
1/4 cup chopped sweet red pepper
    3 tablespoons thinly sliced green onions
    2 tablespoons sugar
    1 jalapeno pepper, seeded and chopped
    1 tablespoon lime juice
1/2 teaspoon minced fresh gingerroot
    2 tablespoons minced fresh cilantro

1. In a shallow bowl, whisk eggs and cayenne. Place flour and macadamia nuts in separate shallow bowls. Coat tilapia with flour, then dip in egg mixture and coat with nuts.

2. Place on a greased baking sheet; drizzle with butter. Bake at 375° for 15-20 minutes or until fish flakes easily with a fork.

3. Meanwhile, in a small serving bowl, combine the pineapple, red pepper, onions, sugar, jalapeno, lime juice and ginger; sprinkle with cilantro. Serve with fish. **Yield:** 4 servings (1-1/2 cups salsa).

Editor's Note: Wear disposable gloves when cutting hot peppers; the oils can burn skin. Avoid touching your face.

Old-Fashioned Glazed Ham

Prep: 15 min. **Bake:** 2 hours 25 min.

Barbara Dalton, Clark, South Dakota

The fruit juices combine with brown sugar to make a sweet gravy that really brings out the meat's flavor. My family looks forward to having this entree every Easter and Christmas.

1/2 fully cooked bone-in ham (6 to 7 pounds)
    2 tablespoons whole cloves
    1 cup packed brown sugar
2/3 cup orange juice
1/2 cup unsweetened pineapple juice
1/3 cup maraschino cherry juice

1. Place ham on a rack in a shallow foil-lined roasting pan. Score the surface of the ham, making diamond shapes 1/2 in. deep; insert a clove into each diamond. Cover and bake at 325° for 2 hours.

2. Meanwhile, in a small saucepan, bring the brown sugar and juices to a boil. Reduce heat; simmer, uncovered, for 30 minutes or until glaze is reduced to 1 cup.

3. Baste ham with 1/3 cup glaze. Bake, uncovered, 25-35 minutes longer or until a thermometer reads 140°, basting with remaining glaze every 10 minutes. **Yield:** 8-10 servings.

Grilled Stuffed Pork Tenderloin

Prep: 20 min. + marinating **Grill:** 25 min.

Bobbie Carr, Lake Oswego, Oregon

We like to serve this stuffed tenderloin with a mixed salad. The grilled pork is easy enough even for your busiest nights.

> ✓ This recipe includes Nutrition Facts & Diabetic Exchanges.

- 2 pork tenderloins (3/4 pound *each*)
- 3/4 cup dry red wine *or* reduced-sodium beef broth
- 1/3 cup packed brown sugar
- 1/4 cup ketchup
- 2 tablespoons reduced-sodium soy sauce
- 2 garlic cloves, minced
- 1 teaspoon curry powder
- 1/2 teaspoon minced fresh gingerroot
- 1/4 teaspoon pepper
- 1-1/4 cups water
- 2 tablespoons butter
- 1 package (6 ounces) stuffing mix

1. Cut a lengthwise slit down the center of each tenderloin to within 1/2 in. of bottom. In a large resealable plastic bag, combine the wine or broth, brown sugar, ketchup, soy sauce, garlic, curry, ginger and pepper; add pork. Seal bag and turn to coat; refrigerate for 2-3 hours.

2. In a small saucepan, bring water and butter to a boil. Stir in stuffing mix. Remove from the heat; cover and let stand for 5 minutes. Cool.

3. Drain and discard marinade. Open tenderloins so they lie flat; spread stuffing down the center of each. Close tenderloins; tie at 1-1/2-in. intervals with kitchen string.

4. Using long-handled tongs, moisten a paper towel with cooking oil and lightly coat the grill rack. Prepare grill for indirect heat using a drip pan. Place pork over drip pan; grill pork, covered, over indirect medium-hot heat for 25-40 minutes or until a meat thermometer reads 160°. Let stand for 5 minutes before slicing. **Yield:** 6 servings.

Nutrition Facts: 1 serving equals 296 calories, 9 g fat (4 g saturated fat), 73 mg cholesterol, 678 mg sodium, 24 g carbohydrate, 1 g fiber, 27 g protein. **Diabetic Exchanges:** 3 lean meat, 1-1/2 starch, 1 fat.

Ham with Mustard-Cream Sauce

Prep/Total Time: 20 min.

Lisa Nelson, Broken Arrow, Oklahoma

This recipe is just too easy to taste so good! It's hard to believe three common ingredients can turn a ham slice into something so uncommonly special.

> 4 boneless fully cooked ham steaks (about 5 ounces *each*)
> 1/4 cup water
> 1/4 cup honey mustard
> 1/2 cup sour cream
> 1/4 cup thinly sliced green onions

1. Place ham steaks in a large skillet. In a small bowl, combine water and mustard; pour over ham. Bring to a boil.

2. Reduce heat; cover and simmer for 3-4 minutes on each side or until heated through. Remove from the heat; stir in sour cream and onions. **Yield:** 4 servings.

Cajun Shrimp Lasagna Roll-Ups

Prep: 30 min. **Bake:** 25 min. + standing

Mary Beth Harris-Murphree, Tyler, Texas

If you enjoy Creole and Cajun dishes, you'll love this one. The seasoning and andouille sausage give it a nice kick, and seafood fans will appreciate the shrimp.

> 1-1/4 pounds uncooked medium shrimp, peeled and deveined
> 1 medium onion, chopped
> 2 tablespoons olive oil
> 4 medium tomatoes, seeded and chopped
> 2 tablespoons Cajun seasoning
> 3 garlic cloves, minced
> 1/4 cup butter, cubed
> 1/4 cup all-purpose flour
> 2 cups milk
> 1-1/2 cups (6 ounces) shredded cheddar cheese
> 1 cup diced fully cooked andouille sausage
> 12 lasagna noodles, cooked and drained
> 4 ounces pepper Jack cheese, shredded
> 1 teaspoon paprika

1. In a large skillet, saute shrimp and onion in oil until shrimp turn pink. Stir in tomatoes and Cajun seasoning; set aside.

2. In a large saucepan, saute garlic in butter for 1 minute. Stir in flour until blended. Gradually add milk. Bring to a boil over medium heat; cook and stir for 2 minutes or until thickened. Remove from the heat; stir in cheddar cheese until smooth. Add sausage; set aside.

3. Spread 1/3 cup shrimp mixture over each noodle. Carefully roll up; place seam side down in a greased 13-in. x 9-in. baking dish. Top with cheese sauce. Sprinkle with pepper Jack cheese and paprika.

4. Cover and bake at 350° for 15 minutes. Uncover; bake 10-15 minutes longer or until bubbly. Let stand 15 minutes before serving. **Yield:** 6 servings.

Caribbean Chutney-Crusted Chops

Prep/Total Time: 30 min.

Josephine Piro, Easton, Pennsylvania

I like to impress my guests with delicious meals, and these lamb chops are one of my best entrees. This recipe started with a jar of chutney I received in a gift basket and didn't know what to do with. Folks think I fuss all day over these sophisticated chops but they're done in 30 minutes flat!

> 1 cup soft bread crumbs
> 1-1/2 teaspoons Caribbean jerk seasoning
> 1/4 cup mango chutney
> 1/2 teaspoon salt
> 1/2 teaspoon pepper
> 4 lamb loin chops (2 inches-thick and 8 ounces each)

1. In a shallow bowl, combine bread crumbs and jerk seasoning; set aside. Combine the chutney, salt and pepper; spread over both sides of lamb chops. Coat with crumb mixture.

2. Place lamb chops on a rack coated with cooking spray in a shallow baking pan. Bake at 450° for 20-25 minutes or until meat reaches desired doneness (for medium-rare, a meat thermometer should read 145°; medium 160°; well-done 170°). **Yield:** 4 servings.

Lemony Vegetables and Pasta

Prep: 25 min. **Cook:** 15 min.

> 1 pound fresh asparagus, trimmed and cut into 1-inch pieces
> 1 medium sweet red pepper, cut into 1-inch pieces
> 1 medium red onion, sliced
> 1 tablespoon olive oil
> 1/2 teaspoon salt
> 1/4 teaspoon pepper
> 4-1/2 cups uncooked bow tie pasta
> 1 tablespoon butter
> 1 tablespoon all-purpose flour
> 3 garlic cloves, minced
> 1/4 teaspoon crushed red pepper flakes
> 1 cup vegetable broth
> 1 cup shredded Parmesan cheese
> 1/2 cup sour cream
> 2 tablespoons lemon juice
> 1 tablespoon grated lemon peel
> 1/2 cup chopped pistachios
> 1/4 cup fresh basil leaves, thinly sliced
> Additional shredded Parmesan cheese

1. In a large bowl, combine the asparagus, red pepper, onion, oil, salt and pepper. Transfer to a greased 15-in. x 10-in. x 1-in. baking pan. Bake at 450° for 10-15 minutes or until golden brown, stirring once.

2. Meanwhile, cook pasta according to package directions. In a large saucepan, melt butter over medium heat.

3. Stir in the flour, garlic and pepper flakes until blended. Whisk in broth until blended. Bring to a boil over medium-high heat; cook and stir for 2 minutes or until thickened and bubbly.

4. Reduce heat. Stir in the cheese, sour cream, lemon juice and peel; heat through. Drain pasta and place in a large bowl.

5. Add cheese sauce and asparagus mixture; toss to coat. Sprinkle with pistachios, basil and additional cheese. **Yield:** 7 servings.

ERIN RENOUF MYLROIE SANTA CLARA, UTAH

My refreshing pasta dish comes together in just 30 minutes. Its simplicity and blend of flavors are typical of authentic Italian cuisine, but still something I can prepare in a hurry.

GRAND PRIZE WINNER

Italian Sausage With Bow Ties

Prep/Total Time: 25 min.

Janelle Moore, Federal Way, Washington

Here's a family favorite that's requested monthly in our house. The Italian sausage paired with creamy tomato sauce tastes out of this world. Not only is this dish simple to make, it also tastes like you slaved over a hot stove for hours.

- 1 package (16 ounces) bow tie pasta
- 1 pound bulk Italian sausage
- 1/2 cup chopped onion
- 1/2 teaspoon crushed red pepper flakes
- 1-1/2 teaspoons minced garlic
- 2 cans (14-1/2 ounces *each*) Italian stewed tomatoes, drained and chopped
- 1-1/2 cups heavy whipping cream
- 1/2 teaspoon salt
- 1/4 teaspoon dried basil
- Shredded Parmesan cheese

1. Cook pasta according to package directions. Meanwhile, in a Dutch oven, cook the sausage, onion and pepper flakes over medium heat for 4-5 minutes or until meat is no longer pink. Add garlic; cook 1 minute longer. Drain.

2. Stir in the tomatoes, cream, salt and basil. Bring to a boil over medium heat. Reduce heat; simmer, uncovered, for 6-8 minutes or until thickened, stirring occasionally. Drain pasta; toss with sausage mixture. Garnish with cheese. **Yield:** 5 servings.

Honey-Soy Pork Chops

Prep: 10 min. + marinating Grill: 10 min.

Edie DeSpain, Logan, Utah

Summer is always a special time for relaxed and casual meals, for patriotic holidays and especially, for picnics in the great outdoors. This hearty grilled entree is perfect for all such occasions—and more.

 This recipe includes Nutrition Facts & Diabetic Exchange.

- 1/4 cup lemon juice
- 1/4 cup honey
- 2 tablespoons reduced-sodium soy sauce
- 1 tablespoon sherry *or* unsweetened apple juice
- 2 garlic cloves, minced
- 4 boneless pork loin chops (4 ounces *each*)

1. In a small bowl, combine the first five ingredients. Pour 1/2 cup into a large resealable plastic bag; add pork chops. Seal bag and turn to coat; refrigerate for 2-3 hours. Cover and refrigerate remaining marinade for basting.

2. Drain and discard marinade. Moisten a paper towel with cooking oil; using long-handled tongs, lightly coat the grill rack.

3. Grill pork, covered, over medium heat or broil 4-5 in. from the heat for 4-5 minutes on each side or until a thermometer reads 145°, basting frequently with remaining marinade. Let meat stand for 5 minutes before serving. **Yield:** 4 servings.

Nutrition Facts: 1 pork chop equals 176 calories, 6 g fat (2 g saturated fat), 55 mg cholesterol, 132 mg sodium, 6 g carbohydrate, trace fiber, 22 g protein. **Diabetic Exchange:** 3 lean meat.

Skillet Sea Scallops

Prep/Total Time: 25 min.

Margaret E. Lowenberg, Kingman, Arizona

You'll want to keep this recipe in mind for a quick-to-fix company dish. Pasta and mixed greens nicely complement the tender, citrus-flavored shellfish.

- 1/2 **cup dry bread crumbs**
- 1/2 **teaspoon salt**
- 1 **pound sea scallops**
- 2 **tablespoons butter**
- 1 **tablespoon olive oil**
- 1/4 **cup white wine** *or* **reduced-sodium chicken broth**
- 2 **tablespoons lemon juice**
- 1 **teaspoon minced fresh parsley**
- 1 **garlic clove, minced**

1. In a large resealable plastic bag, combine bread crumbs and salt. Add the scallops, a few at a time, and shake to coat.

2. In a large skillet over medium-high heat, brown scallops in butter and oil for 1-1/2 to 2 minutes on

each side or until firm and opaque. Remove and keep warm. Add the wine, lemon juice, parsley and garlic to the skillet; bring to a boil. Pour over scallops. Serve immediately. **Yield:** 3-4 servings.

Cheese Enchiladas

Prep: 25 min. **Bake:** 25 min.

Ashley Schackow, Defiance, Ohio

You won't bring home leftovers when you make these easy, crowd-pleasing enchiladas. With a homemade tomato sauce and cheesy filling, they always go fast. You can substitute any type of cheese you wish.

- 2 **cans (15 ounces** *each***) tomato sauce**
- 1-1/3 **cups water**
- 2 **tablespoons chili powder**
- 2 **garlic cloves, minced**
- 1 **teaspoon dried oregano**
- 1/2 **teaspoon ground cumin**
- 16 **flour tortillas (8 inches), warmed**
- 4 **cups (16 ounces) shredded Monterey Jack cheese**
- 2-1/2 **cups (10 ounces) shredded cheddar cheese,** *divided*
- 2 **medium onions, finely chopped**
- 1 **cup (8 ounces) sour cream**
- 1/4 **cup minced fresh parsley**
- 1/2 **teaspoon salt**
- 1/2 **teaspoon pepper**

Shredded lettuce, sliced ripe olives and additional sour cream, optional

1. In a large saucepan, combine the first six ingredients. Bring to a boil. Reduce heat; simmer, uncovered, for 4-5 minutes or until thickened, stirring occasionally. Spoon 2 tablespoons sauce over each tortilla.

2. In a large bowl, combine the Monterey Jack, 2 cups cheddar cheese, onions, sour cream, parsley, salt and pepper. Place about 1/3 cup down the center of each tortilla. Roll up and place seam side down in two greased 13-in. x 9-in. baking dishes. Pour remaining sauce over top.

3. Bake, uncovered, at 350° for 20 minutes. Sprinkle with remaining cheddar cheese. Bake 4-5 minutes longer or until cheese is melted. Garnish with lettuce, olives and sour cream if desired. **Yield:** 16 enchiladas.

1 teaspoon garlic powder
1/4 teaspoon onion powder
1/4 teaspoon pepper
1/2 cup butter, *divided*
1 can (12 ounces) evaporated milk
1 block (8 ounces) brick cheese, cubed
3 packages (10 ounces *each*) frozen chopped spinach, thawed and squeezed dry
2 cups (8 ounces) shredded part-skim mozzarella cheese

1. Cook tortellini according to package directions.

2. Meanwhile, in a large skillet, saute the mushrooms, garlic powder, onion powder and pepper in 1/4 cup butter until the mushrooms are tender. Remove and keep warm.

3. In the same skillet, combine milk and remaining butter. Bring to a gentle boil; stir in brick cheese. Cook and stir until smooth.

4. Drain tortellini; place in a large bowl. Stir in the mushroom mixture and spinach. Add cheese sauce and toss to coat.

5. Transfer to a greased 3-qt. baking dish; sprinkle with mozzarella cheese. Cover; bake at 350° for 15 minutes. Uncover; bake 5-10 minutes longer or until heated through and the mozzarella cheese is melted. **Yield:** 12 servings.

Tortellini Spinach Casserole
Prep: 20 min. **Bake:** 20 min.

Barbara Kellen, Antioch, Illinois

Spinach gives this popular casserole a fresh taste that will delight even those who say they don't like spinach. In fact, people are often surprised at just how good it is! Whenever I bring it to a gathering, it doesn't sit around long.

2 packages (10 ounces *each*) frozen cheese tortellini
1 pound sliced fresh mushrooms

Spaghetti Squash with Red Sauce
Prep: 25 min. **Cook:** 15 min.

✓ This recipe includes Nutrition Facts & Diabetic Exchanges.

1 medium spaghetti squash (about 4 pounds)
2 cups chopped fresh tomatoes
1 cup sliced fresh mushrooms
1 cup diced green pepper
1/2 cup shredded carrot
1/4 cup diced red onion
2 teaspoons Italian seasoning
1/8 teaspoon pepper
1 tablespoon olive oil
2 garlic cloves, minced
1 can (15 ounces) tomato sauce
Grated Parmesan cheese, optional

1. Cut squash in half lengthwise; discard seeds. Place squash, cut side down, on a microwave-safe plate. Microwave, uncovered, on high for 14-16 minutes or until tender.

2. Meanwhile, in a large skillet, saute the tomatoes, mushrooms, green pepper, carrot, onion, Italian seasoning and pepper in oil for 6-8 minutes or until vegetables are tender. Add garlic; cook 1 minute longer. Stir in tomato sauce; heat through.

3. When squash is cool enough to handle, use a fork to separate strands. Place squash on a serving platter; top with sauce. Sprinkle with cheese if desired. **Yield:** 6 servings.

Editor's Note: This recipe was tested in a 1,100-watt microwave.

Nutrition Facts: 3/4 cup squash with 1/3 cup sauce (calculated without Parmesan cheese) equals 135 calories, 4 g fat (1 g saturated fat), 0 cholesterol, 372 mg sodium, 25 g carbohydrate, 6 g fiber, 4 g protein. **Diabetic Exchanges:** 2 vegetable, 1 starch, 1/2 fat.

KATHRYN PEHL PRESCOTT, ARIZONA

This fabulous, meatless main dish is a great way to get the kids to eat lots of vegetables—and a great way for you to use up some of the fresh harvest from your garden.

GRAND
PRIZE
WINNER

Saucy Pork Chops

Prep: 15 min. **Cook:** 4-1/4 hours

Jennifer Ruberg, Two Harbors, Minnesota

I don't always have time to fix dinner so I've come to rely on my slow cooker. Here's my favorite recipes for busy nights.

4 bone-in pork loin chops (8 ounces *each*)
1 teaspoon garlic powder
1/2 teaspoon salt
1/4 teaspoon pepper
2 tablespoons canola oil
2 cups ketchup
1/2 cup packed brown sugar
1 teaspoon Liquid Smoke, optional

1. Sprinkle pork chops with garlic powder, salt and pepper. In a large skillet, brown chops in oil on both sides; drain.

2. In a small bowl, combine the ketchup, brown sugar and Liquid Smoke if desired. Pour half of the sauce into a 3-qt. slow cooker. Top with pork chops and remaining sauce. Cover and cook on low for 4-5 hours or until meat is tender. **Yield:** 4 servings.

Nutrition Facts: 1 serving equals 371 calories, 12 g fat (3 g saturated fat), 28 mg cholesterol, 1,748 mg sodium, 60 g carbohydrate, 2 g fiber, 11 g protein.

Lemon Shrimp Stir-Fry

Prep: 25 min. **Cook:** 10 min.

Caroline Elliott, Grants Pass, Oregon

I got this good-for-you recipe about 10 years ago from a friend. The tasty shrimp and crisp-tender veggies are coated with a mild, lemony sauce that makes this colorful dish a winner.

1 tablespoon cornstarch
1/2 teaspoon sugar
1/2 teaspoon chicken bouillon granules
1/4 teaspoon grated lemon peel
Dash pepper
1/2 cup water
4-1/2 teaspoons lemon juice
1/2 pound uncooked medium shrimp, peeled and deveined
1 tablespoon canola oil
3/4 cup sliced celery
1/2 medium green pepper, cut into strips
1/2 medium sweet red pepper, cut into strips
1 cup sliced fresh mushrooms
3/4 cup fresh sugar snap peas
1 green onion, sliced
1 cup hot cooked long grain rice

1. In a small bowl, combine the first five ingredients. Stir in the water and lemon juice until blended; set bowl aside.

2. In a large skillet or wok, stir-fry shrimp in oil for 1-2 minutes or until no longer pink. Remove with a slotted spoon and keep warm. In the same pan, stir-fry celery and peppers for 2 minutes. Add the mushrooms, peas and onion; stir-fry 3-4 minutes longer or until vegetables are crisp-tender.

3. Stir the cornstarch mixture and add to the pan. Bring to a boil; cook and stir for 2 minutes or until thickened. Add shrimp; heat through. Serve with rice. **Yield:** 2 servings.

Nutrition Facts: 1-1/2 cups shrimp mixture with 1/2 cup rice equals 326 calories, 9 g fat (1 g saturated fat), 168 mg cholesterol, 449 mg sodium, 39 g carbohydrate, 4 g fiber, 24 g protein. **Diabetic Exchanges:** 3 lean meat, 2 starch, 2 vegetable, 1-1/2 fat.

Thai Tofu Lettuce Wraps

Prep/Total Time: 25 min.

Laureen Pittman, Riverside, California

I couldn't keep this yummy, light lunch under wraps! The original recipe featured chicken, but I modified it for my vegetarian husband. Now both of us prefer the Thai-style tofu version.

1/4 cup rice vinegar
1/4 cup canola oil
  2 tablespoons lime juice
  2 tablespoons mayonnaise
  2 tablespoons creamy peanut butter
  1 tablespoon brown sugar
  1 tablespoon soy sauce
  2 teaspoons minced fresh gingerroot
  1 teaspoon sesame oil
  1 teaspoon Thai chili sauce
  1 garlic clove, peeled
1/2 cup minced fresh cilantro, *divided*
  1 package (14 ounces) firm tofu, drained and cut into 1/2-inch cubes
1/2 cup chopped green onions
1/2 cup shredded carrots
  1 small sweet red pepper, diced
3/4 cup dry roasted peanuts, chopped, *divided*
  8 Bibb *or* Boston lettuce leaves

1. For dressing, in a blender, combine the first 11 ingredients; cover and process until smooth. Stir in 1/4 cup cilantro.

2. In a large bowl, combine the tofu, onions, carrots, red pepper, 1/2 cup peanuts and remaining cilantro. Add dressing and toss to coat.

3. Divide among lettuce leaves; sprinkle with remaining peanuts. Fold lettuce over filling. **Yield:** 4 servings.

Citrus Baked Fish

Prep: 5 min. + marinating **Bake:** 15 min.

Phyllis Allen, Vero Beach, Florida

This recipe allows me to combine two things abundant in Florida—fresh fish and orange juice. The orange juice gives the fish a wonderful, tangy flavor.

1/4 cup thawed orange juice concentrate
  1 tablespoon canola oil
  1 teaspoon snipped fresh dill *or* 1/4 teaspoon dill weed
  4 red snapper *or* tilapia fillets (6 ounces *each*)
  2 orange slices, halved
Paprika

1. In a large resealable plastic bag, combine the orange juice concentrate, oil and dill; add fish. Seal bag and turn to coat; refrigerate for at least 15 minutes.

2. Drain and discard marinade. Place the fillets in a greased 15-in. x 10-in. x 1-in. baking pan. Cover and bake at 350° for 15-20 minutes or until fish flakes easily with a fork.

3. Dip cut edges of orange slices in paprika; serve with fish. **Yield:** 4 servings.

Flavorful Fish

To bring out the flavor in fish, marinate the fillets in lemon juice and salt for 15 minutes. It makes the flesh firmer and easier to handle, and gives the fish a fresh taste.

Veggie Lasagna

Prep: 70 min. **Bake:** 1-1/4 hours + standing

Mary Jane Jones, Williamstown, West Virginia

No one will miss the meat when you serve this vegetable-rich lasagna. It has a robust, full-bodied flavor. To save time, prepare the carrot and spinach layers in advance.

   1 package (16 ounces) frozen sliced carrots
1/4 cup finely chopped onion
   2 tablespoons butter
   1 cup ricotta cheese
1/4 teaspoon *each* salt and pepper
SPINACH LAYER:
   2 shallots, chopped
   1 tablespoon olive oil
   2 packages (10 ounces *each*) frozen chopped spinach, thawed and squeezed dry
   1 cup ricotta cheese
   1 egg
1/4 teaspoon *each* salt and pepper
EGGPLANT LAYER:
   1 medium eggplant, peeled and cut into 1/4-inch slices
   3 garlic cloves, minced
   6 tablespoons olive oil
1/2 teaspoon salt
2-1/2 cups marinara sauce

  12 lasagna noodles, cooked and drained
1/4 cup minced fresh basil
   4 cups (16 ounces) part-skim shredded mozzarella cheese
   3 cups grated Parmesan cheese

1. Cook carrots according to package directions; drain and cool. In a small skillet, saute onion in butter until tender. In a food processor, puree the carrots, onion, ricotta, salt and pepper. In the same skillet, saute shallots in oil until tender. In a food processor, puree the shallots, spinach, ricotta, egg, salt and pepper.

2. In a large skillet, cook eggplant and garlic in oil over medium heat in batches for 7-10 minutes or until tender; drain. Sprinkle with salt.

3. Spread 1/2 cup marinara sauce in a greased 13-in. x 9-in. baking dish. Layer with four noodles, carrot mixture, 1/2 cup sauce, 1 tablespoon basil, 1 cup mozzarella and 3/4 cup Parmesan. Top with four noodles, eggplant, 1/2 cup sauce, 1 tablespoon basil, 1 cup mozzarella and 3/4 cup Parmesan.

4. Layer with remaining noodles, spinach mixture, 1/2 cup sauce, 1 tablespoon basil, 1 cup mozzarella and 3/4 cup Parmesan. Top with remaining sauce, basil, mozzarella and Parmesan (dish will be full).

5. Cover and bake at 350° for 1 hour. Uncover; bake 15 minutes longer or until bubbly. Let stand 15 minutes before serving. **Yield:** 12 servings.

Tomato Salmon Bake

Prep/Total Time: 30 min.

Lacey Parker, Cary, North Carolina

I was looking for a healthy alternative to beef and chicken when I found this recipe and decided to personalize it. My husband doesn't usually like fish unless it's fried, but he loves the Italian flavor in this dish. Serve it with a green salad for a great meal any time of year.

    4 **salmon fillets (6 ounces *each*)**
    1 **can (14-1/2 ounces) diced tomatoes, drained**
1/2 **cup sun-dried tomato salad dressing**
    2 **tablespoons shredded Parmesan cheese**
Hot cooked rice

1. Place salmon in a greased 13-in. x 9-in. baking dish. Combine tomatoes and salad dressing; pour over salmon. Sprinkle with cheese.

2. Bake, uncovered, at 375° for 20-25 minutes or until fish flakes easily with a fork. Serve with rice. **Yield:** 4 servings.

Apple-Stuffed Pork Chops

Prep: 30 min. **Bake:** 15 min.

Heather Kenney, Arlington, Virginia

My family has used apples for many great dishes, including this one from my grandmother that I adapted for two. It uses apples, apple butter and apple cider. My boyfriend loves it served with a baked sweet potato and green salad.

    2 **tablespoons apple butter**
    2 **tablespoons cider vinegar**
    1 **tablespoon Dijon mustard**
    2 **to 3 teaspoons minced fresh rosemary**
    2 **boneless butterflied pork chops (6 ounces *each*)**
3/4 **teaspoon salt**
1/4 **teaspoon pepper**
    1 **large tart apple, chopped**
1/3 **cup chopped sweet onion**
    2 **tablespoons butter**
3/4 **cup apple cider *or* juice**

1. In a small bowl, combine the apple butter, vinegar, mustard and rosemary. Flatten pork chops to 1/2-in. thickness; sprinkle with salt and pepper. Brush with apple butter mixture.

2. Combine apple and onion; place over one side of each pork chop. Fold other side of pork over filling and secure with toothpicks.

3. In a small ovenproof skillet, brown chops in butter for 3-4 minutes on each side or until a thermometer reads 145°. Add cider.

4. Bake, uncovered, at 350° for 15-20 minutes or until apples and onions are tender. Remove the chops and keep warm. Bring the pan juices to a boil; cook until reduced by half. Discard toothpicks. Serve pork chops with sauce. **Yield:** 2 servings.

Editor's Note: This recipe was tested with commercially prepared apple butter.

Roasted Vegetable Lasagna

Prep: 50 min. **Bake:** 30 min. + standing

Margaret Welder, Madrid, Iowa

With a vegetarian on my guest list, I was inspired to make this lasagna for a party. Watching the cheese bubble and smelling the veggies roasting, I couldn't wait for the party to start. Everyone went home with the recipe.

- 1 small eggplant
- 2 small zucchini
- 5 plum tomatoes, seeded
- 1 large sweet red pepper
- 1 large onion, cut into small wedges
- 1/4 cup olive oil
- 3 tablespoons minced fresh basil, *divided*
- 3 garlic cloves, minced
- 3/4 teaspoon salt, *divided*
- 1/2 teaspoon pepper, *divided*
- 2/3 cup pitted Greek olives, chopped
- 1/4 cup butter, cubed
- 1/4 cup all-purpose flour
- 2-3/4 cups milk
- 1 bay leaf
- 1/8 teaspoon ground nutmeg
- 5 tablespoons grated Parmesan cheese, *divided*
- 2 tablespoons shredded Asiago cheese
- 3/4 cup shredded part-skim mozzarella cheese
- 6 no-cook lasagna noodles

1. Cut eggplant, zucchini, tomatoes and red pepper into 1-in. pieces; place in a large bowl. Add onion, oil, 2 tablespoons basil, garlic, 1/2 teaspoon salt and 1/4 teaspoon pepper; toss. Transfer to two greased 15-in. x 10-in. x 1-in. baking pans. Bake at 450° for 20-25 minutes or until crisp-tender. Stir in olives.

2. In a large saucepan, melt the butter; stir in flour until smooth. Gradually stir in milk. Add bay leaf and nutmeg. Bring to a boil; cook and stir for 2 minutes or until thickened. Remove from heat.

3. Stir in 3 tablespoons Parmesan, Asiago and remaining basil, salt and pepper. Discard bay leaf. Spread a fourth of the sauce in a greased 11-in. x 7-in. baking dish. Top with 2-1/3 cups vegetables, 1/4 cup mozzarella and three noodles. Repeat layers.

4. Top with a fourth of the sauce, remaining vegetables, mozzarella, sauce and Parmesan. Cover and bake at 375° for 30-40 minutes or until bubbly. Let stand 15 minutes before serving. **Yield:** 8 servings.

Mediterranean Vegetable Pasta

Prep/Total Time: 25 min.

✓ This recipe includes Nutrition Facts.

- 3 ounces uncooked angel hair pasta
- 1 cup chopped zucchini
- 1/2 cup chopped fresh mushrooms
- 1/3 cup chopped green pepper
- 1/4 cup chopped onion
- 2 teaspoons olive oil
- 1 garlic clove, minced
- 1 cup canned Italian diced tomatoes
- 6 pitted ripe olives, halved
- 1/8 teaspoon pepper
- 1/4 cup crumbled reduced-fat feta cheese
- 1 tablespoon shredded Parmesan cheese

1. Cook pasta according to package directions. Meanwhile, in a large skillet, saute the zucchini, mushrooms, green pepper and onion in oil until vegetables are crisp-tender. Add garlic; cook 1 minute longer. Stir in the tomatoes, olives and pepper; heat through.

2. Drain pasta; divide between two plates. Top with vegetable mixture and cheeses. **Yield:** 2 servings.

Nutrition Facts: 2 cups equals 321 calories, 9 g fat (2 g saturated fat), 7 mg cholesterol, 800 mg sodium, 49 g carbohydrate, 4 g fiber, 12 g protein.

JAN CLARK NEW FLORENCE, MISSOURI

I created this fast-to-fix recipe to use up excess zucchini from our garden. Served over delicate angel hair pasta, it creates a colorful and palate-pleasing entree suitable for any occasion.

GRAND
PRIZE
WINNER

PG. 150

PG. 155

PG. 157

SIDES, BREADS & CONDIMENTS

Looking for that perfect something to round out your meal? This chapter has it covered thanks to its hearty collection of home–style side dishes, freshly baked loaves, flavorful salad dressings and more.

PG. 152

Sour Cream Loaves

Prep: 15 min. **Bake:** 40 min. + cooling

Joyce Lemkuil, Branson, Missouri

Cinnamon and nutmeg lend just the right amount of flavor to these moist mini loaves. The batter also works well for muffins.

> ✓ This recipe includes Nutrition Facts.

2/3	cup butter, softened
2/3	cup plus 1 tablespoon sugar, *divided*
1	egg
1/2	teaspoon vanilla extract
1-1/2	cups all-purpose flour
1/2	teaspoon baking soda
1/2	teaspoon salt
1/2	teaspoon ground nutmeg
1/2	teaspoon ground cinnamon, *divided*
1/2	cup sour cream

1. In a large bowl, cream butter and 2/3 cup sugar until light and fluffy. Beat in egg and vanilla. Combine the flour, baking soda, salt, nutmeg and 1/4 teaspoon cinnamon; gradually add to creamed mixture alternately with sour cream.

2. Pour into two 5-3/4-in. x 3-in. x 2-in. loaf pans coated with cooking spray. Combine remaining sugar and cinnamon; sprinkle over batter.

3. Bake at 350° for 40-45 minutes or until a toothpick inserted near the center comes out clean. Cool loaves for 10 minutes before removing from pans to a wire rack. **Yield:** 2 mini loaves (6 slices each).

Nutrition Facts: 1 slice equals 221 calories, 12 g fat (8 g saturated fat), 52 mg cholesterol, 264 mg sodium, 25 g carbohydrate, trace fiber, 3 g protein.

Cherry Cranberry Chutney

Prep/Total Time: 30 min.

Joann Ciboch, St. Joseph, Michigan

I found this recipe in a cookbook compiled by a friend's quilting group. Try it alongside chicken—but don't stop there! It's also good with turkey, ham, pork and venison.

> ✓ This recipe includes Nutrition Facts.

1	cup dried cherries
1/2	cup fresh *or* frozen cranberries
1/2	cup raisins
1/4	cup sugar
1/4	cup cider vinegar
1/4	cup unsweetened apple juice
1/4	cup chopped celery
1-1/2	teaspoons grated lemon peel
1/4 to 3/4	teaspoon crushed red pepper flakes
1/2	cup chopped walnuts, toasted

1. In a small saucepan, combine the first nine ingredients. Bring to a boil. Reduce heat to medium; cover and cook for 15-20 minutes or until celery is tender, stirring occasionally.

2. Remove from the heat; stir in walnuts. Serve chutney warm or at room temperature. Refrigerate leftovers. **Yield:** 2 cups.

Nutrition Facts: 1/4 cup equals 159 calories, 5 g fat (trace saturated fat), 0 cholesterol, 5 mg sodium, 29 g carbohydrate, 2 g fiber, 3 g protein.

Cranberry-Walnut Sweet Potatoes

Prep: 25 min. **Bake:** 1 hour

Mary Wilhelm, Sparta, Wisconsin

For me, the best part of Thanksgiving dinner is the sweet potatoes! But you don't have to wait for Thanksgiving to enjoy this impressive side dish.

> ✓ This recipe includes Nutrition Facts.

    4 large sweet potatoes
1/4 cup finely chopped onion
    1 tablespoon butter
    1 cup fresh *or* frozen cranberries
1/3 cup maple syrup
1/4 cup water
1/4 cup cranberry juice
1/4 teaspoon salt, *divided*
1/2 cup chopped walnuts, toasted
    1 teaspoon Dijon mustard
1/4 teaspoon pepper
    2 tablespoons minced chives

1. Scrub and pierce sweet potatoes. Bake at 400° for 1 hour or until tender.

2. In a small saucepan, saute onion in butter until tender. Add the cranberries, syrup, water, cranberry juice and 1/8 teaspoon salt. Bring to a boil. Reduce heat; cover and simmer for 10-15 minutes or until berries pop, stirring occasionally. Stir in walnuts and mustard; heat through.

3. Cut the potatoes in half lengthwise; sprinkle with pepper and remaining salt. Top each potato half with 2 tablespoons cranberry mixture; sprinkle with chives. **Yield:** 8 servings.

Nutrition Facts: 1/2 potato equals 249 calories, 6 g fat (1 g saturated fat), 4 mg cholesterol, 120 mg sodium, 46 g carbohydrate, 6 g fiber, 5 g protein

Selecting Sweet Potatoes

Sweet potatoes should be firm with no cracks or bruises. If stored in a cool, dark, well-ventilated place, they'll remain fresh for about 2 weeks. Once cooked, sweet potatoes can be stored for up to 1 week in the refrigerator.

Creamed Spinach

Prep/Total Time: 30 min.

Jill Obreiter, Moorpark, California

My twins would not eat anything that even resembled a vegetable, but they would eat seconds—and sometimes thirds—of this fabulous spinach dish.

    1 large onion, finely chopped
    4 green onions, finely chopped
    4 bacon strips, diced
    2 tablespoons plus 2 teaspoons butter
    1 garlic clove, minced
1/2 cup all-purpose flour
1-1/4 teaspoons salt
1/4 teaspoon pepper
2-1/2 cups whole milk
    3 packages (10 ounces *each*) frozen chopped spinach, thawed and squeezed dry
1/2 cup half-and-half cream

1. In a large skillet, cook the onions and bacon in butter over medium heat until bacon is crisp. Add garlic; cook 1 minute longer. Stir in the flour, salt and pepper until blended.

2. Gradually add milk. Bring to a boil; cook and stir for 2 minutes or until thickened. Stir in spinach and cream; cook 3-5 minutes longer or until heated through. **Yield:** 6 servings.

Just Delish Veggie Kabobs

Prep: 30 min. + marinating **Grill:** 10 min.

Agnes Ward, Stratford, Ontario

I first tried these kabobs at my son's cottage this year. They're so tasty, they go with just about any meat! Invite your neighbors over for a grilling get-together and serve these wonderful skewers.

 This recipe includes Nutrition Facts & Diabetic Exchanges.

8 small red potatoes, halved
3 tablespoons unsweetened apple juice
3 tablespoons red wine vinegar

2 tablespoons minced fresh basil
1 tablespoon Dijon mustard
1 tablespoon honey
1 tablespoon reduced-sodium soy sauce
2 teaspoons olive oil
2 garlic cloves, minced
1/4 teaspoon pepper
12 medium fresh mushrooms
1 large sweet red pepper, cut into 1-inch pieces
1 medium zucchini, cut into 1/2-inch slices

1. Place potatoes in a steamer basket; place in a large saucepan over 1 in. of water. Bring to a boil; cover and steam for 7-9 minutes or just until tender. Cool.

2. In a large resealable plastic bag, combine the apple juice, vinegar, basil, mustard, honey, soy sauce, oil, garlic and pepper. Add the mushrooms, red pepper, zucchini and cooked potatoes. Seal bag and turn to coat; refrigerate for 2 hours.

3. Drain and reserve marinade. On four metal or soaked wooden skewers, alternately thread vegetables. Using long-handled tongs, moisten a paper towel with cooking oil and lightly coat the grill rack.

4. Grill the kabobs, covered, over medium heat or broil 4 in. from the heat for 10-15 minutes, turning and basting occasionally with reserved marinade. **Yield:** 4 servings.

Nutrition Facts: 1 kabob equals 168 calories, 3 g fat (trace saturated fat), 0 cholesterol, 258 mg sodium, 32 g carbohydrate, 4 g fiber, 5 g protein. **Diabetic Exchanges:** 1-1/2 starch, 1 vegetable, 1/2 fat.

Sweet Potatoes and Apples Au Gratin

Prep: 25 min. **Bake:** 45 min.

 This recipe includes Nutrition Facts & Diabetic Exchange.

3 cups thinly sliced tart apples (about 3 large)
1 teaspoon lemon juice
3 pounds sweet potatoes (about 5 medium), peeled and thinly sliced
1/4 cup maple syrup
1 tablespoon butter, melted
1/2 teaspoon salt
1/4 teaspoon pepper
1 cup soft bread crumbs
2 teaspoons olive oil
1/4 teaspoon ground cinnamon
1/4 teaspoon ground nutmeg
1/4 teaspoon cider vinegar

1. Place apples in a large bowl; sprinkle with lemon juice. Add the sweet potatoes, syrup, butter, salt and pepper; toss to coat.

2. Transfer to a 3-qt. baking dish coated with cooking spray. Bake, uncovered, at 400° for 35-40 minutes or until apples are tender, stirring once.

3. In a small bowl, combine the bread crumbs, oil, cinnamon, nutmeg and vinegar; sprinkle over potato mixture. Bake 10-15 minutes longer or until topping is golden brown. **Yield:** 12 servings.

Nutrition Facts: 1 serving equals 130 calories, 2 g fat (1 g saturated fat), 3 mg cholesterol, 136 mg sodium, 27 g carbohydrate, 3 g fiber, 2 g protein. **Diabetic Exchange:** 2 starch.

ERIKA VICKERMAN HOPKINS, MINNESOTA

This is a favorite dish of ours that we make every year during the holidays. People on both sides of the family rave about it! The spices go beautifully with both the apples and sweet potatoes and the maple syrup adds a lovely sweetness.

GRAND PRIZE WINNER

Sun-Dried Tomato 'n' Basil Wreath

Prep: 50 min. + rising **Bake:** 20 min.

Teresa Morancie, Brewer, Maine

I added a few creative touches to a family recipe and came up with this bright and pretty wreath. Served with herb butter, it makes a special accompaniment to any meal.

✓ This recipe includes Nutrition Facts & Diabetic Exchanges.

1/2 cup boiling water
1/4 cup sun-dried tomatoes (not packed in oil)
1/2 cup fat-free milk
1/4 cup grated Parmesan cheese
3 tablespoons butter
2 tablespoons sugar
4-1/2 teaspoons minced fresh basil
1/2 teaspoon salt
1 package (1/4 ounce) active dry yeast
2 tablespoons warm water (110° to 115°)
1 egg, beaten
2-1/4 to 2-1/2 cups all-purpose flour
HERB BUTTER:
1 tablespoon butter
2-1/4 teaspoons minced fresh basil
1-1/2 teaspoons grated Parmesan cheese
1-1/2 teaspoons olive oil

1. Pour boiling water over tomatoes; let stand 15 minutes. In a saucepan, combine the next six ingredients. Drain and chop tomatoes; add to pan. Cook and stir mixture over low heat until sugar is dissolved. Remove from heat; cool slightly.

2. In a large bowl, dissolve yeast in warm water. Add tomato mixture, egg and 2 cups flour; beat until smooth. Stir in enough remaining flour to form a soft dough. Knead on a floured surface until smooth, about 6-8 minutes. Place in a bowl coated with cooking spray; turn once to coat top. Cover and let rise until doubled, about 1 hour.

3. In a small saucepan, melt the butter; add the basil, Parmesan and oil. Keep warm. Punch the dough down; divide dough into three portions. Shape each into an 18-in. rope.

4. Brush with half of herb butter. Place ropes on a baking sheet coated with cooking spray; braid and shape into a wreath. Pinch ends to seal. Cover and let rise until doubled, about 40 minutes.

5. Brush with remaining herb butter. Bake at 350° for 20-25 minutes or until golden brown. Remove to a wire rack. **Yield:** 1 loaf (12 slices).

Nutrition Facts: 1 slice equals 155 calories, 6 g fat (3 g saturated fat), 30 mg cholesterol, 207 mg sodium, 21 g carbohydrate, 1 g fiber, 5 g protein. **Diabetic Exchanges:** 1-1/2 starch, 1 fat.

White 'n' Sweet Mashed Potatoes

Prep/Total Time: 30 min.

Gail Drews, Flat Rock, North Carolina

Sweet potatoes are a staple of Southern cooking in North Carolina. Combined with the russet potatoes in this recipe, they take simple mashed potatoes up a notch or two!

✓ This recipe includes Nutrition Facts.

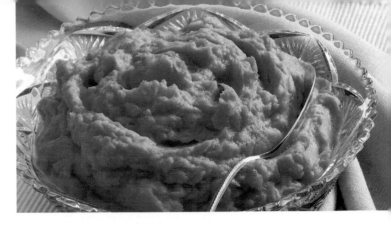

1-1/2 pounds russet potatoes (about 4 medium), peeled and cubed
1-1/2 pounds sweet potatoes (about 4 medium), peeled and cubed
    1 cup milk, warmed
1/4 cup butter, cubed
    1 teaspoon salt
1/2 teaspoon ground cinnamon
1/4 teaspoon ground nutmeg

1. Place russet potatoes and sweet potatoes in a large saucepan and cover with water. Bring to a boil. Reduce heat; cover and simmer for 15-20 minutes or until tender. Drain.

2. In a large bowl, mash the potatoes with the milk, butter, salt, cinnamon and nutmeg until potatoes reach desired consistency. **Yield:** 8 servings.

Nutrition Facts: 3/4 cup equals 172 calories, 7 g fat (4 g saturated fat), 18 mg cholesterol, 354 mg sodium, 26 g carbohydrate, 2 g fiber, 3 g protein.

Hearty Sweet Potato Braids

Prep: 45 min. + rising **Bake:** 30 min.

Suzanne Kesel, Cohocton, New York

We make these hefty loaves yearly. Thyme gives the pretty braids a lovely flavor. For a change, I sometimes use safflower oil in the recipe.

    1 package (1/4 ounce) active dry yeast
1/4 cup warm water (110° to 115°)

1-1/2 cups mashed sweet potatoes, room temperature
    1 cup warm fat-free milk (110° to 115°)
1/4 cup canola oil
    3 tablespoons honey
    1 cup all-purpose flour
1/2 cup yellow cornmeal
    2 teaspoons salt
    1 teaspoon dried thyme
2-3/4 to 3-1/4 cups whole wheat flour
    1 tablespoon cold fat-free milk

1. In a large bowl, dissolve yeast in warm water. Add the sweet potatoes, milk, oil, honey, all-purpose flour, cornmeal, salt, thyme and 2 cups whole wheat flour; beat until smooth. Stir in enough remaining whole wheat flour to form a firm dough.

2. Turn onto a lightly floured surface. Knead until smooth and elastic, about 6-8 minutes. Place in a bowl coated with cooking spray; turn once to coat top. Cover and let rise in a warm place until doubled, about 1 hour.

3. Punch dough down; divide into six equal portions. Shape each into a 20-in. rope. Place three ropes on a baking sheet coated with cooking spray; braid. Pinch ends to seal and tuck under. Repeat with remaining ropes. Cover and let rise in a warm place until doubled, about 35 minutes.

4. Brush loaves with cold milk. Bake at 350° for 30-35 minutes or until golden brown. Remove to wire racks. **Yield:** 2 loaves (12 slices each).

Crumb-Topped Asparagus Casserole

Prep: 20 min. **Bake:** 20 min.

Mrs. E. Allen Orem, Rochester, New York

When we lived on a farm, we had an abundance of fresh vegetables, so I would also make this family favorite with broccoli or green beans instead of asparagus.

- 2 pounds fresh asparagus, trimmed and cut into 1-inch pieces
- 2 cans (10-3/4 ounces *each*) condensed cream of celery soup, undiluted
- 1/2 cup heavy whipping cream
- 1/2 cup mayonnaise
- 1 tablespoon Heinz 57 steak sauce
- 1/4 teaspoon ground cloves
- 1/4 teaspoon ground nutmeg
- 1 cup (4 ounces) shredded cheddar cheese
- 2-1/2 cups crushed seasoned stuffing
- 5 tablespoons butter, melted

1. In a large saucepan, bring 1/2 in. of water to a boil. Add asparagus; cover and boil for 3-5 minutes or until crisp-tender. Drain well. Place in a greased 11-in. x 7-in. baking dish; set aside.

2. In a small bowl, combine the soup, cream, mayonnaise, steak sauce, cloves and nutmeg. Spread over asparagus; sprinkle with cheese.

3. In another small bowl, toss stuffing with butter; sprinkle over casserole. Bake, uncovered, at 350° for 20-25 minutes or until bubbly. **Yield:** 8 servings.

Nutrition Facts: 1 serving (3/4 cup) equals 383 calories, 30 g fat (13 g saturated fat), 62 mg cholesterol, 803 mg sodium, 21 g carbohydrate, 2 g fiber, 8 g protein.

Keeping Asparagus at Its Peak

To keep asparagus fresh longer, place cut stems in a container of cold water and keep refrigerated, changing the water once every 3 days.

Almond-Filled Butterhorns

Prep: 30 min. + rising **Bake:** 10 min./batch

- 3-1/4 teaspoons active dry yeast
- 2 cups warm milk (110° to 115°)
- 4 eggs
- 1 cup mashed potato flakes
- 1 cup butter, softened
- 1/2 cup sugar
- 1-1/8 teaspoons salt
- 7 to 8 cups all-purpose flour
- 1 can (12-1/2 ounces) almond cake and pastry filling

1. In a large bowl, dissolve yeast in milk. Add the eggs, potato flakes, butter, sugar, salt and 4 cups flour. Beat on medium speed for 3 minutes. Beat until smooth. Stir in enough remaining flour to form a soft dough (dough will be sticky).

2. Turn onto a floured surface; knead until smooth and elastic, about 6-8 minutes. Place in a greased bowl, turning once to grease top. Cover and let rise in a warm place until doubled, about 1 hour.

3. Punch dough down. Turn onto a lightly floured surface; divide into thirds. Roll each portion into a 12-in. circle; spread each with filling. Cut each circle into 12 wedges.

4. Roll up wedges from the wide end and place point side down 2 in. apart on greased baking sheets. Curve ends to form a crescent. Cover and let rise until doubled, about 30 minutes.

5. Bake at 375° for 10-12 minutes or until lightly browned. Remove from pans to wire racks. Serve warm. **Yield:** 3 dozen.

Editor's Note: This recipe was tested with Solo brand cake and pastry filling. Look for it in the baking aisle.

LORAINE MEYER BEND, OREGON

I add potato flakes to make my butterhorns moist and tender. The rolls complement any meal wonderfully with just the right touch of sweetness to make them a coffee hour favorite, too. Just remember to hide a few for yourself!

GRAND
PRIZE
WINNER

Lemon Yogurt Bread

Prep: 15 min. **Bake:** 45 min. + cooling

Suzy Horvath, Gladstone, Oregon

This light and luscious quick bread will remind you of pound cake. Its mild lemon flavor and cake-like texture make it perfect for brunch or a midafternoon snack.

✓ This recipe includes Nutrition Facts & Diabetic Exchanges.

1-1/2 cups all-purpose flour
3/4 cup sugar
1/2 teaspoon salt
1/2 teaspoon baking soda
1/4 teaspoon baking powder
1 egg
1 cup (8 ounces) lemon yogurt
1/3 cup canola oil
1 tablespoon lemon juice

1. In a large bowl, combine the flour, sugar, salt, baking soda and baking powder. In another bowl, combine the egg, yogurt, oil and lemon juice. Stir into dry ingredients just until moistened.

2. Pour into an 8-in. x 4-in. loaf pan coated with cooking spray. Bake at 325° for 45-50 minutes or until a toothpick inserted near the center comes out clean. Cool for 10 minutes before removing from pan to a wire rack. **Yield:** 1 loaf (12 slices).

Nutrition Facts: 1 slice equals 177 calories, 7 g fat (1 g saturated fat), 18 mg cholesterol, 176 mg sodium, 26 g carbohydrate, 1 g fiber, 3 g protein. **Diabetic Exchanges:** 1-1/2 starch, 1 fat.

Cheese Potato Puff

Prep: 45 min. **Bake:** 40 min.

Beverly Templeton, Garner, Iowa

I enjoy entertaining and always look for recipes that can be made ahead of time. I got this comforting potato dish from my mother-in-law. It's wonderful because I can prepare it the night before and it contains basic ingredients that everyone loves—like milk and cheddar cheese.

12 medium potatoes, peeled (about 5 pounds)
1 teaspoon salt, *divided*
3/4 cup butter, cubed
2 cups (8 ounces) shredded cheddar cheese
1 cup milk
2 eggs, beaten
Minced chives, optional

1. Place potatoes in a large kettle; cover with water. Add 1/2 teaspoon salt; cook until tender. Drain; mash potatoes until smooth.

2. In a large saucepan, cook and stir the butter, cheese, milk and remaining salt until smooth. Stir into potatoes; fold in eggs. Pour into a greased 3-qt. baking dish. Bake, uncovered, at 350° for 40 minutes or until puffy and golden brown. Sprinkle with chives if desired. **Yield:** 8-10 servings.

Grilled Mushrooms

Prep/Total Time: 15 min.

Melanie Knoll, Marshalltown, Iowa

Mushrooms cooked over hot coals always taste good, but this easy recipe takes the simple ingredient to a whole new level.

✓	This recipe includes Nutrition Facts.

1/2 pound whole fresh medium mushrooms
1/4 cup butter, melted
1/2 teaspoon dill weed
1/2 teaspoon garlic salt

1. Thread mushrooms on skewers. Combine butter, dill and garlic salt; brush over mushrooms.

2. Using long-handled tongs, moisten a paper towel with cooking oil and lightly coat the grill rack. Grill over hot heat or broil 3-4 in. from the heat, for 10-15 minutes, basting and turning every 5 minutes. **Yield:** 4 servings.

Nutrition Facts: 1 serving (1 cup) equals 77 calories, 8 g fat (5 g saturated fat), 20 mg cholesterol, 230 mg sodium, 2 g carbohydrate, trace fiber, 1 g protein.

Save Them for Later

Fresh mushrooms should be used within a few days of purchase. If that's not possible, you can blanch or saute them in a jiffy, then freeze them for up to 1 month for use in homemade soups, sauces and casseroles.

Streusel Fruit Bread

Prep: 20 min. **Bake:** 40 min. + cooling

Robert Logan, Clayton, California

This recipe has been handed down through the years in my family, but over time I've added my own touches. The result is a delightful bread chock-full of dried fruits and nuts.

3/4 cup all-purpose flour
1/3 cup sugar
3/4 teaspoon ground cinnamon

1/4 teaspoon salt
1/4 teaspoon baking soda
1 egg
1/3 cup mashed ripe banana
2 tablespoons canola oil
2 tablespoons light corn syrup
3/4 teaspoon vanilla extract
1/4 cup chopped pecans
2 tablespoons dried cranberries
2 tablespoons chopped dried apricots
TOPPING:
2 tablespoons brown sugar
1 tablespoon all-purpose flour
1-1/2 teaspoons cold butter

1. In a small bowl, combine the flour, sugar, cinnamon, salt and baking soda; set aside. In another bowl, beat the egg, banana, oil, corn syrup and vanilla. Stir into dry ingredients just until moistened. Fold in the pecans, cranberries and apricots.

2. Pour into a 5-3/4-in. x 3-in. x 2-in. loaf pan coated with cooking spray. For topping, combine brown sugar and flour in a small bowl. Cut in butter until crumbly. Sprinkle over batter.

3. Bake at 325° for 40-45 minutes or until a toothpick inserted near the center comes out clean. Cool for 10 minutes before removing from pan to a wire rack. **Yield:** 1 mini loaf (6 slices).

Apricot Nut Bread

Prep: 25 min. **Bake:** 55 min. + cooling

Robert Logan, Clayton, California

My family likes bread, apricots and nuts, so I put all three together to create a recipe. It's fairly easy to make, and everyone loves it. It never lasts long in our house.

✓ This recipe includes Nutrition Facts & Diabetic Exchanges.

    1 **cup boiling water**
1-1/4 **cups chopped dried apricots**
    2 **cups all-purpose flour**
  2/3 **cup sugar**
1-1/2 **teaspoons baking powder**
    1 **teaspoon salt**
  1/4 **teaspoon baking soda**

    1 **egg**
  3/4 **cup apricot nectar**
    2 **tablespoons butter, melted**
  1/4 **cup chopped pecans**
    1 **tablespoon grated orange peel**
GLAZE:
    2 **tablespoons brown sugar**
    1 **tablespoon butter**
1-1/2 **teaspoons fat-free milk**
    2 **tablespoons finely chopped pecans**

1. In a small bowl, pour boiling water over apricots; set aside. In a large bowl, combine the flour, sugar, baking powder, salt and baking soda. Whisk the egg, apricot nectar and butter; stir into dry ingredients just until moistened. Drain apricots; fold into batter with pecans and orange peel.

2. Transfer to an 8-in. x 4-in. loaf pan coated with cooking spray. Bake at 350° for 55-65 minutes or until a toothpick inserted near the center comes out clean. Cool for 10 minutes before removing from pan to a wire rack.

3. For glaze, combine the brown sugar, butter and milk in a small saucepan. Cook and stir over medium heat until butter is melted and mixture is smooth. Cool to room temperature; drizzle over bread. Sprinkle with pecans. **Yield:** 1 loaf (12 slices).

Nutrition Facts: 1 slice equals 233 calories, 6 g fat (2 g saturated fat), 25 mg cholesterol, 320 mg sodium, 42 g carbohydrate, 2 g fiber, 3 g protein. **Diabetic Exchanges:** 2 starch, 1 fruit, 1 fat.

Buttery Sweet Potato Casserole

Prep: 15 min. **Bake:** 20 min.

Sue Miller, Mars, Pennsylvania

Whenever we get together as a family, my kids, nieces and nephews beg me to make this dish. Luckily for me, it goes together in minutes with canned sweet potatoes.

    2 **cans (15-3/4 ounces *each*) sweet potatoes, drained and mashed**
  1/2 **cup sugar**
    1 **egg**
  1/4 **cup butter, melted**
  1/2 **teaspoon ground cinnamon**
Dash salt
TOPPING:
    1 **cup coarsely crushed butter-flavored crackers (about 25 crackers)**
  1/2 **cup packed brown sugar**
  1/4 **cup butter, melted**

1. In a large bowl, combine the first six ingredients. Transfer to a greased 8-in. square baking dish. Combine the topping ingredients; sprinkle over the sweet potato mixture.

2. Bake, uncovered, at 350° for 20-25 minutes or until a thermometer reads 160°. **Yield:** 6-8 servings.

Special Banana Nut Bread

Prep: 25 min. **Bake:** 1 hour + cooling

Beverly Sprague, Baltimore, Maryland

This extra-special banana bread makes a wonderful "thinking of you" gift for friends and neighbors. The recipe makes two loaves, so I can serve one and keep the other one in the freezer for a handy last-minute gift.

   3/4 **cup butter, softened**
      1 **package (8 ounces) cream cheese, softened**
      2 **cups sugar**
      2 **eggs**
1-1/2 **cups mashed ripe bananas (about 4 medium)**
   1/2 **teaspoon vanilla extract**
      3 **cups all-purpose flour**
   1/2 **teaspoon baking powder**
   1/2 **teaspoon baking soda**
   1/2 **teaspoon salt**

      2 **cups chopped pecans,** *divided*
ORANGE GLAZE:
      1 **cup confectioners' sugar**
      3 **tablespoons orange juice**
      1 **teaspoon grated orange peel**

1. In a large bowl, cream the butter, cream cheese and sugar until light and fluffy. Add eggs, one at a time, beating well after each addition. Beat in bananas and vanilla. Combine the flour, baking powder, baking soda and salt; gradually add to creamed mixture. Fold in 1 cup pecans.

2. Transfer to two greased 8-in. x 4-in. loaf pans. Sprinkle with remaining pecans. Bake at 350° for 1 to 1-1/4 hours or until a toothpick inserted near the center comes out clean.

3. In a small bowl, whisk the glaze ingredients; drizzle over loaves. Cool for 10 minutes before removing from pans to wire racks. **Yield:** 2 loaves (12 slices each).

Zucchini Banana Bread

Prep: 15 min. **Bake:** 40 min. + cooling

Donna Hall, Wolfforth, Texas

I got this recipe from a friend and now it's one of my favorites. It makes three small loaves, and they freeze very well.

✔ This recipe includes Nutrition Facts.

1-1/2 cups all-purpose flour
    1 cup sugar
    1 teaspoon ground cinnamon
1/2 teaspoon baking powder
1/2 teaspoon baking soda
1/2 teaspoon salt
    1 egg
    1 cup mashed ripe bananas
1/2 cup canola oil
1/2 teaspoon banana extract
1/2 teaspoon vanilla extract
    1 cup shredded zucchini
1/2 cup chopped walnuts

1. In a large bowl, combine the first six ingredients. In a small bowl, beat the egg, bananas, oil and extracts. Stir into dry ingredients just until moistened. Fold in the zucchini and walnuts.

2. Transfer the batter to three 5-3/4-in. x 3-in. x 2-in. loaf pans coated with cooking spray. Bake at 325° for 40-45 minutes or until a toothpick inserted near the center comes out clean. Cool 10 minutes before removing from the pans to wire racks. **Yield:** 3 mini loaves (6 slices each).

Nutrition Facts: 1 slice equals 175 calories, 9 g fat (1 g saturated fat), 12 mg cholesterol, 116 mg sodium, 23 g carbohydrate, 1 g fiber, 2 g protein.

Creamy Succotash

Prep: 10 min. **Cook:** 20 min. + cooling

Shannon Koene, Blacksburg, Virginia

This is a creation from my sister. When I watched her make it, I didn't think the combination would be very tasty together, but I changed my mind immediately upon tasting it!

✔ This recipe includes Nutrition Facts & Diabetic Exchanges.

    4 cups frozen lima beans
    1 cup water
    4 cups frozen corn
2/3 cup reduced-fat mayonnaise
    2 teaspoons Dijon mustard
1/2 teaspoon onion powder
1/2 teaspoon garlic powder
1/4 teaspoon salt
1/4 teaspoon pepper
    2 medium tomatoes, finely chopped
    1 small onion, finely chopped

1. In a large saucepan, bring lima beans and water to a boil. Reduce heat; cover and simmer for 10 minutes. Add corn; return to a boil. Reduce heat; cover and simmer 5-6 minutes longer or until vegetables are tender. Drain; cool for 10-15 minutes.

2. Meanwhile, in a large bowl, combine the mayonnaise, mustard, onion powder, garlic powder, salt and pepper. Stir in bean mixture, tomatoes and onion. Serve immediately. **Yield:** 10 servings.

Nutrition Facts: 3/4 cup equals 198 calories, 6 g fat (1 g saturated fat), 6 mg cholesterol, 238 mg sodium, 31 g carbohydrate, 6 g fiber, 7 g protein. **Diabetic Exchanges:** 2 starch, 1 fat.

Wholesome Apple-Hazelnut Stuffing

Prep: 20 min. **Bake:** 30 min.

Donna Noel, Gray, Maine

Try this whole grain, fruit and nut stuffing for a delicious new slant on dressing. Herbs balance the sweetness of the apples and give this dish a wonderful flavor.

✓ This recipe includes Nutrition Facts & Diabetic Exchanges.

> 2 celery ribs, chopped
> 1 large onion, chopped
> 1 tablespoon olive oil
> 1 small carrot, shredded
> 3 tablespoons minced fresh parsley *or*
>   1 tablespoon dried parsley flakes
> 1 tablespoon minced fresh rosemary *or*
>   1 teaspoon dried rosemary, crushed
> 2 garlic cloves, minced
> 4 cups cubed day-old whole wheat bread
> 1-1/2 cups shredded peeled tart apples (about
>   2 medium)
> 1/2 cup chopped hazelnuts, toasted
> 1 egg, lightly beaten
> 3/4 cup apple cider *or* unsweetened apple juice
> 1/2 teaspoon coarsely ground pepper
> 1/4 teaspoon salt

1. In a large nonstick skillet, saute celery and onion in oil for 4 minutes. Add the carrot, parsley and rosemary; saute 2-4 minutes longer or until vegetables are tender. Add garlic; cook 1 minute longer.

2. In a large bowl, combine the vegetable mixture, bread cubes, apples and hazelnuts. In a small bowl, combine the egg, cider, pepper and salt. Add to stuffing mixture and mix well.

3. Transfer to an 8-in. square baking dish coated with cooking spray. Cover and bake at 350° for 20 minutes. Uncover; bake 10-15 minutes longer or until a thermometer reads 165°. **Yield:** 6 cups.

Nutrition Facts: 3/4 cup equals 159 calories, 8 g fat (1 g saturated fat), 27 mg cholesterol, 195 mg sodium, 20 g carbohydrate, 4 g fiber, 4 g protein. **Diabetic Exchanges:** 1-1/2 fat, 1 starch.

Nutcracker Bread

Prep: 20 min. **Bake:** 35 min. + cooling

Jacqueline McComas, Paoli, Pennsylvania

Here's a round loaf with a wonderful sugar-and-spice flavor. Turkey, ham or velvety cream cheese-and-jelly sandwiches always taste better on slices of this dense bread.

> 1 cup chopped walnuts, toasted and cooled
> 3/4 cup packed brown sugar
> 2 cups all-purpose flour
> 1-1/4 teaspoons baking powder
> 1/2 teaspoon salt
> 1/4 teaspoon baking soda
> 3 eggs
> 1/2 cup reduced-fat sour cream
> 1/2 cup fat-free milk
> 1 tablespoon cider vinegar

1. In a food processor, combine walnuts and brown sugar; cover and pulse until finely chopped. Transfer to a large bowl. Stir in the flour, baking powder, salt and baking soda.

2. In a small bowl, beat the eggs, sour cream, milk and vinegar. Stir mixture into dry ingredients just until moistened.

3. Transfer to an 8-in. springform pan coated with cooking spray. Bake at 350° for 35-40 minutes or until a toothpick inserted near center comes out clean.

4. Cool on a wire rack for 10 minutes. Remove sides and bottom of pan; cool completely on wire rack. **Yield:** 1 loaf (16 slices).

Slow-Cooked Sausage Dressing

Prep: 20 min. **Cook:** 3 hours

Raquel Haggard, Edmond, Oklahoma

This dressing is so delicious that no one will know it's lower in fat. Best of all, it cooks effortlessly in the slow cooker, so your stovetop and oven are freed up for other dishes!

 This recipe includes Nutrition Facts.

1/2 pound reduced-fat bulk pork sausage
2 celery ribs, chopped
1 large onion, chopped
7 cups seasoned stuffing cubes
1 can (14-1/2 ounces) reduced-sodium chicken broth
1 medium tart apple, chopped
1/3 cup chopped pecans
2 tablespoons reduced-fat butter, melted
1-1/2 teaspoons rubbed sage
1/2 teaspoon pepper

1. In a large nonstick skillet, cook the sausage, celery and onion over medium heat until meat is no longer pink; drain. Transfer to a large bowl; stir in the remaining ingredients.

2. Transfer to a 5-qt. slow cooker coated with cooking spray. Cover; cook on low for 3-4 hours or until stuffing is heated through and apple is tender, stirring once. **Yield:** 8 cups.

Editor's Note: This recipe was tested with Land O'Lakes light stick butter.

Nutrition Facts: 2/3 cup equals 201 calories, 8 g fat (2 g saturated fat), 17 mg cholesterol, 640 mg sodium, 26 g carbohydrate, 3 g fiber, 7 g protein.

Parmesan Herb Loaf

Prep: 15 min. **Bake:** 30 min.

✓ This recipe includes Nutrition Facts.

1-1/4 cups all-purpose flour
3 tablespoons plus 1 teaspoon grated Parmesan cheese, *divided*
1-1/2 teaspoons sugar
1-1/2 teaspoons dried minced onion
1-1/4 teaspoons Italian seasoning, *divided*
1/2 teaspoon baking powder
1/4 teaspoon baking soda
1/4 teaspoon salt
1/2 cup sour cream
2 tablespoons plus 2 teaspoons 2% milk
4-1/2 teaspoons butter, melted
1 egg white, lightly beaten

1. In a small bowl, combine the flour, 3 tablespoons Parmesan cheese, sugar, onion, 1 teaspoon Italian seasoning, baking powder, baking soda and salt. In another bowl, whisk the sour cream, milk and butter. Stir into dry ingredients just until moistened.

2. Turn onto a floured surface; knead for 1 minute. Shape into a round loaf; place on a baking sheet coated with cooking spray. With kitchen scissors, cut a 1/4-in.-deep cross in top of loaf. Brush with egg white. Sprinkle with remaining cheese and Italian seasoning.

3. Bake at 350° for 30-35 minutes or until golden brown. Serve warm. **Yield:** 1 loaf (8 servings).

Nutrition Facts: 1 wedge (prepared with reduced-fat sour cream) equals 257 calories, 9 g fat (6 g saturated fat), 26 mg cholesterol, 466 mg sodium, 35 g carbohydrate, 1 g fiber, 9 g protein.

DIANNE CULLEY NESBIT, MISSISSIPPI

Moist and savory, this loaf is one of my very best quick bread recipes. I like to serve slices with individual ramekins filled with extra virgin olive oil infused with herbs for dipping.

Chocolate-Cherry Banana Bread

Prep: 30 min. **Bake:** 45 min. + cooling

Cindy Beberman, Orland Park, Illinois

I developed this rich, moist bread recipe after looking for a lighter way to use up my extra dried tart cherries.

✓ This recipe includes Nutrition Facts.

1 cup boiling water
2/3 cup dried cherries
1/4 cup butter, softened
3/4 cup sugar
2 egg whites
1 egg
1 large ripe banana, mashed
1/2 cup fat-free sour cream
2 teaspoons vanilla extract
1-1/2 cups all-purpose flour
1/3 cup baking cocoa
1 teaspoon baking powder
1/2 teaspoon baking soda
1/2 teaspoon ground cinnamon
1/4 teaspoon salt
1/4 cup chopped pecans

1. In a small bowl, pour water over cherries; let stand for 15 minutes. Meanwhile, in a large bowl, beat butter and sugar until crumbly, about 2 minutes. Beat in egg whites and egg until smooth.

2. In a small bowl, combine the banana, sour cream and vanilla. Combine the flour, cocoa, baking powder, baking soda, cinnamon and salt; add to butter mixture alternately with banana mixture. Drain cherries and coarsely chop; fold into batter with pecans.

3. Pour into a 9-in. x 5-in. loaf pan coated with cooking spray. Bake at 350° for 45-50 minutes or until a toothpick inserted near center comes out clean. Cool for 10 minutes before removing from pan to a wire rack to cool completely. **Yield:** 1 loaf (16 slices).

Nutrition Facts: 1 slice equals 164 calories, 5 g fat (2 g saturated fat), 22 mg cholesterol, 148 mg sodium, 27 g carbohydrate, 1 g fiber, 3 g protein.

Hearty Red Beans and Rice

Prep: 15 min. + soaking **Cook:** 2 hours

Kathy Jacques, Chesterfield, Michigan

I take this dish to many potlucks and never fail to bring home an empty pot. To get a head start, let the beans soak overnight. Drain them the next day and continue recipe as directed.

✓ This recipe includes Nutrition Facts.

  1 pound dried kidney beans
  2 teaspoons garlic salt
  1 teaspoon Worcestershire sauce
1/4 teaspoon hot pepper sauce
  1 quart water
1/2 pound fully cooked ham, diced
1/2 pound fully cooked smoked sausage, diced
  1 cup chopped onion
1/2 cup chopped celery
  3 garlic cloves, minced
  1 can (8 ounces) tomato sauce
  2 bay leaves
1/4 cup minced fresh parsley
1/2 teaspoon salt
1/2 teaspoon pepper
Hot cooked rice

1. Place beans in a Dutch oven; add water to cover by 2 in. Bring to a boil; boil for 2 minutes. Remove from the heat; cover and let stand for 1 hour to 4 hours or until softened.

2. Drain beans and discard liquid. Add the garlic salt, Worcestershire sauce, hot pepper sauce and water; bring to a boil. Reduce heat; cover and simmer for 1-1/2 hours.

3. Meanwhile, in a large skillet, saute ham and sausage until lightly browned. Remove with a slotted spoon to bean mixture. Saute onion and celery in drippings until tender. Add garlic; cook 1 minute longer. Add to bean mixture. Stir in tomato sauce and bay leaves. Cover and simmer for 30 minutes or until the beans are tender.

4. Discard bay leaves. Measure 2 cups of beans; mash and return to the bean mixture. Stir in the parsley, salt and pepper. Serve over rice. **Yield:** 8-10 servings.

Nutrition Facts: 1 cup (calculated without rice) equals 276 calories, 9 g fat (3 g saturated fat), 27 mg cholesterol, 1,149 mg sodium, 32 g carbohydrate, 8 g fiber, 18 g protein.

Curried Corn on the Cob

Prep: 15 min. + soaking **Grill:** 25 min.

Laura Fall-Sutton, Buhl, Idaho

Here's a delicious new way to enjoy corn on the cob. Don't like goat cheese? Try queso fresco, feta or a sprinkle of Parmesan.

✓ This recipe includes Nutrition Facts & Diabetic Exchanges.

  6 medium ears sweet corn in husks
1/2 cup crumbled goat cheese
  1 tablespoon sugar
  2 teaspoons salt-free seasoning blend
1/2 teaspoon curry powder
1/4 teaspoon salt
1/4 teaspoon pepper

1. Carefully peel back corn husks to within 1 in. of bottoms; remove silk. Rewrap corn in husks and secure with kitchen string. Place in a large kettle; cover with cold water. Soak for 20 minutes; drain.

2. Grill corn, covered, over medium heat for 25-30 minutes or until tender, turning often. In a small bowl, combine the remaining ingredients; spread over warm corn. **Yield:** 6 servings.

Nutrition Facts: 1 ear of corn with 4 teaspoons cheese mixture equals 203 calories, 7 g fat (4 g saturated fat), 15 mg cholesterol, 214 mg sodium, 33 g carbohydrate, 4 g fiber, 8 g protein. **Diabetic Exchanges:** 2 starch, 1 fat.

Mushroom Rice Medley

Prep: 10 min. **Cook:** 1 hour

Sue Mullis, Sharon, Wisconsin

We would never hear the end of it if we failed to have my grandmother's Mushroom Rice Medley for any family gathering. It's the one dish my dad requests most often.

> 3 cups water
> 1/2 cup uncooked brown rice
> 1/2 cup uncooked wild rice
> 1 teaspoon chicken bouillon granules
> 1 teaspoon dried oregano
> 1/2 pound sliced bacon, diced
> 1/2 pound sliced fresh mushrooms
> 1 small onion, chopped
> 1/4 teaspoon salt, optional

1. In a large saucepan, combine water, brown rice, wild rice, bouillon and oregano. Bring to a boil. Reduce heat. Cover and simmer for 50-60 minutes or until rice is tender.

2. In a large skillet, cook bacon over medium heat until crisp. Using a slotted spoon, remove to paper towels. Drain, reserving 2 tablespoons drippings. In the drippings, saute mushrooms and onion until tender. Stir in rice and bacon; heat through. Season with salt if desired. **Yield:** 6 servings.

Nutrition Facts: 1 serving (2/3 cup) equals 201 calories, 7 g fat (2 g saturated fat), 11 mg cholesterol, 440 mg sodium, 27 g carbohydrate, 2 g fiber, 8 g protein.

Duo Tater Bake

Prep: 40 min. **Bake:** 20 min.

> 4 pounds russet *or* Yukon Gold potatoes, peeled and cubed
> 3 pounds sweet potatoes, peeled and cubed
> 2 cartons (8 ounces *each*) spreadable chive and onion cream cheese, *divided*
> 1 cup (8 ounces) sour cream
> 1/4 cup shredded Colby-Monterey Jack cheese
> 1/3 cup milk
> 1/4 cup shredded Parmesan cheese
> 1/2 teaspoon salt
> 1/2 teaspoon pepper
> TOPPING:
> 1 cup (4 ounces) shredded Colby-Monterey Jack cheese
> 1/2 cup chopped green onions
> 1/4 cup shredded Parmesan cheese

1. Place russet potatoes in a Dutch oven and cover with water. Bring to a boil. Reduce heat; cover and cook for 10-15 minutes or until tender.

2. Meanwhile, place sweet potatoes in a large saucepan; cover with water. Bring to a boil. Reduce heat; cover and cook for 10-15 minutes or until tender. Drain; mash with half of the cream cheese and sour cream and all of Colby cheese.

3. Drain russet potatoes; mash with the remaining cream cheese and sour cream. Stir in the milk, Parmesan cheese, salt and pepper.

4. Spread 2-2/3 cups russet potato mixture into each of two greased 11-in. x 7-in. baking dishes. Layer russet potato mixture with 4 cups sweet potato mixture. Repeat layers. Spread with the remaining russet potato mixture.

5. Bake, uncovered, at 350° for 15 minutes or until heated through. Combine topping ingredients; sprinkle over casseroles. Bake 2-3 minutes longer or until cheese is melted. **Yield:** 2 casseroles (10 servings each).

Nutrition Facts: 3/4 cup equals 236 calories, 12 g fat (8 g saturated fat), 38 mg cholesterol, 246 mg sodium, 25 g carbohydrate, 2 g fiber, 5 g protein.

JOAN McCULLOCH ABBOTSFORD, BRITISH COLUMBIA

Cut down on prep time with this creamy potato dish that combines sweet potatoes with regular spuds. I served this for Thanksgiving, and it was a winner with all my family.

GRAND
PRIZE
WINNER

Sides, Breads & Condiments **153**

Herbed Tomatoes And Green Beans

Prep/Total Time: 30 min.

Maryalice Wood, Langley, British Columbia

Looking for new ways to dress up fresh-picked green beans? With just the right amount of oregano and parsley flavor, this colorful side dish is seasoned to please.

✓ This recipe includes Nutrition Facts & Diabetic Exchanges.

    3 green onions, coarsely chopped
    2 teaspoons olive oil
    2 garlic cloves, minced
1/2 pound fresh green beans, trimmed
1/4 cup chicken broth
    2 medium tomatoes, diced
    1 tablespoon minced fresh oregano
    1 tablespoon minced fresh parsley
1/8 teaspoon salt
1/8 teaspoon pepper

1. In a small skillet, saute onions in oil until tender. Add garlic; cook 1 minute longer. Add beans and broth. Bring to a boil. Reduce heat; cover and simmer for 6-9 minutes or until crisp-tender.

2. Stir in the tomatoes and seasonings; heat through. **Yield:** 4 servings.

Nutrition Facts: 2/3 cup equals 59 calories, 3 g fat (trace saturated fat), 0 cholesterol, 144 mg sodium, 9 g carbohydrate, 3 g fiber, 2 g protein. **Diabetic Exchanges:** 2 vegetable, 1/2 fat.

Speedy Spanish Rice

Prep/Total Time: 25 min.

Angie Rorick, Fort Wayne, Indiana

Mexican food is big with our family. In fact, one of my nephews loves this dish so much that he always requests it for his special birthday dinner!

✓ This recipe includes Nutrition Facts & Diabetic Exchanges.

1-1/2 cups uncooked instant brown rice
    1 medium onion, chopped
    1 small green pepper, chopped
    1 tablespoon butter
    1 garlic clove, minced
1-1/2 cups water
    1 tablespoon minced fresh cilantro
    2 teaspoons ground cumin
1-1/2 teaspoons chicken bouillon granules
1/4 teaspoon pepper
    1 cup picante sauce

1. In a large nonstick skillet, saute the rice, onion and green pepper in butter until rice is lightly browned and vegetables are crisp-tender. Add garlic; cook 1 minute longer. Stir in water, cilantro, cumin, bouillon and pepper; bring to a boil. Reduce heat; cover and simmer for 5 minutes.

2. Remove from heat; let stand for 5 minutes. Fluff with a fork. Stir in picante sauce. **Yield:** 4 servings.

Nutrition Facts: 3/4 cup equals 201 calories, 4 g fat (2 g saturated fat), 8 mg cholesterol, 615 mg sodium, 35 g carbohydrate, 3 g fiber, 4 g protein. **Diabetic Exchanges:** 2 starch, 1 vegetable, 1 fat.

Maple-Ginger Root Vegetables

Prep: 35 min. **Bake:** 45 min.

Kelli Ritz, Innisfail, Alberta

My family loves this recipe because it brings out the fabulous flavors of fall vegetables. Even my children enjoy it—especially the drizzle of maple syrup! It's a tasty way to introduce kids to turnips, rutabaga and parsnips, too.

✓ This recipe includes Nutrition Facts & Diabetic Exchange.

  5 **medium parsnips, peeled and sliced**
  5 **small carrots, sliced**
  3 **medium turnips, peeled and cubed**
  1 **large sweet potato, peeled and cubed**
  1 **small rutabaga, peeled and cubed**
  1 **large sweet onion, cut into wedges**
  1 **small red onion, cut into wedges**
  2 **tablespoons olive oil**
  1 **tablespoon minced fresh gingerroot**
  1 **teaspoon salt**
1/2 **teaspoon pepper**
  1 **cup maple syrup**

1. Place the first seven ingredients in a large resealable plastic bag; add the oil, ginger, salt and pepper. Seal bag and shake to coat. Arrange vegetables in a single layer in two 15-in. x 10-in. x 1-in. baking pans coated with cooking spray.

2. Bake, uncovered, at 425° for 25 minutes, stirring once. Drizzle with maple syrup. Bake 20-25 minutes longer or until vegetables are tender, stirring once. **Yield:** 24 servings.

Nutrition Facts: 3/4 cup equals 92 calories, 1 g fat (trace saturated fat), 0 cholesterol, 119 mg sodium, 20 g carbohydrate, 2 g fiber, 1 g protein. **Diabetic Exchange:** 1 starch.

Cherry Tomato Mozzarella Saute

Prep/Total Time: 25 min.

Summer Jones, Pleasant Grove, Utah

Fast to fix and full of flavor, this warm, refreshing side dish makes the most of cherry tomatoes, pairing them with fresh mozzarella cubes and fresh thyme.

✓ This recipe includes Nutrition Facts.

1/4 **cup chopped shallots**
  1 **teaspoon minced fresh thyme**
  2 **teaspoons olive oil**
  1 **garlic clove, minced**
2-1/2 **cups cherry tomatoes, halved**
1/4 **teaspoon salt**
1/4 **teaspoon pepper**
  4 **ounces fresh mozzarella cheese, cut into**
    1/2-inch cubes

1. In a large skillet, saute shallots and thyme in oil until tender. Add garlic; cook 1 minute longer. Add the tomatoes, salt and pepper; heat through. Remove from the heat; stir in cheese. **Yield:** 4 servings.

Nutrition Facts: 1 serving (2/3 cup) equals 129 calories, 9 g fat (4 g saturated fat), 22 mg cholesterol, 198 mg sodium, 7 g carbohydrate, 1 g fiber, 6 g protein.

A Real "Thyme"-Saver

Stripping thyme leaves is a cinch. Just hold the top of the sprig and strip downward (against the grain), using your fingers to remove the leaves. This also works well with rosemary.

Broccoli Tomato Cups

Prep: 20 min. **Bake:** 30 min.

Beatrice Gallo, Richfield Springs, New York

I had an abundance of tomatoes and broccoli one year, so I began experimenting with ways to best use both of them. Now this simple recipe is a family favorite.

- 1-1/2 cups soft bread crumbs, *divided*
- 1 cup grated Parmesan cheese, *divided*
- 6 to 8 medium tomatoes
- 2 cups chopped broccoli
- 1 cup (4 ounces) shredded cheddar cheese
- 3/4 cup mayonnaise
- Salt and pepper to taste

1. Combine 1/2 cup of bread crumbs and 1/4 cup Parmesan cheese; set aside. Cut a thin slice off the top of each tomato; scoop out the pulp and place in a strainer to drain. Place the tomatoes upside down on paper towels.

2. Cook the broccoli until crisp-tender; drain. Chop tomato pulp and place in a large bowl. Add broccoli, cheddar cheese, mayonnaise, salt, pepper and remaining crumbs and Parmesan; mix gently.

3. Stuff the tomatoes with the broccoli mixture; place in a greased 11-in. x 7-in. baking dish. Sprinkle with reserved crumb mixture. Bake, uncovered, at 375° for 30-40 minutes. **Yield:** 6-8 servings.

Campfire Potatoes

Prep: 5 min. **Grill:** 35 min.

JoAnn Dettbarn, Brainerd, Minnesota

Potatoes, onion, cheddar cheese and Worcestershire sauce combine to make a super side dish for any grilled meat. Plus, cooking in the foil makes cleanup a breeze.

- 5 medium potatoes, peeled and thinly sliced
- 1 medium onion, sliced
- 6 tablespoons butter
- 1/3 cup shredded cheddar cheese
- 2 tablespoons minced fresh parsley
- 1 tablespoon Worcestershire sauce
- Salt and pepper to taste
- 1/3 cup chicken broth

1. Place the potatoes and onion on a large piece of heavy-duty foil (about 20 in. x 20 in.); dot with butter. Combine the cheese, parsley, Worcestershire sauce, salt and pepper; sprinkle over potatoes.

2. Fold foil up around potatoes and add broth. Seal the edges of foil well. Grill, covered, over medium heat for 35-40 minutes or until potatoes are tender. **Yield:** 4-6 servings.

Potato Pointers

Don't like to peel and cook potatoes? Next time, make extras to save time later. When the potatoes cool, slice or dice the leftovers, place them in resealable plastic bags and refrigerate until needed for frying, creaming or adding to soups.

Delightful Holiday Bread

Prep: 40 min. + rising **Bake:** 30 min.

Cheri Neustifter, Sturtevant, Wisconsin

The first time I made this braided bread everyone loved it. And no wonder. The interior is tender and the almond-speckled glaze makes it as pretty as it is tasty.

      2 packages (1/4 ounce *each*) active dry yeast
1-3/4 cups warm water (110° to 115°)
      2 eggs
      3 tablespoons sugar
      2 tablespoons almond extract
      2 tablespoons canola oil
1-1/2 teaspoons salt
5-3/4 to 6-1/4 cups all-purpose flour
TOPPING:
      1 egg
      1 tablespoon water
      5 teaspoons sugar
      3 tablespoons sliced almonds

1. In a large bowl, dissolve yeast in warm water. Add the eggs, sugar, extract, oil, salt and 4 cups flour; beat until smooth. Stir in enough remaining flour to form a soft dough (dough will be sticky).

2. Turn onto a lightly floured surface; knead until smooth and elastic, about 6-8 minutes. Place in a large bowl coated with cooking spray; turn once to coat top. Cover and let rise until doubled, about 1 hour.

3. Punch dough down; turn onto a lightly floured surface. Divide into thirds; shape each portion into a 20-in. rope. Place ropes on a large baking sheet coated with cooking spray; braid. Pinch ends together, forming a round loaf. Cover and let rise until doubled, about 40 minutes.

4. Beat egg and water; brush over loaf. Sprinkle with sugar and almonds. Bake at 350° for 30-35 minutes or until golden brown. Remove to a wire rack to cool. **Yield:** 1 loaf (24 slices).

Creamy Broccoli With Cashews

Prep/Total Time: 20 min.

Karen Ann Bland, Gove, Kansas

Looking for a veggie side dish that's something special? The sour-cream sauce in my broccoli casserole makes it a little different from the usual, and the cashews lend a nice crunch. It's great with a wide variety of entrees.

      9 cups fresh broccoli florets
  1/4 cup chopped onion
      2 tablespoons butter
      1 cup (8 ounces) sour cream
      2 teaspoons honey
      1 teaspoon cider vinegar
  1/2 teaspoon salt
  1/2 teaspoon paprika
  1/2 cup coarsely chopped cashews

1. Place broccoli in a steamer basket; place in a large saucepan over 1 in. of water. Bring to a boil; cover and steam for 3-4 minutes or until crisp-tender.

2. Meanwhile, in a small skillet, saute onion in butter until tender. Remove from the heat; stir in the sour cream, honey, vinegar, salt and paprika.

3. Transfer broccoli to a serving bowl. Add sour cream mixture and toss to coat. Sprinkle with chopped cashews. **Yield:** 6 servings.

PG. 164

PG. 160

PG. 169

COOKIES, BARS & CANDY

Go ahead...take one for each hand. How can you resist with all the tempting goodies showcased here? Chocolaty, gooey, fruity...there's something to satisfy every sweet tooth.

PG. 168

Hazelnut-Espresso Sandwich Cookies

Prep: 45 min. + chilling **Bake:** 10 min./batch + cooling

Cindy Beberman, Orland Park, Illinois

The inspiration for this cute cookie came from my sister's description of a hazelnut cookie she tried in Italy. She declared my version a wonderful approximation!

  1 cup butter, softened
1-1/4 cups sugar
  1 egg
  1 egg yolk
  4 teaspoons instant espresso granules
  2 teaspoons vanilla extract
2-1/2 cups all-purpose flour
  1/2 teaspoon salt
  1/2 teaspoon baking powder
  1 cup finely ground hazelnuts
FILLING:
1-3/4 cups semisweet chocolate chips, *divided*
1-1/4 cups milk chocolate chips
  1 cup heavy whipping cream

1. In a large bowl, cream butter and sugar until light and fluffy. Beat in the egg, yolk, espresso granules and vanilla. Combine the flour, salt and baking powder; gradually add to creamed mixture and mix well. Stir in hazelnuts.

2. Divide dough into thirds; flatten each portion into a circle. Wrap each portion in plastic wrap; refrigerate for 1 hour or until easy to handle.

3. On a lightly floured surface, roll out one portion of dough to 1/8-in. thickness. Cut with a floured 1-1/2-in. cookie cutter; place 1/2 in. apart on ungreased baking sheets. Repeat with the remaining dough; chill and reroll scraps.

4. Bake at 375° for 6-8 minutes or until edges begin to brown. Remove to wire racks to cool.

5. For filling, place 3/4 cup semisweet chocolate chips and milk chocolate chips in a small bowl. In a small saucepan, bring cream just to a boil. Pour over chocolate; whisk until smooth. Refrigerate for 1-1/2 hours or until filling reaches spreading consistency, stirring occasionally.

6. Spread filling over the bottom of half of the cookies; top with remaining cookies. In a microwave, melt remaining semisweet chips; stir until smooth. Drizzle over cookies. Let stand until set. Store in an airtight container in the refrigerator. **Yield:** 3 dozen.

Chocolate Thumbprint Cookies

Prep: 25 min. + chilling **Bake:** 10 min. + cooling

Laura Bryant German, W. Warren, Massachusetts

Rolled in nuts and topped with a chocolate kiss, these quick bites are an absolute gem of a cookie—and irresistible!

- 1/2 **cup butter, softened**
- 2/3 **cup sugar**
- 1 **egg,** *separated*
- 2 **tablespoons milk**
- 1 **teaspoon vanilla extract**
- 1 **cup all-purpose flour**
- 1/3 **cup baking cocoa**
- 1/4 **teaspoon salt**
- 1 **cup finely chopped walnuts**

FILLING:
- 1/2 **cup confectioners' sugar**
- 1 **tablespoon butter, softened**
- 2 **teaspoons milk**
- 1/4 **teaspoon vanilla extract**
- 26 **milk chocolate kisses**

1. In a large bowl, cream butter and sugar until light and fluffy. Beat in the egg yolk, milk and vanilla. Combine the flour, cocoa and salt; gradually add to creamed mixture and mix well. Cover and refrigerate for 1 hour or until or until easy to handle.

2. In a small bowl, whisk egg white until foamy. Shape dough into 1-in. balls; dip in egg white, then roll in nuts. Place on greased baking sheets. Using a wooden spoon handle, make an indentation in center of each cookie. Bake at 350° for 10-12 minutes or until center is set.

3. For filling, combine the confectioners' sugar, butter, milk and vanilla; stir until smooth. Spoon or pipe 1/4 teaspoon into each warm cookie; gently press a chocolate kiss in the center. Carefully remove from pans to wire racks to cool. **Yield:** 2 dozen.

Chocolate Pecan Bars

Prep: 25 min. **Bake:** 25 min. + cooling

Carole Fraser, North York, Ontario

These chewy, chocolaty bars are great for any special occasion—and always a big hit with everyone. They're also easy to prepare, elegant to look at and make a big batch.

- 2/3 **cup butter, softened**
- 1/3 **cup sugar**
- 2 **cups all-purpose flour**

FILLING:
- 6 **ounces semisweet chocolate, chopped**
- 1-1/4 **cups light corn syrup**
- 1-1/4 **cups sugar**
- 4 **eggs, lightly beaten**
- 1-1/4 **teaspoons vanilla extract**
- 2-1/4 **cups chopped pecans**

GLAZE:
- 4 **ounces semisweet chocolate, chopped**
- 1-1/4 **teaspoons shortening**

1. In a small bowl, cream butter and sugar until light and fluffy. Beat in flour. Press into a greased 15-in. x 10-in. x 1-in. baking pan. Bake at 350° for 12-15 minutes or until golden brown.

2. Meanwhile, in a large saucepan, melt chocolate with corn syrup over low heat; stir until smooth. Remove from the heat. Stir in the sugar, eggs and vanilla. Add pecans.

3. Spread chocolate mixture evenly over hot crust. Bake for 25-30 minutes or until firm around the edges. Cool on a wire rack.

4. In a microwave, melt chocolate and shortening; stir until smooth. Drizzle over bars. **Yield:** 4 dozen.

Toffee-Almond Cookie Slices

Prep: 15 min. Bake: 40 min. + cooling

Julie Plummer, Sykesville, Maryland

Make your coffee break something special with these crispy, cookie-like treats. They also make a lovely gift. Simply bake up a batch, wrap several slices in bright cellophane and add stickers and curly ribbons for last-minute gifts.

 1 package (17-1/2 ounces) sugar cookie mix
 1/2 cup all-purpose flour
 1/2 cup butter, softened
 1 egg
 1/3 cup slivered almonds, toasted
 1/3 cup miniature semisweet chocolate chips
 1/3 cup English toffee bits *or* almond brickle chips

1. In a large bowl, combine the sugar cookie mix, flour, butter and egg. Stir in the almonds, chocolate chips and toffee bits.

2. Divide dough in half. On an ungreased baking sheet, shape each portion into a 10-in. x 2-1/2-in. rectangle. Bake at 350° for 25-30 minutes or until lightly browned.

3. Carefully remove to wire racks; cool for 10 minutes. Transfer to a cutting board; with a serrated knife, cut each rectangle diagonally into 15 slices.

4. Place cut side down on ungreased baking sheets. Bake for 15-20 minutes or until golden brown. Remove to wire racks to cool. Store the cookies in an airtight container. **Yield:** 2-1/2 dozen.

Chocolaty Double Crunchers

Prep: 20 min. Bake: 10 min./batch + cooling

Cheryl Johnson, Upper Marlboro, Maryland

I first tried these fun cookies at a family picnic when I was a child. Packed with oats, cornflakes and coconut, they quickly became a regular at our house. Now, years later, I'm still making them for my own family.

 1/2 cup butter, softened
 1/2 cup sugar
 1/2 cup packed brown sugar
 1 egg
 1/2 teaspoon vanilla extract
 1 cup all-purpose flour
 1/2 teaspoon baking soda
 1/4 teaspoon salt
 1 cup quick-cooking oats
 1 cup crushed cornflakes
 1/2 cup flaked coconut
FILLING:
 2 packages (3 ounces *each*) cream cheese, softened
 1-1/2 cups confectioners' sugar
 2 cups (12 ounces) semisweet chocolate chips, melted

1. In a large bowl, cream butter and sugars until light and fluffy. Beat in egg and vanilla. Combine the flour,

baking soda and salt; gradually add to creamed mixture and mix well. Stir in oats, cornflakes and coconut.

2. Shape into 1-in. balls and place 2 in. apart on greased baking sheets. Flatten with a glass dipped lightly in flour. Bake at 350° for 8-10 minutes or until lightly browned. Remove to wire racks to cool.

3. For filling, beat cream cheese and sugar until smooth. Beat in chocolate. Spread about 1 tablespoon on half of the cookies and top each with another cookie. Store in refrigerator. **Yield:** 2 dozen.

Spice Cookies
With Pumpkin Dip

Prep: 20 min. **Bake:** 10 min./batch

Kelly McNeal, Derby, Kansas

My husband and two kids are sure to eat the first dozen of these cookies, warm from the oven, before the next tray is even baked! A co-worker gave me the recipe for the pumpkin dip, which everyone loves to eat with the cookies.

 This recipe includes Nutrition Facts.

1-1/2 **cups butter, softened**
    2 **cup sugar**
    2 **eggs**
  1/2 **cup molasses**
    4 **cups all-purpose flour**
    4 **teaspoons baking soda**
    2 **teaspoons ground cinnamon**
    1 **teaspoon** *each* **ground ginger and cloves**
    1 **teaspoon salt**
PUMPKIN DIP:
    1 **package (8 ounces) cream cheese, softened**
    2 **cups pumpkin pie filling**
    2 **cups confectioners' sugar**
  1/2 **to 1 teaspoon ground cinnamon**
  1/4 **to 1/2 teaspoon ground ginger**

1. In a large bowl, cream butter and sugar until light and fluffy. Beat in eggs and molasses. Combine the flour, baking soda, cinnamon, ginger, cloves and salt; add to the creamed mixture and mix well. Let the dough chill overnight.

2. Shape dough into 1/2-in. balls; roll in sugar. Place 2 in. apart on ungreased baking sheets. Bake at 375° for 6 minutes or until edges begin to brown. Cool for 2 minutes before removing to a wire rack.

3. For dip, beat cream cheese in a large bowl until smooth. Beat in pumpkin pie filling. Add the sugar, cinnamon and ginger and mix well. Serve with cookies. Store leftover dip in the refrigerator.
Yield: about 20 dozen cookies (3 cups dip).

Nutrition Facts: 3 cookies equals 108 calories, 5 g fat (3 g saturated fat), 18 mg cholesterol, 147 mg sodium, 16 g carbohydrate, trace fiber, 1 g protein.

Marshmallow Puffs

Prep: 10 min. + chilling

Dody Cagenello, Simsbury, Connecticut

With peanut butter, chocolate and marshmallows, these treats were very popular with our three children as they were growing up. Today, they're just as popular with our two grandchildren.

  36 **large marshmallows**
1-1/2 **cups semisweet chocolate chips**
  1/2 **cup chunky peanut butter**
    2 **tablespoons butter**

1. Line a 9-in. square pan with foil; butter the foil. Arrange marshmallows in pan. In a microwave, melt the chocolate chips, peanut butter and butter; stir until smooth. Pour and spread over the marshmallows. Chill completely. Cut between the marshmallows.
Yield: 3 dozen.

Editor's Note: This recipe was tested in a 1,100-watt microwave.

Peanut Butter Brownie Bars

Prep: 20 min. **Bake:** 25 min. + chilling

Radelle Knappenberger, Oviedo, Florida

A brownie mix base makes this a no-fuss treat that will appeal to adults and children alike. Creamy peanut butter, crunchy nuts and crisp cereal make the bars fun to bite into.

        1 package fudge brownie mix (13-inch x 9-inch pan size)
       12 peanut butter cups, chopped
      1/2 cup salted peanuts, chopped
        2 cups (12 ounces) semisweet chocolate chips
    1-1/4 cups creamy peanut butter
        1 tablespoon butter
    1-1/2 cups crisp rice cereal
        1 teaspoon vanilla extract
      1/8 teaspoon salt

1. Prepare brownie batter according to package directions. Spread into a greased 13-in. x 9-in. baking pan. Bake at 350° for 20-25 minutes or until a toothpick inserted near the center comes out with moist crumbs.

2. Sprinkle with peanut butter cups and peanuts. Bake 4-6 minutes longer or until chocolate is melted. Cool on a wire rack.

3. Meanwhile, in a microwave-save bowl, melt the chocolate chips, peanut butter and butter; stir until smooth. Stir in the cereal, vanilla and salt. Carefully spread over brownies. Cover and refrigerate for at least 2 hours before cutting. **Yield:** 3 dozen.

Almost a Candy Bar

Prep: 15 min. **Bake:** 15 min. + chilling

Barb Wyman, Hankinson, North Dakota

Because I love candy bars and marshmallows, this recipe was a cinch to invent—and I've yet to find anyone who doesn't enjoy it! With all the different layers and flavors, these bars seem to please just about everyone.

        1 tube (16-1/2 ounces) refrigerated chocolate chip cookie dough
        4 nutty s'mores trail mix bars (1.23 ounces each), chopped
        1 package (10 to 11 ounces) butterscotch chips
    2-1/2 cups miniature marshmallows
        1 cup chopped walnuts
    1-1/2 cups miniature pretzels
        1 package (10 ounces) peanut butter chips
      3/4 cup light corn syrup
      1/4 cup butter, cubed
        1 package (11-1/2 ounces) milk chocolate chips

1. Let dough stand at room temperature for 5-10 minutes to soften. In a large bowl, combine dough and trail mix bars. Press into an ungreased 13-in. x 9-in. baking pan. Bake, uncovered, at 350° for 10-12 minutes or until golden brown.

2. Sprinkle with butterscotch chips and marshmallows. Bake 3-4 minutes longer or until marshmallows begin to brown. Sprinkle with walnuts; arrange pretzels over the top. In a small saucepan, melt the peanut butter chips, corn syrup and butter; spoon over bars.

3. In a microwave, melt chocolate chips; stir until smooth. Spread or drizzle over bars. Refrigerate for 1 hour or until firm before cutting. **Yield:** 3 dozen.

Lemon Butter Cookies

Prep: 20 min. + chilling **Bake:** 10 min./batch

Judy McCreight, Springfield, Illinois

These tender cutouts have a slight lemony flavor that makes them stand out from the rest. They're very easy to roll out compared to other sugar cookies I've worked with. I know you'll enjoy them as much as we do.

    1 cup butter, softened
    2 cups sugar
    2 eggs, lightly beaten
1/4 cup whole milk
    2 teaspoons lemon extract
1/2 teaspoon salt
4-1/2 cups all-purpose flour
    2 teaspoons baking powder
1/4 teaspoon baking soda
Colored sugar, optional

1. In a large bowl, cream butter and sugar until light and fluffy. Beat in the eggs, milk and extract. Combine dry ingredients; gradually add to creamed mixture and mix well. Cover and chill for 2 hours.

2. Roll out on a lightly floured surface to 1/8-in. thickness. Cut with a 2-in. cookie cutter dipped in flour. Place 2 in. apart on ungreased baking sheets. Sprinkle with colored sugar if desired.

3. Bake at 350° for 8-9 minutes or until the edges just begin to brown. Remove to wire racks to cool. **Yield:** about 13 dozen.

No-Mess Melted Chocolate

Here's another handy way to melt chocolate chips. Seal chips in a resealable plastic bag and place in a pan of hot water. After a few minutes, knead the bag to smooth chocolate, cut a hole in one corner and pipe out the chocolate.

Peanut Butter S'more Bars

Prep: 10 min. **Bake:** 20 min. + chilling

Julie Wischmeier, Brownstown, Indiana

I originally whipped up these bars to bring something new and colorful to my Christmas cookie trays. When I give them to my kids' teachers, they're gone in a flash! I can make them ahead when convenient because they freeze so well. You can use M&Ms in different colors for holidays year-round.

    1 tube (16-1/2 ounces) refrigerated peanut
      butter cookie dough
3-1/2 cups miniature marshmallows
  3/4 cup milk chocolate chips
    2 teaspoons shortening
1-1/2 cups milk chocolate M&M's

1. Let dough stand at room temperature for 5-10 minutes to soften. Cut into 24 slices; arrange side by side in an ungreased 13-in. x 9-in. baking pan. Pat together to close gaps.

2. Bake at 350° for 18-20 minutes or until lightly browned and edges are firm. Sprinkle with marshmallows; bake 2-3 minutes longer or until marshmallows are puffy.

3. In a microwave, melt chocolate chips and shortening; stir until smooth. Sprinkle M&M's over marshmallow layer; drizzle with melted chocolate. Chill until set before cutting. **Yield:** 2 dozen.

1 teaspoon vanilla extract
2-1/2 cups all-purpose flour
1 tablespoon ground cinnamon
1 teaspoon baking soda
1 teaspoon salt
1 teaspoon pumpkin pie *or* apple pie spice
2 cups quick-cooking oats
2 cups raisins
1-1/2 cups chopped pecans

1. In a large bowl, cream butter and sugars. Beat in the eggs, milk and vanilla. Combine the flour, cinnamon, baking soda, salt and pie spice; add to creamed mixture and mix well. Stir in the oats, raisins and nuts; mix well.

2. Drop by tablespoonfuls 2 in. apart onto greased baking sheets. Bake at 350° for 10-12 minutes or until light golden brown. Remove cookies to wire racks to cool. **Yield:** 5-6 dozen.

Chewy Pecan Cookies

Prep: 25 min. **Bake:** 10 min./batch

Janice Jackson, Haleyville, Alabama

For a classic Southern treat, don't pass up these soft and chewy cookies that have the taste of pecan pie.

1 cup butter, softened
1 cup sugar
3/4 cup packed brown sugar
3 eggs
1/4 cup milk

It's Not Just for Ice Cream

An ice cream scoop is great for making uniformly sized drop cookies. (A 1 tablespoon-sized scoop will result in a 2-in. cookie.) Scoop the dough, even off the top with a flat-edge spatula and release onto the baking sheet.

Rustic Nut Bars

Prep: 20 min. **Bake:** 35 min. + cooling

1 tablespoon plus 3/4 cup cold butter, *divided*
2-1/3 cups all-purpose flour
1/2 cup sugar
1/2 teaspoon baking powder
1/2 teaspoon salt
1 egg, lightly beaten
TOPPING:
2/3 cup honey
1/2 cup packed brown sugar
1/4 teaspoon salt
6 tablespoons butter, cubed
2 tablespoons heavy whipping cream
1 cup chopped hazelnuts, toasted
1 cup roasted salted almonds
1 cup salted cashews, toasted
1 cup pistachios, toasted

1. Line a 13-in. x 9-in. baking pan with foil; grease the foil with 1 tablespoon butter. Set aside.

2. In a large bowl, combine the flour, sugar, baking powder and salt; cut in remaining butter until mixture resembles coarse crumbs. Stir in egg until blended (mixture will be dry).

3. Press firmly onto the bottom of prepared pan. Bake at 375° for 18-20 minutes or until edges are golden brown. Cool on a wire rack.

4. In a large heavy saucepan, bring the honey, brown sugar and salt to a boil over medium heat until sugar is smooth; stirring often. Boil without stirring for 2 minutes. Add butter and cream. Bring to a boil; cook and stir for 1 minute or until smooth. Remove from the heat; stir in the hazelnuts, almonds, cashews and pistachios. Spread over crust.

5. Bake at 375° for 15-20 minutes or until topping is bubbly. Cool completely on a wire rack. Using foil, lift bars out of pan. Discard foil; cut into squares. **Yield:** about 3 dozen.

BARBARA DRISCOLL WEST ALLIS, WISCONSIN

People always comment on the buttery, shortbread-like crust and wildly nutty topping of these chewy, gooey bars. They're just as delicious as they look!

GRAND
PRIZE
WINNER

Pecan Caramels

Prep: 20 min. **Cook:** 35 min. + cooling

Patsy Howell, Peru, Indiana

I changed the original recipe for these creamy, nutty caramels by substituting condensed milk for part of the whipping cream and cutting back on the sugar. They're absolutely delightful and I guarantee you cannot eat just one piece!

✓ | This recipe includes Nutrition Facts.

   1 **tablespoon butter, softened**
   1 **cup sugar**
   1 **cup light corn syrup**
   2 **cups heavy whipping cream,** *divided*
   1 **can (14 ounces) sweetened condensed milk**
   2 **cups chopped pecans**
   1 **teaspoon vanilla extract**

1. Line a 13-in. x 9-in. pan with foil; grease the foil with butter. Set aside.

2. In a large heavy saucepan, combine the sugar, corn syrup and 1 cup cream. Bring to a boil over medium heat. Cook and stir until smooth and blended, about 10 minutes. Stir in milk and remaining cream. Bring to a boil over medium-low heat, stirring constantly. Cook and stir until a candy thermometer reads 238° (soft-ball stage), about 25 minutes.

3. Remove from the heat; stir in pecans and vanilla. Pour into prepared pan (do not scrape saucepan). Cool. Using foil, lift candy out of pan; cut into 1-in. squares. Wrap individually in waxed paper. **Yield:** about 2-1/2 pounds.

Editor's Note: We recommend that you test your candy thermometer before each use by bringing water to a boil; the thermometer should read 212°. Adjust your recipe temperature up or down based on your test.

Nutrition Facts: 1 piece equals 66 calories, 4 g fat (2 g saturated fat), 9 mg cholesterol, 12 mg sodium, 7 g carbohydrate, trace fiber, 1 g protein.

Three-Chocolate Fudge

Prep: 35 min. + chilling

Betty Grantham, Hanceville, Alabama

I make this fudge at Christmastime to give to friends and neighbors. The tradition started years ago, when I made more candy than my husband, three sons and I could eat, so we were glad to share it—and still do!

3-1/3 cups sugar
   1 cup butter
   1 cup packed dark brown sugar
   1 can (12 ounces) evaporated milk
  32 large marshmallows, halved
   2 cups (12 ounces) semisweet chocolate chips
   2 milk chocolate candy bars (7 ounces *each*), broken
   2 ounces semisweet chocolate, chopped
   1 teaspoon vanilla extract
   2 cups chopped pecans

1. In a large saucepan, combine first four ingredients. Cook and stir over medium heat until sugar is dissolved. Bring to a rapid boil; boil for 5 minutes, stirring constantly. Remove from the heat; stir in marshmallows until melted.

2. Stir in chocolate chips until melted. Add chocolate bars and chopped chocolate; stir until melted. Fold in vanilla and pecans; mix well. Pour into a greased 15-in. x 10- in. x 1-in. pan. Chill until firm. Cut into squares. **Yield:** 5-1/2 pounds.

Glazed Peanut Butter Bars

Prep: 15 min. **Bake:** 20 min. + cooling

Janis Luedtke, Westminster, Colorado

Memories of lunchtime at school and my Aunt Shelly's kitchen come to mind whenever I bite into these sweet, chewy bars I enjoyed as a child. They're also an all-time favorite with my husband—and so easy to make.

3/4 cup butter, softened
3/4 cup creamy peanut butter
3/4 cup sugar
3/4 cup packed brown sugar
  2 eggs
  2 teaspoons water
1-1/2 teaspoons vanilla extract
1-1/2 cups all-purpose flour
1-1/2 cups quick-cooking oats
3/4 teaspoon baking soda
1/2 teaspoon salt
GLAZE:
1-1/4 cups milk chocolate chips
1/2 cup butterscotch chips
1/2 cup creamy peanut butter

1. In a large bowl, cream the butter, peanut butter and sugars until light and fluffy, about 4 minutes. Beat in the eggs, water and vanilla. Combine the flour, oats, baking soda and salt; gradually add to creamed mixture and mix well.

2. Spread into a greased 15-in. x 10-in. x 1-in. baking pan. Bake at 325° for 18-22 minutes or until lightly browned.

3. For glaze, in a microwave, melt chips and peanut butter; stir until smooth. Pour over warm bars; spread evenly. Cool completely on a wire rack before cutting. **Yield:** 4 dozen.

3 cups all-purpose flour
1-1/2 cups sugar, *divided*
1 teaspoon baking powder
1/4 teaspoon salt
1/4 teaspoon ground cinnamon
1 cup shortening
2 eggs, lightly beaten
1 teaspoon almond extract
1 tablespoon cornstarch
4 cups fresh *or* frozen raspberries

1. In a large bowl, combine the flour, 1 cup sugar, baking powder, salt and cinnamon. Cut in shortening until mixture resembles coarse crumbs. Stir in eggs and extract. Press two-thirds of the mixture into a greased 13-in. x 9-in. baking dish.

2. In a large bowl, combine cornstarch and remaining sugar; add berries and gently toss. Spoon over crust. Sprinkle with remaining crumb mixture.

3. Bake at 375° for 35-45 minutes or until bubbly and golden brown. Cool on a wire rack. Cut into bars. Store in the refrigerator. **Yield:** 3 dozen.

Editor's Note: If using frozen raspberries, do not thaw before tossing with cornstarch mixture.

Nutrition Facts: 1 serving (1 each) equals 131 calories, 6 g fat (1 g saturated fat), 12 mg cholesterol, 31 mg sodium, 18 g carbohydrate, 1 g fiber, 2 g protein.

Raspberry Patch Crumb Bars

Prep: 30 min. **Bake:** 35 min. + cooling

Leanna Thorne, Lakewood, Colorado

To give these fresh, fruity bars even more crunch, add a sprinkling of nuts to the yummy crumb topping. They're light enough for everyone to enjoy!

 This recipe includes Nutrition Facts.

Peach Almond Bars

Prep: 25 min. **Bake:** 20 min. + cooling

Justine Furman-Olshan, Willow Street, Pennsylvania

These luscious treats are a favorite in my family. And at under 200 calories a serving, you can afford to indulge!

✓ This recipe includes Nutrition Facts.

1 tube (16-1/2 ounces) refrigerated sugar
  cookie dough
1 jar (18 ounces) peach preserves
1-1/2 cups slivered almonds, *divided*
4 egg whites
1/2 cup sugar

1. Let dough stand at room temperature for 5-10 minutes to soften. Press into an ungreased 13-in. x 9-in. baking pan. Bake at 350° for 12-15 minutes or until golden brown.

2. Spread preserves over crust. Sprinkle with 3/4 cup almonds. In a large bowl, beat egg whites on medium speed until soft peaks form. Gradually beat in sugar, 1 tablespoon at a time, on high until stiff glossy peaks form and sugar is dissolved.

3. Spread meringue evenly over almonds. Sprinkle with remaining almonds. Bake for 20-25 minutes or until lightly browned. Cool on a wire rack. Store in the refrigerator. **Yield:** 2 dozen.

Nutrition Facts: 1 serving (1 each) equals 196 calories, 7 g fat (1 g saturated fat), 6 mg cholesterol, 91 mg sodium, 31 g carbohydrate, 1 g fiber, 3 g protein.

Fancy Sugar Cookie Bars

Prep: 10 min. **Bake:** 20 min. + cooling

Shirley Dehler, Columbus, Wisconsin

Looking for a quick and easy way to transform plain old refrigerated cookie dough into something special enough for unexpected guests? Try this recipe! I dress up the bars with chocolate chips, coconut and whatever nuts I have on hand.

 This recipe includes Nutrition Facts.

> 1 tube (16-1/2 ounces) refrigerated sugar cookie dough
> 1 cup semisweet chocolate chips
> 1/2 cup flaked coconut
> 1/4 cup chopped pecans

1. Let dough stand at room temperature for 5-10 minutes to soften. Press into an ungreased 13-in. x 9-in. baking pan. Bake at 350° for 10-12 minutes or until golden brown.

2. Sprinkle with chocolate chips, coconut and pecans. Bake 10 minutes longer. Cool on a wire rack. **Yield:** 2 dozen.

Nutrition Facts: 1 each equals 137 calories, 8 g fat (3 g saturated fat), 6 mg cholesterol, 88 mg sodium, 17 g carbohydrate, 1 g fiber, 1 g protein.

Presentation Pizzazz

Triangle-shaped bars give a festive look to any cookie platter. Simply cut the bars into squares, then cut each square in half diagonally.

Peanut Butter 'n' Jelly Bars

Prep: 10 min. **Bake:** 15 min. + cooling

Carolyn Mulloy, Davison, Michigan

My two young sons are crazy about these simple, fast-to-fix cookie bars. So as a busy mom, I rely on this fun dessert often.

> 1 tube (16-1/2 ounces) refrigerated peanut butter cookie dough
> 1/2 cup peanut butter chips
> 1 can (16 ounces) buttercream frosting
> 1/4 cup creamy peanut butter
> 1/4 cup seedless raspberry jam *or* grape jelly

1. Let dough stand at room temperature for 5-10 minutes to soften. Press into an ungreased 13-in. x 9-in. baking dish; sprinkle with peanut butter chips.

2. Bake at 375° for 15-18 minutes or until lightly browned and edges are firm to the touch. Cool on a wire rack.

3. In a small bowl, beat frosting and peanut butter until smooth. Spread over bars. Drop jam by teaspoonfuls over frosting; cut through frosting with a knife to swirl the jam. **Yield:** 2 dozen.

1/4 teaspoon salt
1 cup fresh raspberries
FROSTING:
6 ounces bittersweet chocolate, chopped
3/4 cup heavy whipping cream
2 tablespoons seedless raspberry jam
1 teaspoon vanilla extract
12 fresh raspberries

Raspberry Truffle Brownies

Prep: 30 min. **Bake:** 25 min. + chilling

Agnes Ward, Stratford, Ontario

Each of these rich, fudge-like brownies is bursting with fresh, plump red raspberries and topped with a dreamy, bittersweet ganache. What's not to love?

6 ounces bittersweet chocolate, chopped
1/2 cup butter, cubed
2 eggs
1 cup sugar
1 teaspoon vanilla extract
1 cup all-purpose flour
1/4 teaspoon baking soda

1. In a microwave, melt chocolate and butter; stir until smooth. In a large bowl, beat eggs, sugar and vanilla. Stir in chocolate mixture. Combine flour, baking soda and salt; gradually add to chocolate mixture until combined. Gently fold in raspberries.

2. Spread into a greased 9-in. square baking pan. Bake at 350° for 25-30 minutes or until a toothpick inserted near the center comes out clean (do not overbake). Cool on a wire rack.

3. For frosting, in a microwave-safe bowl, combine the chocolate, cream and jam. Microwave at 50% power for 2-3 minutes or until smooth, stirring twice. Transfer to a small bowl; stir in vanilla. Place in a bowl of ice water; stir for 3-5 minutes. With a hand mixer, beat on medium speed until soft peaks form.

4. Cut a small hole in a corner of a heavy-duty resealable plastic bag; insert #825 star tip. Fill with 1/2 cup frosting. Spread remaining frosting over brownies. Cut into 12 bars.

5. Pipe a chocolate rosette in the center of each brownie; top with a raspberry. Cover and refrigerate for 30 minutes or until frosting is set. Refrigerate leftovers. **Yield:** 1 dozen.

Editor's Note: This recipe was tested in a 1,100-watt microwave.

Chocolate Coconut Candies

Prep: 30 min. + chilling

1-3/4 cups confectioners' sugar
1-3/4 cups flaked coconut
1 cup chopped almonds
1/2 cup sweetened condensed milk
2 cups (12 ounces) semisweet chocolate chips
2 tablespoons shortening
Optional ingredients: flaked coconut, chopped almonds, sliced almonds and sprinkles

1. In a large bowl, combine the confectioners' sugar, coconut, almonds and milk. Shape into 1-in. balls. Refrigerate until firm, about 20 minutes.

2. In a microwave, melt semisweet chips and shortening on high for about 1 minute; stir. Microwave at additional 10- to 20-second intervals, stirring until smooth.

3. Dip balls in chocolate; allow excess to drip off. Coat or garnish with ingredients of your choice. Place on waxed paper; let stand until set. Store in an airtight container. **Yield:** 2-1/2 dozen.

MARY ANN MARINO WEST PITTSBURGH, PENNSYLVANIA

These candies disappear just as fast as I put them out. Good thing they're a snap to whip up! People always comment on what a beautiful presentation they make on any cookie plate. I suggest mounding them high and sprinkling with coconut—then watch them vanish!

GRAND
PRIZE
WINNER

Cookies, Bars & Candy **173**

PG. 178

PG. 182

PG. 198

CAKES & PIES

Settling on a scrumptious dessert is as easy as pie! In this chapter, you can choose from the best of the best in luscious desserts, including cupcakes and tortes, so selecting a mealtime finale is always a piece of cake!

PG. 199

Apple Harvest Cake

Prep: 20 min. **Bake:** 40 min. + cooling

E. Bartuschat, Abington, Massachusetts

Tender apple slices and subtle flavors of orange, vanilla and cinnamon mingle in this old-fashioned cake that is very popular with my family and friends.

2-1/4 cups sugar, *divided*
1 cup canola oil
4 eggs
1/4 cup orange juice
2-1/2 teaspoons vanilla extract
3 cups all-purpose flour
3 teaspoons baking powder
1/2 teaspoon salt
4 medium tart apples, peeled and cubed
2 teaspoons ground cinnamon
Whipped cream and additional cinnamon, optional

1. In a large bowl, beat 2 cups sugar, oil, eggs, orange juice and vanilla until well blended. Combine the flour, baking powder and salt; gradually beat into sugar mixture until blended. Stir in apples.

2. Spread half of the batter into a greased 13-in. x 9-in. baking dish. Combine cinnamon and remaining sugar; sprinkle over batter. Carefully spread remaining batter over the top.

3. Bake at 350° for 40-50 minutes or until a toothpick inserted near the center comes out clean. Cool on a wire rack. Garnish with whipped cream and additional cinnamon if desired. **Yield:** 12-15 servings.

Coconut Cream Dream Cake

Prep: 30 min. **Bake:** 20 min. + cooling

3/4 cup sugar
2 tablespoons shortening
2 tablespoons butter, softened
1 egg
1 egg yolk
3/4 teaspoon vanilla extract
1 cup all-purpose flour
1 teaspoon baking powder
1/2 teaspoon salt
1/2 cup 2% milk
FROSTING/FILLING:
1/2 cup sugar
4 teaspoons water
2 teaspoons light corn syrup
1 egg white
1/4 teaspoon cream of tartar
1/4 teaspoon vanilla extract
1 cup cold 2% milk
1/2 teaspoon coconut extract
1/2 cup instant vanilla pudding mix
6 tablespoons flaked coconut, *divided*

1. In a small bowl, cream the sugar, shortening and butter until light and fluffy. Beat in egg and yolk. Add vanilla. Combine the flour, baking powder and salt; add to creamed mixture alternately with milk. Beat just until combined.

2. Pour into two 6-in. round baking pans coated with cooking spray. Bake at 350° for 20-25 minutes or until a toothpick comes out clean. Cool for 10 minutes; remove from pans to wire racks. Cool completely.

3. In a double boiler over simmering water, combine the sugar, water, corn syrup, egg white and cream of tartar. With a portable mixer, beat on low speed for 1 minute. Continue beating on low over low heat until frosting reaches 160°, about 5 minutes. Pour into a small bowl; add vanilla. Beat on high until stiff peaks form, about 7 minutes.

4. In a bowl, whisk the milk, extract and pudding mix for 2 minutes. Let stand for 2 minutes or until soft-set. Finely chop 1/4 cup coconut; fold into pudding mix.

5. Split each cake into two horizontal layers. Spread a third of the pudding over one cake layer; repeat layers twice. Top with remaining cake. Frost top and sides. Toast remaining coconut; sprinkle over top. Store in the refrigerator. **Yield:** 6 servings.

TIP: Prepare the remaining pudding according to package directions for a quick and easy dessert.

PAMELA SHANK PARKERSBURG, WEST VIRGINIA

This pretty four-layer cake is easy to make with an instant pudding filling and 7-minute frosting. It tastes like coconut cream pie, so it's like getting the best of two desserts in one.

GRAND
PRIZE
WINNER

Caramel Nut Torte

Prep: 30 min. **Bake:** 20 min. + cooling

Karla Stichter, New Paris, Indiana

This recipe caught my eye many years ago because it uses apple cider. My father has a small orchard and we all help pick, wash and sort the apples before they're pressed into cider. We love this delicious cake after a busy day of harvesting.

>   3 eggs, *separated*
> 1/4 cup apple cider *or* juice
>   1 teaspoon vanilla extract
> 1/2 teaspoon baking powder
> 1/4 teaspoon ground cinnamon
> 2/3 cup sugar, *divided*
>   1 cup graham cracker crumbs
> 1/2 cup ground almonds
> **CARAMEL SAUCE:**
> 1/4 cup packed brown sugar
> 1-1/2 teaspoons cornstarch
>   3 tablespoons butter
>   2 tablespoons plus 2 teaspoons apple cider *or* juice, *divided*
>   4 ounces cream cheese, softened
> **FROSTING:**
> 1/2 cup heavy whipping cream
>   1 tablespoon sugar
> 1/4 teaspoon vanilla extract

1. Line two 6-in. round baking pans with parchment paper; coat with cooking spray. In a small bowl, lightly beat egg yolks. Set aside 1 tablespoon. Add cider, vanilla, baking powder, cinnamon and 1/2 cup sugar to remaining yolks.

2. In another bowl, beat egg whites on medium until soft peaks form. Beat in remaining sugar, about 1 tablespoon at a time, on high until stiff peaks form and sugar is dissolved. Fold a fourth of the whites into batter; then fold in remaining whites. Fold in crumbs and almonds.

3. Gently spoon into prepared pans. Bake at 325° for 20-25 minutes or until cake springs back when lightly touched. Cool for 10 minutes; remove from pans to wire racks. Cool completely.

4. In a saucepan, combine the brown sugar, cornstarch, butter and 2 tablespoons cider. Bring to a boil over medium heat, stirring constantly. Cook and stir for 2 minutes or until thickened. Stir a small amount into reserved yolk; return all to pan. Bring to a gentle boil, stirring constantly. Cool.

5. In a small bowl, beat cream cheese until fluffy. Beat in 2 tablespoons caramel sauce until smooth. Spread over one cake; top with remaining cake. Add the remaining cider to remaining caramel sauce to achieve drizzling consistency.

6. Beat cream until it begins to thicken. Add sugar and vanilla; beat until soft peaks form. Frost top and sides of cake. Drizzle the frosting with caramel sauce. **Yield:** 6 servings.

Blitz Torte

Prep: 25 min. **Bake:** 20 min. + cooling

Caroline Krueger, Ripon, Wisconsin

In the 1930s, my three siblings and I always got to select the birthday cake we wanted, and I always chose my mother's Blitz Torte. Years later, I created a downsized version that is equally lovely and light.

        5 tablespoons butter, softened
    2/3 cup confectioners' sugar
        3 egg yolks
    1/2 teaspoon vanilla extract
    2/3 cup all-purpose flour
    1/2 teaspoon baking powder
    1/3 cup 2% milk
MERINGUE:
        2 egg whites
    1/3 cup sugar
    1/4 cup sliced almonds
FILLING:
    1/4 cup sugar
        2 teaspoons cornstarch
    1/2 cup 2% milk
        2 tablespoons beaten egg
    1/2 teaspoon vanilla extract

1. In a small bowl, cream butter and confectioners' sugar until light and fluffy. Add yolks, one at a time, beating well after each. Stir in vanilla. Combine flour and baking powder; add to creamed mixture alternately with milk. Pour into two 6-in. round baking pans coated with cooking spray; set aside.

2. In a small bowl, beat egg whites on medium speed until soft peaks form. Gradually beat in sugar, 1 tablespoon at a time, on high until stiff glossy peaks form and sugar is dissolved. Spread evenly over batter. Sprinkle with almonds. Bake at 350° for 20-25 minutes or until meringue is lightly browned. Cool on wire racks.

3. In a small saucepan, combine sugar and cornstarch; whisk in milk and egg. Bring to a boil over medium heat; cook and stir for 1-2 minutes or until thickened. Remove from the heat; stir in vanilla. Cool.

4. Run a knife around edge of baking pans. Using two large spatulas, carefully remove one cake to a serving plate, meringue side up. Carefully spread with filling. Top with second cake, meringue side up. Store in the refrigerator. **Yield:** 4 servings.

Walnut Banana Cupcakes

Prep: 25 min. **Bake:** 20 min. + cooling

Rachel Krupp, Perkiomenville, Pennsylvania

What makes these tender banana cupcakes extra special is the nutmeg, so make sure that it's fresh. They're amazingly good, and I get requests for them all the time.

    1/4 cup butter, softened
    3/4 cup sugar
        2 eggs
    1/2 cup mashed ripe banana
        1 teaspoon vanilla extract
        1 cup all-purpose flour
    1/2 teaspoon baking soda
    1/2 teaspoon ground nutmeg
    1/4 teaspoon salt
    1/4 cup sour cream
CREAM CHEESE FROSTING:
        4 ounces cream cheese, softened
    1/2 teaspoon vanilla extract
    1-3/4 cups confectioners' sugar
        3 tablespoons chopped walnuts

1. In a large bowl, cream butter and sugar until light and fluffy. Add eggs, one at a time, beating well after each addition. Beat in banana and vanilla. Combine the flour, baking soda, nutmeg and salt; gradually add to creamed mixture alternately with sour cream, mixing well after each addition.

2. Fill paper-lined muffin cups half full. Bake at 350° for 18-22 minutes or until a toothpick inserted near the center comes out clean. Cool for 10 minutes before removing from pan to a wire rack to cool completely.

3. For frosting, in a small bowl, beat cream cheese and vanilla until smooth. Gradually beat in confectioners' sugar. Frost cupcakes; sprinkle with walnuts. Store in the refrigerator. **Yield:** 1 dozen.

Almond Praline Cakes

Prep: 20 min. **Bake:** 20 min.

Kendra Doss, Kansas City, Missouri

Cute and chocolaty, these mini cakes are moist and rich with a crunchy almond crust. The original recipe was so good that I just had to pare it down. This new recipe is just as delicious!

2 tablespoons butter
1/3 cup packed brown sugar
2 tablespoons 2% milk
1/4 cup chopped almonds
BATTER:
  2 tablespoons butter, softened
1/2 cup sugar
  1 egg
1/4 teaspoon vanilla extract
1/2 cup all-purpose flour
  2 tablespoons baking cocoa
1/2 teaspoon baking powder
1/4 teaspoon baking soda
1/3 cup 2% milk

1. In a small saucepan, melt butter over medium heat. Stir in brown sugar and milk. Cook and stir until sugar is dissolved, about 1 minute. Pour into four 8-oz. ramekins or custard cups coated with cooking spray. Sprinkle with almonds; set aside.

2. In a small bowl, cream butter and sugar until light and fluffy. Beat in egg and vanilla. Combine the flour, cocoa, baking powder and baking soda; gradually add to creamed mixture alternately with milk. Spoon over almonds.

3. Bake at 350° for 20-25 minutes or until a toothpick comes out clean. Cool on a wire rack for 5 minutes. Carefully run a knife around the edge of ramekins to loosen. Invert cakes onto dessert plates. Serve warm or at room temperature. **Yield:** 4 servings.

Special Mocha Cupcakes

Prep: 25 min. **Bake:** 20 min. + cooling

  1 cup sugar
1/2 cup cold brewed coffee
1/2 cup canola oil
  2 eggs
  3 teaspoons cider vinegar
  3 teaspoons vanilla extract
1-1/2 cups all-purpose flour
1/3 cup baking cocoa
  1 teaspoon baking soda
1/2 teaspoon salt
MOCHA FROSTING:
  3 tablespoons milk chocolate chips
  3 tablespoons semisweet chocolate chips
1/3 cup butter, softened
  2 cups confectioners' sugar
  1 to 2 tablespoons brewed coffee
1/2 cup chocolate sprinkles

1. In a large bowl, beat the sugar, coffee, oil, eggs, vinegar and vanilla until well blended. In a small bowl, combine the flour, cocoa, baking soda and salt; gradually beat into coffee mixture until blended.

2. Fill paper-lined muffin cups three-fourths full. Bake at 350° for 20-25 minutes or until a toothpick inserted near the center comes out clean. Cool for 10 minutes before removing from pan to a wire rack to cool.

3. For frosting, in a microwave, melt chips and butter; stir until smooth. Transfer to a large bowl. Gradually beat in confectioners' sugar and enough coffee to achieve desired consistency. Pipe frosting onto cupcakes. Top with sprinkles; gently press down. **Yield:** 1 dozen.

MARY BILYEU ANN ARBOR, MICHIGAN

Topped with a fluffy frosting and chocolate sprinkles, these extra-rich, extra-delicious cupcakes smell wonderful while baking and taste even better!

GRAND
PRIZE
WINNER

Peanut Butter Chocolate Cupcakes

Prep: 30 min. **Bake:** 25 min. + cooling

Julie Small, Claremont, New Hampshire

I didn't have any luck finding a recipe for peanut butter-filled chocolate cupcakes (my two favorite flavors). So I made my trusted chocolate cupcake recipe and experimented on my own with different fillings until I found one I liked.

> 1 package (3 ounces) cream cheese, softened
> 1/4 cup creamy peanut butter
> 2 tablespoons sugar
> 1 tablespoon 2% milk

BATTER:
> 2 cups sugar
> 1-3/4 cups all-purpose flour
> 1/2 cup baking cocoa
> 1-1/2 teaspoons baking powder
> 1 teaspoon salt
> 1/4 teaspoon baking soda
> 2 eggs
> 1 cup water
> 1 cup 2% milk

> 1/2 cup canola oil
> 2 teaspoons vanilla extract

FROSTING:
> 1/3 cup butter, softened
> 2 cups confectioners' sugar
> 6 tablespoons baking cocoa
> 3 to 4 tablespoons 2% milk

1. In a small bowl, beat cream cheese, peanut butter, sugar and milk until smooth; set aside.

2. In a large bowl, combine sugar, flour, cocoa, baking powder, salt and baking soda. In another bowl, whisk the eggs, water, milk, oil and vanilla. Stir into dry ingredients just until moistened (batter will be thin).

3. Fill paper-lined jumbo muffin cups half full with batter. Drop scant tablespoonfuls of peanut butter mixture into the center of each; cover peanut butter mixture with remaining batter.

4. Bake at 350° for 25-30 minutes or until a toothpick inserted into cake comes out clean. Cool 10 minutes; remove from pans to wire racks. Cool completely.

5. In a large bowl, combine the frosting ingredients until smooth; frost cupcakes. Store cupcakes in the refrigerator. **Yield:** 1 dozen jumbo cupcakes.

Coconut Pecan Cupcakes

Prep: 50 min. **Bake:** 20 min. + cooling

Tina Harrison, Prairieville, Louisiana

I created this recipe for my best friend, who loves Italian cream cake so much, she worries about portion control!

- 5 **eggs**, *separated*
- 1/2 cup **butter**, softened
- 1/2 cup **shortening**
- 2 cups **sugar**
- 3/4 teaspoon **vanilla extract**
- 1/4 teaspoon **almond extract**
- 1-1/2 cups **all-purpose flour**
- 1/4 cup **cornstarch**
- 1/2 teaspoon **baking soda**
- 1/2 teaspoon **salt**
- 1 cup **buttermilk**
- 2 cups **flaked coconut**
- 1 cup **finely chopped pecans**

FROSTING:
- 1 package (8 ounces) **cream cheese**, softened
- 1/4 cup **butter**, softened
- 1/2 teaspoon **vanilla extract**
- 1/4 teaspoon **almond extract**
- 3-3/4 cups **confectioners' sugar**
- 3/4 cup **chopped pecans**

1. Let eggs stand at room temperature for 30 minutes. In a large bowl, cream butter, shortening and sugar until light and fluffy. Add egg yolks, one at a time, beating well after each addition. Stir in extracts.

2. Combine flour, cornstarch, baking soda and salt; add to creamed mixture alternately with buttermilk, beating well after each addition. In a small bowl, beat egg whites on high speed until stiff peaks form. Fold into batter. Stir in coconut and pecans.

3. Fill paper-lined muffin cups three-fourths full. Bake at 350° for 20-25 minutes or until a toothpick inserted near the center comes out clean. Cool 10 minutes; remove from pans to wire racks to cool completely.

4. In a large bowl, combine frosting ingredients until smooth; frost cupcakes. Store frosted cupcakes in the refrigerator. **Yield:** 2 dozen.

Pecan Sour Cream Cake

Prep: 20 min. **Bake:** 35 min. + cooling

Rachel Yoder, Middlebury, Indiana

There's a surprise, sweet streusel filling inside this tender cake drizzled with cinnamon frosting.

- 1/2 cup **butter**, softened
- 2/3 cup **sugar**
- 3 **eggs**
- 2 tablespoons **maple syrup**
- 2 teaspoons **vanilla extract**
- 1-1/2 cups **all-purpose flour**
- 1/4 cup **ground pecans**, toasted
- 1/2 teaspoon **baking soda**
- 3/4 cup **sour cream**

FILLING:
- 1/4 cup **ground pecans**, toasted
- 4 teaspoons **brown sugar**
- 1-1/2 teaspoons **all-purpose flour**
- 1/2 teaspoon **ground cinnamon**

GLAZE:
- 1/2 cup **confectioners' sugar**
- 1/4 teaspoon **ground cinnamon**
- 2 to 3 teaspoons **2% milk**

1. In a small bowl, cream butter and sugar until light and fluffy. Beat in the eggs, syrup and vanilla. Combine the flour, pecans and baking soda; add to creamed mixture alternately with sour cream.

2. Pour 2 cups batter into an 8-in. fluted tube pan coated with cooking spray. Combine the filling ingredients; sprinkle over batter. Top with remaining batter.

3. Bake at 350° for 35-40 minutes or until a toothpick inserted near the center comes out clean. Cool for 15 minutes; remove from pan to a wire rack to cool completely. Combine glaze ingredients; drizzle over cake. **Yield:** 6 servings.

Honey Pecan Pie

Prep: 25 min. **Bake:** 45 min. + cooling

Cathy Hudak, Wadsworth, Ohio

Looking for a sweet ending to a special meal? This pretty pecan pie with a traditional sugary filling and honey-glazed pecans is perfect! A store-bought crust makes it fast and easy.

        4 eggs
        1 cup chopped pecans
        1 cup light corn syrup
    1/4 cup sugar
    1/4 cup packed brown sugar
        2 tablespoons butter, melted
        1 teaspoon vanilla extract
    1/2 teaspoon salt
        1 unbaked pastry shell (9 inches)
TOPPING:
        3 tablespoons butter
    1/3 cup packed brown sugar
        3 tablespoons honey
1-1/2 cups pecan halves

1. In a large bowl, combine the eggs, pecans, corn syrup, sugars, butter, vanilla and salt. Pour into pastry shell. Bake at 350° for 30 minutes.

2. In a small saucepan, melt butter over medium heat. Stir in brown sugar and honey until combined. Stir in pecan halves until coated. Spoon over pie.

3. Bake 15-20 minutes longer or until a knife inserted near the center comes out clean. Cool completely on a wire rack. Refrigerate leftovers. **Yield:** 8 servings.

Maple Cream Meringue Pie

Prep: 35 min. **Bake:** 15 min. + chilling

Nicole Hardy, St Albans, Vermont

My dessert won first place in the pie category at the annual Vermont Maple Festival. It's simple to make and uses more maple syrup than most other maple cream pies.

        2 tablespoons cornstarch
    1/4 cup water
        1 cup maple syrup
        1 cup heavy whipping cream
        2 egg yolks, lightly beaten
        3 tablespoons butter
        1 pastry shell (9 inches), baked
        3 egg whites
    1/2 teaspoon vanilla extract
    1/4 teaspoon cream of tartar
        6 tablespoons sugar

1. In a small saucepan, combine cornstarch and water until smooth. Stir in syrup and cream. Cook and stir over medium-high heat until thickened and bubbly. Reduce heat to medium; cook, stirring constantly, 2 minutes longer. Remove from the heat.

2. Stir a small amount of hot filling into egg yolks; return all to the pan, stirring constantly. Bring to a gentle boil; cook and stir 2 minutes longer. Remove from the heat. Gently stir in butter. Pour mixture into pastry shell.

3. In a large bowl, beat egg whites, vanilla and cream of tartar on medium speed until soft peaks form. Gradually beat in sugar, 1 tablespoon at a time, on high until stiff glossy peaks form and sugar is dissolved. Spread evenly over hot filling, sealing edges to crust.

4. Bake at 350° for 12-15 minutes or until meringue is golden brown. Cool on a wire rack for 1 hour. Refrigerate for at least 3 hours before serving. Store leftovers in the refrigerator. **Yield:** 8 servings.

Raspberry Patch Cream Pie

Prep: 35 min. + chilling

Allison Anderson, Raymond, Washington

Our family simply loves raspberries. This layered pie keeps the flavor and firmness of the berries intact—and keeps everyone coming back for seconds!

- 1 cup graham cracker crumbs
- 1/2 cup sugar
- 5 tablespoons butter, melted

FILLING:
- 1 package (8 ounces) cream cheese, softened
- 1/4 cup confectioners' sugar
- 2 teaspoons 2% milk
- 1 teaspoon vanilla extract

TOPPING:
- 3/4 cup sugar
- 3 tablespoons cornstarch
- 1-1/3 cups cold water
- 1/4 cup raspberry gelatin powder
- 3 cups fresh raspberries

1. In a small bowl, combine the cracker crumbs, sugar and butter. Press onto the bottom and up the sides of an ungreased 9-in. pie plate. Bake at 350° for 9-11 minutes or until set. Cool on a wire rack.

2. For filling, in a small bowl, combine the cream cheese, confectioners' sugar, milk and vanilla. Carefully spread over crust.

3. For topping, in a small saucepan, combine the sugar, cornstarch and water until smooth. Bring to a boil; cook and stir for 2 minutes or until thickened. Remove from the heat; stir in gelatin until dissolved. Cool to room temperature. Refrigerate until slightly thickened.

4. Arrange raspberries over filling. Spoon gelatin mixture over berries. Refrigerate until set. **Yield:** 6-8 servings.

Creamy Banana Pie

Prep: 30 min. + chilling

Rita Pribyl, Waukesha, Wisconsin

Here's a delectable pie I adapted from a recipe I found years ago. It's so creamy and just bursting with banana flavor!

- 1 envelope unflavored gelatin
- 1/4 cup cold water
- 3/4 cup sugar
- 1/4 cup cornstarch
- 1/2 teaspoon salt
- 2-3/4 cups milk
- 4 egg yolks, beaten
- 2 tablespoons butter
- 1 tablespoon vanilla extract

- 4 medium firm bananas, *divided*
- 1 cup heavy whipping cream, whipped
- 1 pastry shell (10 inches), baked

Juice and grated peel of 1 lemon
- 1/2 cup apple jelly

1. Soften gelatin in cold water; set aside. In a saucepan, combine the sugar, cornstarch and salt. Whisk in the milk until smooth. Cook and stir over medium-high heat until thickened and bubbly. Reduce heat; cook and stir 2 minutes longer. Remove from the heat.

2. Stir a small amount of hot filling into yolks. Return all to the pan, stirring constantly. Bring to a gentle boil. Cook and stir 2 minutes longer. Remove from the heat; stir in softened gelatin until dissolved. Stir in butter and vanilla. Cover the surface of custard with plastic wrap and chill until no longer warm.

3. Slice 3 bananas; fold into custard along with whipped cream. Spoon into pie shell. Cover and refrigerate until set, about 4-5 hours.

4. Just before serving, place lemon juice in a small bowl and slice the remaining banana into it. Melt jelly in a saucepan over low heat. Drain banana; pat dry and arrange over filling. Brush banana with the jelly. Sprinkle with grated lemon peel. Serve immediately. Refrigerate leftovers. **Yield:** 8 servings.

Editor's Note: The filling is very light in color. It is not topped with additional whipped cream.

Chocolate Cream Cheese Cupcakes

Prep: 30 min. **Bake:** 25 min. + cooling

Vivian Morris, Cleburne, Texas

Here is a tried-and-true favorite that I've been making for years. The combination of flavors is irresistible.

        1 package (8 ounces) cream cheese, softened
    1-1/2 cups sugar, *divided*
        1 egg
        1 teaspoon salt, *divided*
        1 cup (6 ounces) semisweet chocolate chips
    1-1/2 cups all-purpose flour
      1/4 cup baking cocoa
        1 teaspoon baking soda
        1 cup water
      1/3 cup canola oil
        1 tablespoon white vinegar
FROSTING:
    3-3/4 cups confectioners' sugar
        3 tablespoons baking cocoa
      1/2 cup butter, melted
        6 tablespoons milk
        1 teaspoon vanilla extract
      1/3 cup chopped pecans

1. For filling, in a small mixing bowl, beat cream cheese and 1/2 cup sugar until smooth. Beat in egg and 1/2 teaspoon salt until combined. Fold in chocolate chips; set aside.

2. In a bowl, combine the flour, cocoa, baking soda, and remaining sugar and salt. In another bowl, whisk the water, oil and vinegar; stir into dry ingredients just until moistened.

3. Fill paper-lined muffin cups half full with batter. Drop filling by heaping tablespoonfuls into the center of each. Bake at 350° for 24-26 minutes or until a toothpick inserted in cake comes out clean. Cool for 10 minutes before removing from pans to wire racks to cool completely.

4. For frosting, in a large mixing bowl, combine confectioners' sugar, cocoa, butter, milk and vanilla; beat until blended. Frost cupcakes; sprinkle with pecans. Store in the refrigerator. **Yield:** 20 cupcakes.

Berry-Topped White Cupcakes

Prep: 30 min. **Bake:** 20 min. + cooling

Judith Kenninger, Brownsburg, Indiana

Guests absolutely devour these tender white cupcakes topped with cream cheese frosting and a berry garnish.

        5 egg whites
      1/2 cup plus 2 tablespoons butter, softened
        1 cup sugar, *divided*
      3/4 teaspoon vanilla extract
    2-1/4 cups cake flour
    2-1/4 teaspoons baking powder
      1/2 teaspoon salt
      3/4 cup milk
ICING:
        4 ounces cream cheese, softened
      1/3 cup butter, softened
        2 cups confectioners' sugar
      1/2 teaspoon lemon juice
Assorted fresh fruit

1. Place egg whites in a large bowl; let stand at room temperature for 30 minutes. In another bowl, cream butter and 3/4 cup sugar until light and fluffy. Beat in vanilla. Combine the flour, baking powder and salt; add to creamed mixture alternately with milk, beating well after each addition.

2. Beat egg whites on medium speed until soft peaks form. Gradually beat in remaining sugar, about 2 tablespoons at a time, on high until stiff glossy peaks form and sugar is dissolved. Fold a fourth of the egg whites into batter; fold in remaining whites.

3. With a spoon, gently fill foil- or paper-lined muffin cups two-thirds full. Bake at 350° for 18-22 minutes. Cool for 10 minutes before removing from pans to wire racks to cool completely.

4. For icing, in a small bowl, beat cream cheese and butter until smooth. Gradually beat in confectioners' sugar and lemon juice. Frost cupcakes. Top with fruit. **Yield:** 22 cupcakes.

Delightful Devil's Food Cake

Prep: 25 min. **Bake:** 25 min. + cooling

Betty Knorr, Chandler, Arizona

There's more than chocolate in this luscious, small-sized layer cake. The creamy ricotta cheese filling is flavored with orange juice, mini chocolate chips and bits of candied cherries.

1 cup sugar
3/4 cup plus 2 tablespoons all-purpose flour
6 tablespoons baking cocoa
1 teaspoon baking soda
1/2 teaspoon salt
1 egg
1/2 cup buttermilk
1/2 cup brewed coffee
1/4 cup canola oil
1 teaspoon vanilla extract
FILLING:
3/4 cup ricotta cheese
2 tablespoons sugar
4 teaspoons orange juice concentrate
2 tablespoons chopped red candied cherries
2 tablespoons miniature semisweet chocolate chips
FROSTING:
3/4 cup heavy whipping cream
3 to 4 tablespoons confectioners' sugar
4-1/2 teaspoons baking cocoa
3/4 teaspoon vanilla extract

1. In a small bowl, combine the sugar, flour, cocoa, baking soda and salt. Whisk the egg, buttermilk, coffee, oil and vanilla; add to dry ingredients until combined.

2. Coat a 9-in. round baking pan with cooking spray and dust with flour. Add batter. Bake at 350° for 25-30 minutes or until a toothpick comes out clean. Cool for 10 minutes; remove from pan to a wire rack. Cool completely.

3. For filling, combine ricotta, sugar and orange juice concentrate; fold in cherries and chips. Cut cake in half vertically. Spread filling over one half; top with remaining half.

4. In a bowl, beat cream until soft peaks form. Gradually beat in confectioners' sugar, cocoa and vanilla until stiff peaks form. Frost top and sides of cake. Store in the refrigerator. **Yield:** 6 servings.

Dark Chocolate Pecan Cake

Prep: 30 min. **Bake:** 25 min. + cooling

Laura Draper, Garfield, Washington

Made in a mini loaf pan, this doubly good chocolate cake has two nutty praline layers and two layers of fluffy whipped cream. It's the only cake my husband really likes.

        1 tablespoon butter
        3 tablespoons brown sugar
    1-1/2 teaspoons heavy whipping cream
        3 tablespoons chopped pecans
BATTER:
        2 tablespoons shortening
        1/4 cup sugar
        2 tablespoons beaten egg
        1/8 teaspoon vanilla extract
        6 tablespoons cake flour
        2 tablespoons baking cocoa
        1/4 teaspoon baking soda
        1/8 teaspoon baking powder
        1/8 teaspoon salt
        3 tablespoons water
TOPPING:
        1/4 cup heavy whipping cream
        2 teaspoons confectioners' sugar
        1/8 teaspoon vanilla extract

1. Line a 5-3/4-in. x 3-in. x 2-in. loaf pan with parchment paper; coat with cooking spray. In a small saucepan, melt butter; stir in brown sugar and cream. Cook and stir over low heat until sugar dissolves. Pour into prepared pan. Top with chopped pecans. Cover and refrigerate.

2. In a small bowl, cream shortening and sugar until light and fluffy. Beat in egg and vanilla. Combine the flour, cocoa, baking soda, baking powder and salt; add to creamed mixture alternately with water. Beat just until combined.

3. Pour over pecans. Bake at 325° for 25-30 minutes or until a toothpick comes out clean. Cool completely in pan.

4. In a small bowl, beat cream until it begins to thicken. Add confectioners' sugar and vanilla; beat until stiff peaks form. Remove cake from pan; split into two horizontal layers. Place bottom cake layer, nut side up, on a serving plate. Spread with half of the topping. Top with the remaining cake layer and topping. **Yield:** 2 servings.

Rhubarb Dessert Cake

Prep: 10 min. **Bake:** 30 min. + cooling

Loraine Meyer, Bend, Oregon

I've shared this recipe with many people since it was passed on to me by a relative. In fact, I freeze rhubarb when it's in season just so I can make this year-round.

    2 tablespoons butter, melted
    1 cup packed brown sugar

        4 cups sliced fresh *or* frozen rhubarb
    1-1/2 cups sugar
    1-1/2 cups all-purpose flour
    1-1/2 teaspoons baking powder
        1/8 teaspoon salt
        3 eggs
        1/2 cup water
        1 teaspoon vanilla extract
Whipped cream *or* vanilla ice cream

1. In a greased 13-in. x 9-in. baking dish, combine butter and brown sugar. Top with rhubarb.

2. In a large bowl, combine the sugar, flour, baking powder and salt. In another bowl, whisk the eggs, water and vanilla; stir into dry ingredients just until moistened. Pour over rhubarb.

3. Bake at 350° for 30-35 minutes or until cake springs back when lightly touched. Cool for 10 minutes on a wire rack. Serve warm or at room temperature with whipped cream or ice cream. **Yield:** 12 servings.

Editor's Note: If using frozen rhubarb, measure rhubarb while still frozen, then thaw completely. Drain in a colander, but do not press liquid out.

Pineapple Upside-Down Cupcakes

Prep: 30 min. Bake: 30 min. + cooling

Barbara Hahn, Park Hills, Missouri

I have baked cupcakes for years since serving as a room mother for my three children. These easy-to-make, jumbo treats make an attractive dessert for special occasions.

- 6 tablespoons butter, cubed
- 1 cup packed light brown sugar
- 2 tablespoons light corn syrup
- 1 small pineapple, peeled, cored and cut into 1/2-inch slices
- 12 maraschino cherries, well drained
- 3 eggs
- 2 cups sugar
- 1 cup canola oil
- 1 cup (8 ounces) sour cream
- 2 teaspoons vanilla extract
- 2-1/2 cups all-purpose flour
- 1/2 teaspoon baking powder
- 1/2 teaspoon baking soda
- 1/2 teaspoon salt
- Whipped topping, optional

1. Line the bottom of 12 greased jumbo muffin cups with waxed paper; grease the paper and set aside.

2. In a small saucepan, melt butter over low heat; stir in brown sugar and corn syrup. Cook and stir over medium heat until sugar is dissolved. Remove from the heat. Spoon 1 tablespoonful into each muffin cup; top each with a pineapple slice and a cherry.

3. In a large bowl, beat eggs and sugar until thickened and lemon-colored. Beat in the oil, sour cream and vanilla until smooth. Combine the flour, baking powder, baking soda and salt. Add to egg mixture and mix well.

4. Fill muffin cups two-thirds full. Bake at 350° for 28-32 minutes or until a toothpick inserted near the center comes out clean. Cool cupcakes for 5 minutes before inverting onto wire racks to cool completely. Garnish with whipped topping if desired. **Yield:** 1 dozen jumbo cupcakes.

Apple Cakes with Lemon Sauce

Prep: 15 min. Bake: 30 min.

Mary Shivers, Ada, Oklahoma

Perfect for dessert or brunch, these rich mini apple cakes are irresistible served with a steaming cup of coffee.

- 2 tablespoons shortening
- 1/4 cup sugar
- 1 egg white
- 1/2 cup all-purpose flour
- 1/4 teaspoon baking soda
- 1/4 teaspoon ground cinnamon
- 1/8 teaspoon salt
- 1/8 teaspoon ground nutmeg
- 1 cup shredded peeled apple
- 1/4 cup chopped pecans

LEMON SAUCE:

- 2 tablespoons plus 2 teaspoons sugar
- 1 teaspoon cornstarch
- 1/4 cup cold water
- 1-1/2 teaspoons lemon juice
- 1-1/2 teaspoons butter

1. In a small bowl, beat shortening and sugar until crumbly, about 2 minutes. Beat in egg white until combined. Combine flour, baking soda, cinnamon, salt and nutmeg; add to shortening mixture just until combined. Fold in the apple and pecans (batter will be thick).

2. Divide between two 8-oz. ramekins or custard cups coated with cooking spray. Bake at 325° for 28-30 minutes or until a toothpick comes out clean.

3. In a small microwave-safe bowl, combine the sugar, cornstarch and water until smooth. Microwave, uncovered, on high for 2-3 minutes or until thickened, stirring every 30 seconds. Stir in lemon juice and butter until blended. Spoon over warm cakes. **Yield:** 2 servings.

Editor's Note: This recipe was tested in a 1,100-watt microwave.

Cherry Gingerbread Cupcakes

Prep: 30 min. **Bake:** 20 min. + cooling

Laura McAllister, Morganton, North Carolina

A sweet frosting with a hint of lemon complements these little spice cakes, each with a maraschino cherry hidden in the center. They're one of my dad's favorite desserts and a sure way of getting him to come over for a cup of coffee.

- 1/2 cup shortening
- 1 cup sugar
- 2 eggs
- 1 cup molasses
- 3 cups all-purpose flour
- 1 teaspoon baking soda
- 1 teaspoon ground ginger
- 1 teaspoon ground cinnamon
- 1 cup buttermilk
- 1/2 cup chopped walnuts
- 24 maraschino cherries, well drained

LEMON CREAM CHEESE FROSTING:
- 4 ounces cream cheese, softened
- 1/4 cup butter, softened
- 1 teaspoon vanilla extract
- 1 teaspoon grated lemon peel
- 1-3/4 to 2 cups confectioners' sugar

1. In a large bowl, cream shortening and sugar until light and fluffy. Add eggs, one at a time, beating well after each addition. Beat in molasses. Combine the flour, baking soda, ginger and cinnamon; gradually add to creamed mixture alternately with buttermilk, beating well after each addition. Stir in walnuts.

2. Fill paper-lined muffin cups two-thirds full; place a cherry in the center of each. Bake at 375° for 20-24 minutes or until a toothpick inserted near the center comes out clean. Cool for 10 minutes before removing from pans to wire racks to cool completely.

3. For frosting, in a small bowl, beat cream cheese and butter until fluffy; add vanilla and lemon peel. Gradually beat in confectioners' sugar until smooth. Frost cupcakes. **Yield:** 2 dozen.

Frost Cupcakes...Fast!

To quickly frost cupcakes, place frosting in a bowl and bring to a spreadable consistency. If it's too stiff, add milk a teaspoon at a time until it reaches desired consistency. Dip the cupcake into the frosting, twist slightly and lift up.

Chocolate-Cherry Ice Cream Pie

Prep: 15 min. + freezing

- 1 bottle (7-1/4 ounces) chocolate hard-shell ice cream topping, *divided*
- 1 graham cracker crust (9 inches)
- 1 jar (10 ounces) maraschino cherries, drained
- 1 quart vanilla ice cream, softened
- 2 packages (1-1/2 ounces *each*) peanut butter cups, chopped

1. Following package directions, drizzle half of the ice cream topping over crust; gently spread to coat bottom and sides. Freeze until firm.

2. Meanwhile, set aside six cherries for garnish; chop remaining cherries. In a large bowl, combine ice cream and chopped cherries. Spread into prepared crust. Sprinkle with peanut butter cups; drizzle with remaining ice cream topping.

3. Garnish with reserved cherries. Cover and freeze for 2 hours or until firm. Remove from the freezer 15 minutes before serving. **Yield:** 6 servings.

KIMBERLY WEST PRAIRIEVILLE, LOUISIANA

No one would ever dream that the fancy taste and look of this luscious freezer pie could come from only five simple ingredients! It makes for an unbelievably easy dessert—perfect for an elegant dinner party or as a cool, high-energy kids' treat on a sweltering day.

GRAND PRIZE WINNER

Mocha Nut Torte

Prep: 40 min. + chilling **Bake:** 20 min. + cooling

Megan Shepherdson, Winnipeg, Manitoba

My husband doesn't like chocolate cake, but this spectacular three-layer torte is one he looks forward to. I've used this recipe for special occasions, such as birthdays, for many years.

>   7 eggs, *separated*
>   1 cup sugar, *divided*
>   1 teaspoon vanilla extract
> 1-1/4 cups ground walnuts
> 1-1/4 cups ground pecans
>   1/4 cup dry bread crumbs
>   1 teaspoon baking powder
>   3/4 teaspoon salt, *divided*

FILLING:
>   1 cup heavy whipping cream
>   1/2 cup confectioners' sugar
>   1 teaspoon vanilla extract

MOCHA FROSTING:
>   1/4 cup butter, cubed
>   4 ounces unsweetened chocolate, chopped
>   1/2 cup brewed coffee
>   2 teaspoons vanilla extract
>   3 to 3-1/4 cups confectioners' sugar

Pecan halves, optional

1. Line three 9-in. round baking pans with waxed paper; set aside. Place egg whites in a large bowl; let stand at room temperature for 30 minutes.

2. Meanwhile, in another bowl, beat egg yolks until slightly thickened. Gradually add 1/2 cup sugar, beating until thick and lemon-colored. Beat in vanilla. Combine nuts, crumbs, baking powder and 1/2 teaspoon salt; stir into yolk mixture until combined.

3. Add remaining salt to egg whites; beat on medium speed until soft peaks form. Gradually beat in remaining sugar, about 2 tablespoons at a time, on high until stiff glossy peaks form and sugar is dissolved. Gradually fold into batter just until blended. Divide among prepared pans.

4. Bake at 375° for 20-25 minutes or until tops spring back when lightly touched. Invert pans; cool for 20 minutes. Remove from pans to wire racks; cool completely. Remove waxed paper.

5. In a small bowl, beat cream until it begins to thicken. Add the confectioners' sugar and vanilla extract; beat until stiff peaks form. Cover; refrigerate until assembling.

6. In a large saucepan, melt butter and chocolate over low heat. Remove from the heat. Stir in coffee, vanilla and enough confectioners' sugar to achieve frosting consistency. Spread filling between layers. Frost top and sides of cake. Garnish with pecans if desired. **Yield:** 12 servings.

Banana Nut Cake

Prep: 20 min. **Bake:** 30 min. + cooling

Marlene Saunders, Lincoln, Nebraska

Sweet, buttery frosting and a sprinkling of chopped nuts top this yummy cake that's loaded with banana and pecan flavor. Serve it with a cup of coffee or a cold glass of milk.

- 1/2 cup butter, softened
- 1 cup sugar
- 2 eggs
- 1/2 teaspoon vanilla extract
- 1-1/4 cups all-purpose flour
- 3/4 teaspoon baking soda
- 1/2 teaspoon salt
- 3/4 cup mashed ripe banana
- 1/2 cup chopped pecans, toasted

BUTTER PECAN FROSTING:
- 1/2 cup butter, softened
- 1/4 cup 2% milk
- 1 teaspoon vanilla extract

Dash salt
- 2 to 2-1/2 cups confectioners' sugar
- 1 cup finely chopped pecans, toasted

Additional chopped pecans, optional

1. In a large bowl, cream butter and sugar until light and fluffy. Add eggs, one at a time, beating well after each addition. Beat in vanilla. Combine the flour, baking soda and salt; add to creamed mixture just until combined. Fold in banana and pecans.

2. Pour into a greased 8-in. square baking dish. Bake at 350° for 30-35 minutes or until a toothpick inserted near the center comes out clean. Cool on a wire rack.

3. In a small bowl, cream butter until light and fluffy. Beat in the milk, vanilla, salt and enough confectioners' sugar to achieve spreading consistency. Stir in toasted pecans. Frost cake. Garnish with additional pecans if desired. **Yield:** 9 servings.

Caramel-Pecan Apple Pie

Prep: 45 min. **Bake:** 55 min. + cooling

Jean Castro, Santa Rosa, California

You'll love the aroma in your kitchen—and the smiles on people's faces—when you make this scrumptious pie that's drizzled with caramel sauce. It takes me back home to Virginia and being at my granny's table.

- 7 cups sliced peeled tart apples
- 1 teaspoon lemon juice
- 1 teaspoon vanilla extract

- 3/4 cup chopped pecans
- 1/3 cup packed brown sugar
- 3 tablespoons sugar
- 4-1/2 teaspoons ground cinnamon
- 1 tablespoon cornstarch
- 1/4 cup caramel ice cream topping, room temperature
- 1 unbaked pastry shell (9 inches)
- 3 tablespoons butter, melted

STREUSEL TOPPING:
- 3/4 cup all-purpose flour
- 2/3 cup chopped pecans
- 1/4 cup sugar
- 6 tablespoons cold butter
- 1/4 cup caramel ice cream topping, room temperature

1. In a large bowl, toss apples with lemon juice and vanilla. Combine the pecans, sugars, cinnamon and cornstarch; add to apple mixture and toss to coat. Pour caramel topping over bottom of pastry shell; top with apple mixture (shell will be full). Drizzle with butter.

2. In a small bowl, combine the flour, pecans and sugar. Cut in butter until mixture resembles coarse crumbs. Sprinkle over filling.

3. Bake at 350° for 55-65 minutes or until filling is bubbly and topping is browned. Immediately drizzle with caramel topping. Cool on a wire rack. **Yield:** 8 servings.

Tastes Like Eggnog Cake

Prep: 30 min. **Bake:** 25 min. + cooling

Lisa Barrett, Durango, Colorado

My holiday eggnog cake starts with a convenient boxed mix and comes out perfect every time. It always gets compliments, and most people think I spend hours in the kitchen making it! My husband's colleagues request it every Christmas.

    1 **package (18-1/4 ounces) yellow cake mix**
    1 **teaspoon ground nutmeg**
1/4 **teaspoon ground ginger**
FROSTING:
1-1/2 **cups heavy whipping cream**
    3 **tablespoons confectioners' sugar**
    1 **teaspoon rum extract**

1. Prepare cake batter according to package directions, adding nutmeg and ginger to dry ingredients. Pour into a greased 13-in. x 9-in. baking pan.

2. Bake at 350° for 25-30 minutes or until a toothpick inserted near the center comes out clean. Cool on a wire rack.

3. For the frosting, in a small bowl, beat cream and confectioners' sugar until stiff peaks form. Fold in the rum extract. Spread frosting over the cake. Store in the refrigerator. **Yield:** 12-15 servings.

Elegant Chocolate Torte

Prep: 50 min. **Bake:** 30 min. + cooling

1/3 **cup all-purpose flour**
    3 **tablespoons sugar**
1/4 **teaspoon salt**
1-3/4 **cups 2% milk**
    1 **cup chocolate syrup**
    1 **egg, lightly beaten**
    1 **tablespoon butter**
    1 **teaspoon vanilla extract**
BATTER:
1/2 **cup butter, softened**
1-1/4 **cups sugar**
    4 **eggs**
    1 **teaspoon vanilla extract**
1-1/4 **cups all-purpose flour**
1/3 **cup baking cocoa**
3/4 **teaspoon baking soda**
1/4 **teaspoon salt**
1-1/2 **cups chocolate syrup**
1/2 **cup water**
FROSTING:
    2 **cups heavy whipping cream**
1/4 **cup chocolate syrup**
1/4 **teaspoon vanilla extract**

1. For filling, in a small saucepan, combine the flour, sugar and salt. Stir in milk and syrup until smooth. Bring to a boil over medium heat, stirring constantly; cook and stir for 1-2 minutes or until thickened.

2. Remove from heat. Stir a small amount of hot mixture into egg; return all to the pan, stirring constantly. Bring to a gentle boil; cook and stir for 2 minutes. Remove from heat; stir in butter and vanilla. Cool to room temperature, stirring often.

3. In a large bowl, cream butter and sugar until light and fluffy. Add eggs, one at a time, beating well after each. Stir in vanilla. Combine dry ingredients; add to creamed mixture alternately with syrup and water. Beat just until combined.

4. Pour into two greased and floured 9-in. round baking pans. Bake at 350° for 30-35 minutes or until a toothpick inserted near the center comes out clean. Cool for 10 minutes; remove from pans to wire racks to cool.

5. Cut each cake in half horizontally. Place one bottom layer on a serving plate; spread with a third of the filling. Repeat layers twice. Top with remaining cake. In a large bowl, beat frosting ingredients until stiff peaks form; spread or pipe over top and sides of cake. **Yield:** 16 servings.

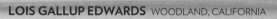

LOIS GALLUP EDWARDS WOODLAND, CALIFORNIA

When I want to serve a really special dessert, I turn to this incredible recipe. The tender, four-layer chocolate cake has a yummy pudding-like filling. Instead of the whipped cream frosting, you could also use chocolate-flavored whipped topping.

Lemon Curd Cupcakes

Prep: 40 min. + chilling **Bake:** 20 min. + cooling

Kerry Barnett-Amundson, Ocean Park, Washington

Homemade lemon curd flavors these tender cupcakes that were made for my brother-in-law's 66th birthday. Lemon fans will give these a big thumbs-up.

      3 tablespoons plus 1-1/2 teaspoons sugar
      3 tablespoons lemon juice
4-1/2 teaspoons butter
      1 egg, lightly beaten
      1 teaspoon grated lemon peel
BATTER:
   3/4 cup butter, softened
      1 cup sugar
      2 eggs
      1 teaspoon vanilla extract
      1 teaspoon grated lemon peel
1-1/2 cups cake flour
   1/2 teaspoon baking powder
   1/4 teaspoon baking soda
   1/4 teaspoon salt
   2/3 cup buttermilk
FROSTING:
      2 tablespoons butter, softened
   1/2 teaspoon vanilla extract
Pinch salt
      2 cups confectioners' sugar
      2 to 4 tablespoons milk
Edible flowers *or* additional grated lemon peel,
      optional

1. For lemon curd, in a heavy saucepan, cook and stir the sugar, lemon juice and butter until smooth. Stir a small amount of hot mixture into egg; return all to pan. Bring to a gentle boil, stirring constantly; cook 2 minutes longer or until thickened. Stir in lemon peel. Cool for 10 minutes. Cover and chill for 1-1/2 hours or until thickened.

2. In a large bowl, cream butter and sugar until light and fluffy. Add eggs, one at a time, beating well after each. Add vanilla and lemon peel. Combine the flour, baking powder, baking soda and salt; add to creamed mixture alternately with buttermilk.

3. Fill paper-lined muffin cups three-fourths full. Bake at 350° for 20-25 minutes or until a toothpick comes out clean. Cool for 10 minutes; remove from pan to a wire rack to cool completely.

4. Cut a small hole in the corner of a pastry or plastic bag; insert a small round pastry tip. Fill bag with lemon curd. Insert tip 1 in. into center of each cupcake; fill with curd just until tops of cupcakes begin to crack.

5. In a small bowl, combine the butter, vanilla, salt, confectioners' sugar and enough milk to achieve frosting consistency. Frost cupcakes. Store in the refrigerator. Garnish with flowers or lemon peel if desired. **Yield:** 1 dozen.

Editor's Note: You can find confectionery roses in the cake decorating aisle at your grocery store.

Chip Lover's Cupcakes

Prep: 30 min. **Bake:** 20 min. + cooling

Donna Scully, Middletown, Delaware

Making chocolate chip cookies is a challenge with three teenagers who are always grabbing a sample of the dough. Their love of cookie dough inspired the recipe for these cupcakes that adults will enjoy, too.

- 1 package (18-1/4 ounces) white cake mix
- 1/4 cup butter, softened
- 1/4 cup packed brown sugar
- 2 tablespoons sugar
- 1/3 cup all-purpose flour
- 1/4 cup confectioners' sugar
- 1/4 cup miniature semisweet chocolate chips

BUTTERCREAM FROSTING:
- 1/2 cup butter, softened
- 1/2 cup shortening
- 4-1/2 cups confectioners' sugar
- 4 tablespoons 2% milk, *divided*
- 1-1/2 teaspoons vanilla extract
- 1/4 cup baking cocoa
- 18 miniature chocolate chip cookies

1. Prepare cake batter according to package directions; set aside. For filling, in a small bowl, cream butter and sugars until light and fluffy. Gradually beat in the flour and confectioners' sugar until blended. Fold in the chocolate chips.

2. Fill paper-lined muffin cups half full with cake batter. Drop filling by tablespoonfuls into the center of each; cover with remaining batter.

3. Bake at 350° for 20-22 minutes or until a toothpick inserted in cake comes out clean. Cool for 10 minutes before removing cupcakes from pans to wire racks to cool completely.

4. For frosting, in a large bowl, cream the butter, shortening and confectioners' sugar until smooth. Beat in 3 tablespoons milk and vanilla until creamy. Set aside 1 cup frosting; frost cupcakes with remaining frosting.

5. Stir baking cocoa and remaining milk into reserved frosting. Cut a small hole in a corner of a pastry or plastic bag; insert star tip. Fill bag with chocolate frosting. Pipe a rosette on top of each cupcake; garnish with a cookie. **Yield:** 1-1/2 dozen.

Mint-Chocolate Ice Cream Cake

Prep: 15 min. + freezing

Kathy Morrow, Hubbard, Ohio

Truly impressive, my versatile ice cream cake is pretty enough for company, and simple enough for a weeknight treat.

- 1 package (16 ounces) Suzy Q's
- 3 cups mint chocolate chip ice cream, softened
- 12 cream-filled chocolate sandwich cookies, crushed, *divided*
- 2 cups whipped topping
- 1/2 teaspoon mint extract, optional

1. Line an 8-in. x 4-in. loaf pan with plastic wrap. Place four Suzy Q's in pan, completely covering the bottom. Spread ice cream over Suzy Q's; sprinkle with half of the cookie crumbs. Press remaining Suzy Q's on top. Cover and freeze for at least 3 hours.

2. Just before serving, remove from the freezer and invert onto a serving plate. Remove pan and plastic wrap. Combine whipped topping and extract if desired; frost top and sides of cake. Sprinkle with remaining cookie crumbs. **Yield:** 10 servings.

Chocolate Cherry Lincoln Log

Prep: 30 min. **Bake:** 10 min. + freezing

Marilyn Jensen, Cody, Wyoming

The first time I made this festive cake roll was for Lincoln's birthday–but it's a great dessert for any holiday or special meal. Feel free to change the ice cream flavor.

- 3 eggs
- 1 cup sugar
- 1/3 cup water
- 1 teaspoon vanilla extract
- 1 cup all-purpose flour
- 1/3 cup baking cocoa
- 1 teaspoon baking powder
- 1/4 teaspoon salt
- Confectioners' sugar
- 1 quart cherry ice cream, softened

FROSTING:
- 1 ounce unsweetened chocolate
- 1 tablespoon butter
- 1-1/4 cups confectioners' sugar
- 2 to 3 tablespoons milk

1. Line a greased 15-in. x 10-in. x 1-in. baking pan with waxed paper; grease the paper and set aside. In a large bowl, beat eggs for 3 minutes. Gradually add sugar; beat for 2 minutes or until mixture becomes thick and lemon-colored. Stir in water and vanilla. Combine the flour, cocoa, baking powder and salt; fold into egg mixture (batter will be thin).

2. Spread evenly into prepared pan. Bake at 375° for 10-13 minutes or until cake springs back when lightly touched. Cool for 5 minutes. Invert onto a kitchen towel dusted with confectioners' sugar. Gently peel off waxed paper. Roll up cake in the towel jelly-roll style, starting with a short side. Cool completely on a wire rack.

3. For frosting, in microwave-safe bowl, melt chocolate and butter; stir until smooth. Gradually beat in confectioners' sugar and enough milk to achieve desired consistency.

4. Unroll cake; spread ice cream evenly over cake to within 1/2 in. of edges. Roll up again. Place seam side down on a serving platter. Spread with frosting. Cover and freeze overnight. **Yield:** 14 servings.

Raspberry Peach Cupcakes

Prep: 25 min. **Bake:** 15 min. + cooling

Arlene Butler, Ogden, Utah

These easy cupcakes have an appealing combination of fresh fruit and white chocolate. The luscious lemon buttercream frosting adds a zippy citrus tang.

- 1 cup white baking chips
- 6 tablespoons butter, cubed
- 1 package (18-1/4 ounces) white cake mix
- 1 cup 2% milk
- 3 eggs
- 1 teaspoon vanilla extract
- 1 cup fresh raspberries
- 1/2 cup chopped peeled fresh peaches *or* frozen unsweetened peach slices, thawed and chopped

LEMON FROSTING:
- 1/2 cup butter, softened
- 3 cups confectioners' sugar
- 2 tablespoons lemon juice

Fresh raspberries and peach pieces, optional

1. In a microwave, melt white baking chips and butter; stir until smooth.

2. In a large bowl, combine the cake mix, milk, eggs, vanilla and melted chips; beat on low speed for 30 seconds. Beat on medium for 2 minutes. Fold in raspberries and peaches.

3. Fill paper-lined muffin cups three-fourths full. Bake at 350° for 15-20 minutes or until a toothpick inserted near the center comes out clean. Cool for 10 minutes before removing from pans to wire racks to cool completely.

4. For frosting, in a small bowl, beat the butter, confectioners' sugar and lemon juice until smooth. Frost cupcakes. Top with fruit if desired. **Yield:** 2 dozen.

Editor's Note: This recipe was tested with Betty Crocker cake mix.

Black 'n' Blue Berry Crumb Pie

Prep: 15 min. **Bake:** 55 min. + cooling

Linda Palmer, Greenville, Ohio

Here's a very simple recipe for a mouthwatering, fresh-tasting pie that features two kinds of berries. The brown-sugar crumb topping adds buttery, old-time crunchiness and flavor to this summery dessert.

    1 sheet refrigerated pie pastry
    3 cups fresh blackberries
    2 cups fresh blueberries
    3/4 cup sugar
    1/4 cup cornstarch
    1/8 teaspoon ground nutmeg
TOPPING:
    1/2 cup all-purpose flour
    1/4 cup packed brown sugar
    1/4 cup cold butter

1. Unroll pastry into a 9-in. pie plate. Trim pastry to 1/2 in. beyond edge of plate; flute edges.

2. In a large bowl, combine blackberries and blueberries. Combine sugar, cornstarch and nutmeg; sprinkle over berries and toss gently. Pour into crust.

3. In a small bowl, combine flour and brown sugar; cut in butter until crumbly. Sprinkle over filling.

4. Bake at 375° for 55-60 minutes or until filling is set (cover edges with foil during the last 15 minutes to prevent overbrowning if necessary). Cool on a wire rack. **Yield:** 6-8 servings.

Texas Chocolate Cupcakes

Prep: 30 min. **Bake:** 15 min. + cooling

Cathy Bodkins, Dayton, Virginia

I never thought about putting caramel icing on chocolate cupcakes, but boy, was I wrong. My mother-in-law passed down this recipe. It's to die for!

    2 cups all-purpose flour
    2 cups sugar
    1 teaspoon salt
    1/2 teaspoon baking soda
    1/4 cup baking cocoa
    1 cup water
    1 cup canola oil
    1/2 cup butter, cubed
    2 eggs
    1/3 cup buttermilk
    1 teaspoon vanilla extract
CARAMEL ICING:
    1 cup packed brown sugar
    1/2 cup butter, cubed
    1/4 cup milk
    2 to 2-1/4 cups confectioners' sugar

1. In a large bowl, combine flour, sugar, salt and baking soda. In a large saucepan over medium heat, bring the cocoa, water, oil and butter to a boil. Gradually add to dry ingredients and mix well. Combine the eggs, buttermilk and vanilla; gradually add to batter and mix well (batter will be very thin).

2. Fill paper-lined muffin cups three-fourths full. Bake at 350° for 15-20 minutes or until a toothpick inserted near the center comes out clean. Cool 10 minutes. Remove from pans to wire racks to cool completely.

3. For icing, in a heavy saucepan, combine the brown sugar, butter and milk. Cook and stir over low heat until sugar is dissolved. Increase heat to medium. Do not stir. Cook for 3-6 minutes or until bubbles form in center of mixture and syrup turns amber. Remove from the heat; transfer to a small bowl. Cool to room temperature. Gradually beat in confectioners' sugar until smooth. Frost cupcakes. **Yield:** 2 dozen.

PG. 203

PG. 218

PG. 210

JUST DESSERTS

Save room for dessert—or better yet, enjoy dessert first! It's easy to do when you're dazzled with this decadent assortment of prize–winning cheesecakes, tarts, crisps and cobblers. Go ahead. Indulge!

PG. 212

Mock Apple Pie Squares

Prep: 30 min. **Bake:** 25 min. + cooling

Lynn Hamilton, Naperville, Illinois

No one ever guesses these sweet "apple" squares are made with zucchini. In fact, there isn't one bit of apple in them! The recipe makes a big batch and uses economical ingredients.

> 4 cups all-purpose flour
> 2 cups sugar
> 1/2 teaspoon salt
> 1-1/2 cups cold butter, cubed
> **FILLING:**
> 8 cups sliced peeled zucchini
> 2/3 cup lemon juice
> 1 cup sugar
> 1 teaspoon ground cinnamon
> 1/4 teaspoon ground nutmeg
> 1/2 cup chopped walnuts
> 1/2 cup golden raisins

1. In a large bowl, combine the flour, sugar and salt. Cut in butter until mixture resembles coarse crumbs. Press half of the crumb mixture into a greased 15-in. x 10-in. x 1-in. baking pan. Bake at 375° for 10-12 minutes or until lightly browned. Set remaining crumb mixture aside.

2. Meanwhile, in a large saucepan, bring zucchini and lemon juice to a boil. Reduce heat; cover and simmer for 5-6 minutes or until tender. Drain. Stir in the sugar, cinnamon, nutmeg and 1/2 cup reserved crumb mixture. Cook and stir for 2-3 minutes. Stir in walnuts and raisins.

3. Spread filling evenly over crust. Sprinkle with remaining crumb mixture. Bake for 25-30 minutes or until golden brown. Cool on a wire rack. Cut into squares. **Yield:** about 2-1/2 dozen.

Rustic Caramel Apple Tart

Prep: 20 min. + chilling **Bake:** 25 min.

Betty Fulks, Onia, Arkansas

Like an apple pie without the pan, this scrumptious tart has a crispy crust that cuts nicely and a yummy caramel topping.

> 2/3 cup all-purpose flour
> 1 tablespoon sugar

> 1/8 teaspoon salt
> 1/4 cup cold butter, cubed
> 6-1/2 teaspoons cold water
> 1/8 teaspoon vanilla extract
> **FILLING:**
> 1-1/2 cups chopped peeled tart apples
> 3 tablespoons sugar
> 1 tablespoon all-purpose flour
> **TOPPING:**
> 1 teaspoon sugar
> 1/4 teaspoon ground cinnamon
> 2 tablespoons caramel ice cream topping, warmed

1. In a large bowl, combine the flour, sugar and salt; cut in butter until crumbly. Gradually add water and vanilla, tossing with a fork until dough forms a ball. Cover and refrigerate for at least 30 minutes.

2. On a lightly floured surface, roll dough into a 10-in. circle. Transfer to a parchment paper-lined baking sheet. Combine the filling ingredients; spoon over pastry to within 2 in. of edges. Fold up edges of pastry over filling, leaving center uncovered. Combine sugar and cinnamon; sprinkle over filling.

3. Bake at 400° for 25-30 minutes or until crust is golden and filling is bubbly. Using parchment paper, slide tart onto a wire rack. Drizzle with caramel topping. Serve warm. **Yield:** 4 servings.

Mixed Nut Chocolate Tart

Prep: 20 min. **Bake:** 35 min. + cooling

Debbie Cross, Sharon, Pennsylvania

A buttery shortbread crust holds a delectable filling made with chocolate and a mix of chopped pistachios, almonds and pecans. This is one impressive yet easy-to-prepare dessert. I guarantee it will be one of your most-requested recipes!

1-1/2 cups all-purpose flour
1/4 cup sugar
1/2 cup plus 1 tablespoon cold butter
6 tablespoons heavy whipping cream
1-1/2 teaspoons vanilla extract
FILLING:
1 cup pistachios
1 cup pecan halves
3/4 cup unblanched almonds
3 eggs
3/4 cup light corn syrup
1/4 cup packed brown sugar
1/4 cup butter, melted
1-1/2 teaspoons almond extract
1 teaspoon vanilla extract
1 cup milk chocolate chips
Whipped cream

1. In a small bowl, combine flour and sugar; cut in butter until mixture resembles fine crumbs. Add cream and vanilla, tossing with a fork until dough forms a ball. Press onto the bottom and up the sides of an ungreased fluted 11-in. tart pan with removable bottom; set aside.

2. Place nuts in a food processor; cover and process until chopped. In a large bowl, whisk the eggs, corn syrup, brown sugar, butter and extracts until smooth. Stir in chocolate chips and nut mixture; pour into crust.

3. Place pan on a baking sheet. Bake at 350° for 35-40 minutes or until center is set. Cool on a wire rack. Store in the refrigerator. Garnish with whipped cream. **Yield:** 12-14 servings.

Peanut Butter Pudding Dessert

Prep: 25 min. **Bake:** 25 min. + chilling

Barbara Schindler, Napoleon, Ohio

Here's a fun, layered dessert that appeals to all ages. If you want it even nuttier, you can use chunky peanut butter; and if you're not a fan of cashews, substitute your favorite nuts.

1 cup all-purpose flour
1/2 cup cold butter, cubed
1-1/2 cups chopped cashews, *divided*
1 package (8 ounces) cream cheese, softened
1/3 cup creamy peanut butter
1 cup confectioners' sugar
1 carton (12 ounces) frozen whipped topping, thawed, *divided*
2-2/3 cups cold milk
1 package (3.9 ounces) instant chocolate pudding mix
1 package (3.4 ounces) instant vanilla pudding mix
1 milk chocolate candy bar (1.55 ounces), coarsely chopped

1. Place flour and butter in a food processor; cover and process until mixture resembles coarse crumbs. Add 1 cup cashews; pulse a few times until combined.

2. Press into a greased 13-in. x 9-in. baking dish. Bake at 350° for 25-28 minutes or until golden brown. Cool completely on a wire rack.

3. In a small bowl, beat the cream cheese, peanut butter and confectioners' sugar until smooth. Fold in 1 cup whipped topping. Spoon over crust.

4. In another bowl, whisk milk and both pudding mixes for 2 minutes. Let stand for 2 minutes or until soft-set. Spread over cream cheese layer. Top with remaining whipped topping. Sprinkle with chopped candy bar and remaining cashews. Cover and refrigerate for at least 1 hour before serving. **Yield:** 12-16 servings.

Frosty Raspberry Parfaits

Prep: 35 min. + freezing

Clare Hafferman, Kalispell, Montana

These elegant, fruity parfaits are a traditional part of our Fourth of July buffet every year. For patriotic color, try garnishing with a mix of blueberries and raspberries.

 This recipe includes Nutrition Facts.

4 cups fresh *or* frozen raspberries, thawed, *divided*
4 egg yolks, lightly beaten
1/2 cup sugar
1 teaspoon vanilla extract
1 cup heavy whipping cream, whipped
Additional fresh raspberries, optional

1. Place 2 cups raspberries in a food processor; cover and process until blended. Press through a fine mesh strainer; discard seeds and pulp.

2. In a small saucepan, combine egg yolks and sugar; stir in raspberry puree until smooth. Cook and stir over medium heat until mixture reaches at least 160° and coats the back of a metal spoon. Remove from the heat; stir in vanilla. Transfer to a bowl. Refrigerate until chilled.

3. Fold in whipped cream. Coarsely mash remaining raspberries. In six freezer-proof parfait glasses, layer 1 tablespoon mashed berries and 1/4 cup cream mixture. Repeat layers. Cover and freeze for 6 hours or overnight. Garnish with additional raspberries if desired. **Yield:** 6 servings.

Nutrition Facts: 1 parfait equals 215 calories, 11 g fat (6 g saturated fat), 169 mg cholesterol, 13 mg sodium, 27 g carbohydrate, 6 g fiber, 3 g protein.

Peach Blackberry Cobbler

Prep: 40 min. **Bake:** 40 min.

✓ This recipe includes Nutrition Facts.

12 medium peaches, peeled and sliced
1/3 cup all-purpose flour
1/4 cup honey
3 tablespoons lemon juice
1/4 teaspoon salt
3 cups fresh blackberries
TOPPING:
2 cups all-purpose flour
1/2 cup sugar
1 teaspoon baking powder
1/2 teaspoon salt
1/4 teaspoon baking soda
1/3 cup cold butter, cubed
1-1/4 cups buttermilk
1 tablespoon coarse sugar

1. In a large bowl, combine the peaches, flour, honey, lemon juice and salt; let stand for 15 minutes. Fold in blackberries. Transfer to a 13-in. x 9-in. baking dish coated with cooking spray.

2. For topping, in a large bowl, combine the flour, sugar, baking powder, salt and baking soda. Cut in butter until crumbly. Make a well in the center; pour in buttermilk. Stir just until a soft dough forms. Drop by tablespoonfuls over fruit mixture; sprinkle with coarse sugar.

3. Bake at 400° for 40-45 minutes or until filling is bubbly and a toothpick inserted in topping comes out clean. Serve warm. **Yield:** 12 servings.

Nutrition Facts: 1 serving equals 263 calories, 6 g fat (3 g saturated fat), 15 mg cholesterol, 286 mg sodium, 51 g carbohydrate, 5 g fiber, 4 g protein.

MARGUERITE SHAEFFER SEWELL, NEW JERSEY

What could be more tempting than a freshly baked cobbler starring ripe peaches and blackberries? Every bite of this tried-and-true favorite is like a taste of summer.

GRAND PRIZE WINNER

Frozen Cheesecake Bites

Prep: 1 hour + freezing **Bake:** 40 min. + freezing

Frank Millard, Janesville, Wisconsin

It only takes one of these rich nibbles to cure your cheesecake cravings...but your guests are sure to ask for more.

✓ This recipe includes Nutrition Facts.

> 3 **packages (8 ounces *each*) cream cheese,**
> **softened**
> 1-1/4 **cups sugar, *divided***
> 1-1/2 **teaspoons vanilla extract**
> 1/2 **teaspoon salt**
> 4 **eggs, lightly beaten**
> 9 **ounces semisweet chocolate, chopped**
> 3/4 **cup heavy whipping cream**
> 1/2 **cup graham cracker crumbs**
> 1/2 **cup milk chocolate English toffee bits**

1. Line the bottom of a 9-in. springform pan with parchment paper; coat paper and sides of pan with cooking spray. Set aside. In a large bowl, beat the cream cheese, 1 cup sugar, vanilla and salt until smooth. Add eggs; beat on low speed just until combined. Pour into prepared pan.

2. Place the pan on a baking sheet. Bake at 325° for 40-45 minutes or until center is almost set. Cool on a wire rack for 10 minutes. Carefully run a knife around edge of pan to loosen; cool 1 hour longer. Cover pan and freeze overnight.

3. Remove from the freezer and let stand for 30 minutes or until easy to handle. Meanwhile, in a small saucepan over low heat, melt chocolate with cream; stir until blended. Remove from the heat. Transfer to a large bowl; cover and refrigerate until mixture reaches spreading consistency, stirring occasionally.

4. In a small bowl, combine cracker crumbs and remaining sugar. Using a melon baller, scoop out 1-in. balls of cheesecake; place on parchment paper-lined baking sheets. Top each with a heaping teaspoonful of chocolate mixture. Sprinkle crumb mixture over half of the balls and toffee bits over the remaining balls. Cover and freeze for 2 hours or until firm. **Yield:** 5-1/2 dozen.

Nutrition Facts: 1 cheesecake bite equals 55 calories, 3 g fat (2 g saturated fat), 21 mg cholesterol, 47 mg sodium, 6 g carbohydrate, trace fiber, 1 g protein.

Frosty Pistachio Delight

Prep: 25 min. + freezing

Sandie Davenport, Farmer City, Illinois

I love the simple make-ahead convenience of this refreshing dessert drizzled with fudge topping. When having guests, I make the pie the night before, freeze it—and have time to enjoy their company!

2-1/2 cups chocolate graham cracker crumbs
  2/3 cup butter, melted
    1 carton (1-3/4 quarts) vanilla ice cream, softened
    2 packages (3.4 ounces *each*) instant pistachio pudding mix
    1 cup plus 2 tablespoons pistachios, chopped, *divided*
    3 drops green food coloring, optional
    1 carton (8 ounces) frozen whipped topping, thawed
    1 jar (11-3/4 ounces) hot fudge ice cream topping, warmed

1. In a small bowl, combine cracker crumbs and butter. Press into a greased 13-in. x 9-in. baking dish. Bake at 350° for 7-9 minutes or until set. Cool on a wire rack.

2. In a large bowl, combine the ice cream, pudding mixes, 1 cup pistachios and food coloring if desired. Fold in whipped topping. Spread over crust. Cover and freeze for at least 4 hours.

3. Remove from the freezer 10 minutes before serving. Drizzle with fudge topping; sprinkle with remaining pistachios. **Yield:** 15 servings.

Strawberry Tart

Prep: 20 min. **Bake:** 10 min. + chilling

Dawn Tringali, Hamilton Square, New Jersey

Here's the perfect ending to any summertime meal. This fast-fixing, creamy tart boasts a crunchy chocolate layer tucked right next to the crust. You could also make individual tartlets instead of one big one dessert.

    1 sheet refrigerated pie pastry
    3 ounces German sweet chocolate, melted
    2 packages (8 ounces *each*) cream cheese, softened
    3 tablespoons heavy whipping cream
    2 teaspoons vanilla extract
1-3/4 cups confectioners' sugar
2-1/2 cups sliced fresh strawberries
  1/4 cup red currant jelly

1. Press pastry onto the bottom and up the sides of an ungreased 9-in. fluted tart pan with a removable bottom. Place on a baking sheet. Bake at 450° for 10-12 minutes or until crust is golden brown. Cool on a wire rack.

2. Spread melted chocolate over bottom of crust. Cover and refrigerate for 5-10 minutes or until almost set. Meanwhile, in a large bowl, beat the cream cheese, cream and vanilla until smooth. Gradually beat in confectioners' sugar. Spread over chocolate layer.

3. Arrange strawberries over filling; brush with jelly. Cover and refrigerate for at least 2 hours. Remove sides of pan before serving. **Yield:** 6-8 servings.

Triple-Berry Cobbler

Prep: 20 min. **Bake:** 25 min.

Edna Woodard, Fredericksburg, Texas

*I combined several recipes to come up with this one winner!
It's incredibly versatile and lends itself nicely to other fruits
depending on the season and availability.*

 This recipe includes Nutrition Facts.

1/2 cup sugar
  3 tablespoons cornstarch
1/4 teaspoon ground cinnamon
  1 cup water
  1 cup fresh *or* frozen cranberries, thawed
  1 cup fresh blueberries
  1 cup fresh blackberries
TOPPING:
1/4 cup sugar
  2 tablespoons butter, softened
1/3 cup fat-free milk
1/4 teaspoon vanilla extract
2/3 cup all-purpose flour
3/4 teaspoon baking powder
1/4 teaspoon salt

1. In a small heavy saucepan, combine the sugar, cornstarch, cinnamon and water until smooth. Bring to a boil; cook and stir for 2 minutes or until thickened. Remove from the heat; stir in berries. Transfer to an 8-in. square baking dish coated with cooking spray.

2. For topping, in a small bowl, beat sugar and butter until crumbly, about 2 minutes. Beat in milk and vanilla. Combine the flour, baking powder and salt; stir into butter mixture just until blended. Drop by tablespoonfuls over fruit mixture.

3. Bake at 375° for 25-30 minutes or until filling is bubbly and a toothpick inserted in topping comes out clean. Serve warm. **Yield:** 6 servings.

Nutrition Facts: 1 serving equals 235 calories, 4 g fat (2 g saturated fat), 10 mg cholesterol, 195 mg sodium, 49 g carbohydrate, 3 g fiber, 2 g protein.

Strawberry Mallow Pops

Prep: 20 min. + freezing

Arlene Pickard, Redvers, Saskatchewan

*These strawberry pops are especially popular with our family
on hot, summer days. It's fun biting into the frosty bits of fruit
and marshmallow.*

  1 package (8 ounces) cream cheese, softened
1/4 cup honey
  2 packages (10 ounces *each*) frozen sweetened
    sliced strawberries, thawed
  3 cups miniature marshmallows
  1 cup heavy whipping cream, whipped

1. In a small bowl, beat cream cheese and honey until smooth. Add strawberries with juice; beat until blended. Fold in marshmallows and whipped cream.

2. Pour 1/4 cupfuls into 24 plastic molds or 3-oz. paper cups; top with holders or insert Popsicle sticks into cups. Freeze until firm. **Yield:** 2 dozen.

Jumbleberry Crumble

Prep: 10 min. + standing **Bake:** 45 min.

Mary Ann Dell, Phoenixville, Pennsylvania

A friend shared her recipe for this delicious, down-home dessert with me. The blend of juicy berries and a crumbly cinnamon-sugar topping just seems to appeal to everyone!

> 3 cups halved fresh strawberries
> 1-1/2 cups fresh raspberries
> 1-1/2 cups fresh blueberries
> 2/3 cup sugar
> 3 tablespoons quick-cooking tapioca
> 1/2 cup all-purpose flour
> 1/2 cup quick-cooking oats
> 1/2 cup packed brown sugar
> 1 teaspoon ground cinnamon
> 1/3 cup butter, melted

1. In a large bowl, combine the strawberries, raspberries and blueberries. Combine sugar and tapioca; sprinkle over berries and toss gently. Pour into a greased 11-in. x 7-in. baking dish; let stand for 15 minutes.

2. Meanwhile, in a small bowl, combine the flour, oats, brown sugar and cinnamon. Stir in butter; sprinkle over berry mixture.

3. Bake at 350° for 45-50 minutes or until filling is bubbly and topping is golden brown. Serve warm. **Yield:** 6-8 servings.

Nutrition Facts: 1 piece equals 290 calories, 8 g fat (5 g saturated fat), 20 mg cholesterol, 84 mg sodium, 54 g carbohydrate, 4 g fiber, 2 g protein.

Caramel Apple-Pear Crisp

Prep: 20 min. **Bake:** 40 min. + standing

Amanda Pettit, Logan, Ohio

A fall favorite, this lightened-up crisp is packed with a healthy combination of fresh pears and apples, and just the right amount of tasty walnuts in the topping. You'll love it!

> 3 medium pears, peeled and sliced
> 2 medium tart apples, peeled and sliced
> 2 tablespoons sugar
> 1/4 teaspoon ground allspice
> 1/3 cup sugar-free caramel topping
> **TOPPING:**
> 1/4 cup quick-cooking oats
> 1/4 cup packed brown sugar
> 2 tablespoons all-purpose flour
> 3 tablespoons cold reduced-fat butter
> 1/4 cup chopped walnuts
> 3/4 cup reduced-fat whipped topping

1. In a large bowl, combine the pears, apples, sugar and allspice. Transfer to an 8-in. square baking dish coated with cooking spray. Drizzle with caramel topping.

2. For topping, in a small bowl, combine the oats, brown sugar and flour. Cut in butter until crumbly; stir in walnuts. Sprinkle over fruit mixture.

3. Bake at 375° for 40-45 minutes or until topping is golden brown and fruit is tender. Let stand for 15 minutes. Spoon cooking juices over each serving; garnish with whipped topping. **Yield:** 6 servings.

Editor's Note: This recipe was tested with Land O'Lakes light stick butter.

Chocolate-Covered Cheesecake Squares

Prep: 1-1/2 hours + freezing

Esther Neustaeter, La Crete, Alberta

Satisfy your sweet tooth with these bite-size cheesecakes! They're party favorites and perfect for the holidays, when portion control is tough with so many sweets to choose from.

>   1 cup graham cracker crumbs
> 1/4 cup finely chopped pecans
> 1/4 cup butter, melted
> **FILLING:**
>   2 packages (8 ounces *each*) cream cheese, softened
> 1/2 cup sugar
> 1/4 cup sour cream
>   2 eggs, lightly beaten
> 1/2 teaspoon vanilla extract
> **COATING:**
>   24 ounces semisweet chocolate, chopped
>   3 tablespoons shortening

1. Line a 9-in. square baking pan with foil and grease the foil. In a small bowl, combine the graham cracker crumbs, pecans and butter. Press into prepared pan; set aside.

2. In a large bowl, beat the cream cheese, sugar and sour cream until smooth. Add eggs; beat on low speed just until combined. Stir in vanilla. Pour over crust.

3. Bake at 325° for 35-40 minutes or until center is almost set. Cool on a wire rack. Refrigerate until chilled. Freeze overnight.

4. In a microwave, melt chocolate and shortening; stir until smooth. Cool slightly.

5. Using foil, lift cheesecake out of pan. Gently peel off foil; cut into 49 squares. Remove a few pieces at a time for dipping; keep remaining squares refrigerated until ready to dip.

6. Using a toothpick, completely dip squares, one at a time, in melted chocolate; allow excess to drip off. Place on waxed paper-lined baking sheets; spoon about 1 teaspoon chocolate over each. (Reheat chocolate if needed to finish dipping.)

7. Let stand for 20 minutes or until set. Store cheesecake squares in an airtight container in the refrigerator or freezer. **Yield:** 49 squares.

Giant Peanut Butter Ice Cream Sandwich

Prep: 30 min. **Bake:** 20 min. + freezing

JoAnn Belack, Bradenton, Florida

Who doesn't like peanut butter, chocolate, ice cream and cookies? This over-the-top dessert combines all four!

- 2 packages (16 ounces *each*) ready-to-bake refrigerated peanut butter cup cookie dough
- 6 whole chocolate graham crackers, crushed
- 1 cup cold milk
- 1 cup heavy whipping cream
- 1 package (3.4 ounces) instant vanilla pudding mix
- 1 package (8 ounces) cream cheese, softened
- 1-1/3 cups creamy peanut butter
- 3 cups vanilla ice cream, softened
- 1/4 cup Nutella

1. Let dough stand at room temperature for 5-10 minutes to soften. Press into two ungreased 9-in. springform pans; sprinkle with graham cracker crumbs. Bake at 350° for 20-25 minutes or until set. Cool completely.

2. In a large bowl, whisk the milk, cream and pudding mix for 2 minutes. Let stand for 2 minutes or until soft-set. In another large bowl, beat cream cheese and peanut butter until smooth. Add pudding and ice cream; beat until smooth.

3. Spread over one cookie crust. Remove sides of second pan; place crust, crumb side down, over filling. Cover and freeze for 4 hours or until firm.

4. Remove from the freezer 15 minutes before serving. Place Nutella in a small microwave-safe bowl; cover and microwave at 50% power for 1-2 minutes or until smooth, stirring twice. Remove sides of pan; cut dessert into slices. Drizzle with Nutella. **Yield:** 12 servings.

Editor's Note: Look for chocolate hazelnut spread in the peanut butter section.

Praline Chocolate Dessert

Prep: 25 min. + chilling **Bake:** 10 min. + cooling

Korrie Bastian, Clearfield, Utah

Praline and cream cheese layered between a rich cookie crumb crust and chocolate ganache make this dessert a showstopper.

- 2 cups cream-filled chocolate sandwich cookie crumbs
- 1/2 cup butter, melted
- 1 cup chopped pecans

PRALINE:
- 1-1/2 cups butter, cubed
- 1 cup packed brown sugar
- 1 teaspoon vanilla extract

FILLING:
- 2 packages (8 ounces *each*) cream cheese, softened
- 1/2 cup confectioners' sugar
- 1/3 cup packed brown sugar

GANACHE:
- 1 cup (6 ounces) semisweet chocolate chips
- 1/2 cup heavy whipping cream

Pecan halves

1. In a small bowl, combine cookie crumbs and butter. Press onto the bottom of a greased 9-in. springform pan. Place on a baking sheet. Bake at 350° for 10 minutes. Cool on a wire rack. Sprinkle with pecans.

2. In a large saucepan over medium heat, bring butter and brown sugar to a boil, stirring constantly. Reduce heat; simmer, uncovered, for 10 minutes. Remove from the heat; stir in vanilla. Pour over pecans. Refrigerate for 1-2 hours or until set.

3. In a large bowl, beat filling ingredients until smooth. Spread over praline layer. Refrigerate for 1-2 hours or until set.

4. For ganache, place chocolate chips in a small bowl. In a small saucepan, bring cream just to a boil. Pour over chocolate; whisk until smooth. Spread over filling. Refrigerate for 1-2 hours or until set.

5. Carefully run a knife around edge of pan to loosen; remove sides of pan. Garnish with pecan halves. Refrigerate leftovers. **Yield:** 14-16 servings.

Frosty Lemon-Strawberry Dessert

Prep: 15 min. + freezing

Gail Marshall, Fort Lauderdale, Florida

This fun frosty treat is so simple, cool and refreshing on a hot summer day. Top with fresh berries if you like!

- 1 quart fresh strawberries, hulled
- 1/2 gallon vanilla ice cream, softened
- 1 can (12 ounces) frozen lemonade concentrate, thawed
- 2 teaspoons grated lemon peel

1. Place strawberries in a food processor; cover and process until pureed. Transfer to a large bowl; add the ice cream, lemonade concentrate and lemon peel. Beat until blended.

2. Pour into an ungreased 13-in. x 9-in. dish. Cover and freeze overnight. Remove from the freezer 15 minutes before serving. **Yield:** 12 servings.

Apple Turnovers

Prep: 50 min. + chilling **Bake:** 20 min.

- 1 cup all-purpose flour
- 1/2 teaspoon salt
- 1/2 cup cold butter, *divided*
- 1/4 cup ice water
- **FILLING:**
- 1/3 cup sugar
- 2 teaspoons cornstarch
- 1/8 teaspoon ground cinnamon
- 2 medium tart apples, peeled and thinly sliced
- 1 teaspoon lemon juice
- 2 tablespoons beaten egg
- 1-1/2 teaspoons water
- **GLAZE:**
- 1/4 cup confectioners' sugar
- 1 teaspoon water

1. In a small bowl, combine flour and salt; cut in 1/4 cup butter until crumbly. Gradually add water, tossing with a fork until a ball forms. On a lightly floured surface, roll dough into a 12-in. x 6-in. rectangle.

2. Cut remaining butter into thin slices. Starting at a short side of dough, arrange half of the butter slices over two-thirds of rectangle to within 1/2 in. of edges. Fold unbuttered third of dough over middle third. Fold remaining third over the middle, forming a 6-in. x 4-in. rectangle. Roll dough into a 12-in. x 6-in. rectangle.

3. Repeat steps of butter layering and dough folding, ending with a 6-in. x 4-in. rectangle. Wrap in plastic wrap; refrigerate for 15 minutes. Roll dough into a 12-in. x 6-in. rectangle. Fold in half lengthwise and then widthwise. Wrap in plastic wrap; refrigerate for 1 hour.

4. Meanwhile, in a small saucepan, combine the sugar, cornstarch and cinnamon. Add apples and lemon juice; toss to coat. Bring to a boil over medium heat, stirring constantly. Reduce heat; simmer, uncovered, for 5-10 minutes or until apples are tender, stirring often. Remove from the heat.

5. In a small bowl, combine egg and water. Roll dough into a 12-in. square; cut into four squares. Brush with half of the egg mixture. Spoon about 1/4 cup filling on half of each square; fold dough over filling. Press edges with a fork to seal. Place on an ungreased baking sheet. Brush with remaining egg mixture. With a sharp knife, cut three small slits in the top of each turnover.

6. Bake at 450° for 17-22 minutes or until golden brown. Remove to a wire rack. Combine the glaze ingredients; drizzle glaze over turnovers. Serve warm. **Yield:** 4 servings.

Quick Apple Turnovers: Substitute 1 sheet frozen puff pastry, thawed, for the dough. Skip steps 1-3. Proceed as directed in steps 4-6. Check doneness after 15 minutes.

Blueberry Turnovers: Omit filling. In a saucepan, combine 1/4 cup blueberries, 1 tablespoon sugar, 1-1/2 teaspoons cornstarch and 1 teaspoon grated lemon peel. Mash well with a fork. Bring to a boil over low heat; cook and stir for 2 minutes or until thickened. Remove from the heat. Stir in 1 tablespoon butter and 3/4 cup blueberries. Fill and bake turnovers as directed.

DOROTHY BAYES SARDIS, OHIO

*These traditional turnovers are tender and flaky, with apple pie-like filling and a light glaze.
I like to freeze any extras and warm them up in the microwave to enjoy with my coffee.*

GRAND
PRIZE
WINNER

Coffee Ice Cream Cookie Cups

Prep: 30 min. **Bake:** 15 min. + freezing

Marcus Dooley, Red Oak, Texas

I invented this special treat for my sister's birthday party. Everyone had compliments and wanted more. I've also tried it with peanut butter cookie dough and different flavored ice creams, but I like coffee the best.

> 1 tube (16-1/2 ounces) refrigerated chocolate chip cookie dough
> 2 cups coffee ice cream
> Whipped cream and chocolate syrup
> 1/3 cup English toffee bits *or* almond brickle chips

1. Let dough stand at room temperature for 5-10 minutes to soften. Cut into 12 slices; press onto the bottoms and up the sides of greased muffin cups.

2. Bake at 350° for 12-14 minutes or until golden brown. Cool on a wire rack. Spoon ice cream into each cup. Cover; freeze for 1-2 hours or until firm.

3. Remove cups from pan. Garnish with whipped cream and chocolate syrup. Sprinkle with toffee bits. **Yield:** 12 servings.

Cream Cheese Ice Cream

Prep: 20 min. + chilling **Process:** 20 min./batch + freezing

Johnnie McLeod, Bastrop, Louisiana

This is hands-down the best homemade ice cream I've ever eaten! It tastes like cheesecake with a refreshing hint of lemon.

> 2-1/2 cups half-and-half cream
> 1 cup milk
> 1-1/4 cups sugar
> 2 eggs, lightly beaten
> 12 ounces cream cheese, cubed
> 1 tablespoon lemon juice
> 1 teaspoon vanilla extract

1. In a large saucepan, heat the cream and milk to 175°; stir in sugar until dissolved. Whisk a small amount of hot mixture into the eggs. Return all to the pan, whisking constantly. Cook and stir over low heat until mixture reaches at least 160° and coats the back of a metal spoon.

2. Remove from the heat. Whisk in cream cheese until smooth. Cool quickly by placing pan in a bowl of ice water; stir for 2 minutes. Stir in lemon juice and vanilla. Press plastic wrap onto surface of custard. Refrigerate for several hours or overnight.

3. Fill cylinder of ice cream freezer two-thirds full; freeze according to manufacturer's directions. Refrigerate remaining mixture until ready to freeze. Transfer to a freezer container; freeze for 2-4 hours before serving. **Yield:** 1-1/2 quarts.

Peanut Ice Cream Delight

Prep: 50 min. + freezing

Barb Rader, Brock, Nebraska

A cookie crust topped with ice cream, peanuts, homemade caramel and chocolate sauce...no wonder this dessert was such a hit at my future daughter-in-law's bridal shower!

- 1 package (16.6 ounces) cream-filled chocolate sandwich cookies, crushed
- 1/3 cup butter, melted
- 1/2 gallon vanilla ice cream, softened
- 1-1/2 cups salted peanuts

CARAMEL SAUCE:
- 1 cup packed brown sugar
- 1 cup heavy whipping cream
- 1/2 cup butter, cubed
- 1 teaspoon vanilla extract

CHOCOLATE SAUCE:
- 1 can (12 ounces) evaporated milk
- 1 cup (6 ounces) semisweet chocolate chips
- 1/2 cup butter, cubed
- 2 cups confectioners' sugar
- 1 teaspoon vanilla extract

1. In a bowl, combine cookie crumbs and butter; press onto the bottom and up the sides of an ungreased 13-in. x 9-in. dish. Spread ice cream over crust; sprinkle with peanuts. Cover and freeze for at least 1 hour.

2. For caramel sauce, in a small saucepan, combine the brown sugar, cream and butter. Bring to a boil; cook and stir for 1 minute. Remove from the heat; stir in vanilla. Cool. Drizzle over peanuts. Cover and freeze for at least 1 hour.

3. For chocolate sauce, in a large saucepan, combine the milk, chocolate chips and butter. Cook and stir over low heat until melted and smooth. Stir in confectioners' sugar. Bring to a boil. Reduce heat; simmer, uncovered, for 8-10 minutes or until thickened, stirring frequently. Remove from the heat; stir in vanilla. Cool.

4. Drizzle over dessert. Cover and freeze for 2 hours or until firm. **Yield:** 12-15 servings.

Granola-Topped Pear Crisp

Prep: 20 min. Bake: 25 min.

Pat Habiger, Spearville, Kansas

Lots of crunchy topping and just the right touch of sweetness make this a delicious dish. With fruit and granola, it's perfect for brunch or breakfast!

 This recipe includes Nutrition Facts.

- 4 medium pears, peeled and thinly sliced
- 2 tablespoons cornstarch
- 1/2 cup peach preserves, warmed

TOPPING:
- 1/3 cup all-purpose flour
- 1/3 cup sugar
- 3/4 teaspoon ground cinnamon
- 1/4 teaspoon salt
- 1/8 teaspoon ground nutmeg
- 3 tablespoons cold butter
- 1 cup granola with fruit and nuts

1. Place pears in a large bowl; sprinkle with cornstarch and toss to coat. Gently stir in preserves just until combined. Transfer to an 11-in. x 7-in. baking dish coated with cooking spray.

2. For topping, in a small bowl, combine the flour, sugar, cinnamon, salt and nutmeg. Cut in butter until crumbly; stir in granola. Sprinkle over fruit mixture.

3. Bake at 375° for 25-30 minutes or until the topping is golden brown and the fruit is tender. Serve crisp warm. **Yield:** 8 servings.

Nutrition Facts: 1 serving equals 244 calories, 7 g fat (3 g saturated fat), 11 mg cholesterol, 132 mg sodium, 46 g carbohydrate, 3 g fiber, 2 g protein.

Chocolate Chip Cookie Dessert

Prep: 25 min. **Bake:** 15 min. + freezing

Carol Marnach, Sioux Falls, South Dakota

Drizzled with melted chocolate, this frosty family favorite couldn't be much easier to prepare. My husband and three sons love it so much that we even use our grill to make it on camping trips or during the hot summer months when I don't like turning on the oven.

- 1 tube (16-1/2 ounces) refrigerated chocolate chip cookie dough
- 1/2 cup caramel ice cream topping
- 1/2 cup cold 2% milk

- 1 package (3.4 ounces) instant vanilla pudding mix
- 1 carton (8 ounces) frozen whipped topping, thawed
- 3/4 cup chopped nuts
- 3/4 cup English toffee bits *or* almond brickle chips
- 3 ounces semisweet chocolate, chopped
- 3 tablespoons butter

1. Let dough stand at room temperature for 5-10 minutes to soften. Press into an ungreased 13-in. x 9-in. baking pan. Bake at 350° for 14-16 minutes or until golden brown. Cool completely on a wire rack.

2. Spread caramel topping over crust. In a large bowl, whisk milk and pudding mix for 2 minutes. Let stand for 2 minutes or until soft-set.

3. Fold in the whipped topping, nuts and toffee bits. Spread over caramel layer. Cover and freeze for 4 hours or until firm.

4. In a microwave, melt chocolate and butter; stir until smooth. Drizzle over pudding layer. Cut into squares. **Yield:** 16 servings.

Sweet Use of Leftovers

Pour leftover melted chocolate into a small nonstick pan and refrigerate until hardened. Then chop the chocoalte block into chunks to use in recipes that call for chocolate chips.

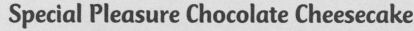

Special Pleasure Chocolate Cheesecake

Prep: 20 min. **Bake:** 40 min. + chilling

- 1 package (18 ounces) ready-to-bake refrigerated triple-chocolate cookie dough
- 1 package (8 ounces) milk chocolate toffee bits, *divided*
- 1 package (9-1/2 ounces) Dove dark chocolate candies
- 3 packages (8 ounces *each*) cream cheese, softened
- 1 can (14 ounces) sweetened condensed milk
- 3/4 cup (6 ounces) vanilla yogurt
- 4 eggs, lightly beaten
- 1 teaspoon vanilla extract

Whipped cream

1. Let dough stand at room temperature for 5-10 minutes to soften. Press nine portions of dough into an ungreased 13-in. x 9-in. baking dish (save remaining dough for another use). Set aside 2 tablespoons toffee bits for garnish; sprinkle remaining toffee bits over dough.

2. In a small microwave-safe bowl, heat chocolate candies at 70% power for 15 seconds; stir. Microwave in 5-second intervals until melted; stir until smooth.

3. In a large bowl, beat the cream cheese, milk and yogurt until smooth. Add eggs; beat on low speed just until combined. Fold in vanilla and melted chocolate. Pour over crust.

4. Bake at 350° for 40-45 minutes or until center is almost set. Cool on a wire rack. Refrigerate for 4 hours or overnight.

5. Garnish cheesecake with whipped cream and reserved toffee bits. Refrigerate leftovers. **Yield:** 24 servings.

BENJAMIN & SUE ELLEN CLARK WARSAW, NEW YORK

When I have time, I enjoy making cheesecakes. In fact, I've come up with a couple of my own recipes. I like this fail-proof dessert because it's so easy to prepare and has just the right mix of ingredients to make it a favorite with just about everyone!

GRAND
PRIZE
WINNER

Blueberry Squares

Prep: 25 min. **Bake:** 10 min. + chilling

Barbara Robbins, Chandler, Arizona

I've made these easy berry squares for many years and they never fail to bring raves from people of all ages. I like the convenience of being able to make them a day ahead of time.

- 1 **cup crushed vanilla wafers (about 30 wafers)**
- 2 **tablespoons butter, melted**

- 3/4 **cup sugar**
- 1/4 **cup cornstarch**
- 1/4 **cup cold water**
- 3 **cups fresh blueberries,** *divided*
- 3 **tablespoons lemon juice**
- 1 **teaspoon grated lemon peel**
- 1 **cup heavy whipping cream**
- 2 **tablespoons confectioners' sugar**
- 1-1/2 **cups miniature marshmallows**

1. In a small bowl, combine wafers and butter. Press into a greased 8-in. square baking dish. Bake at 350° for 8-10 minutes or until lightly browned. Cool on a wire rack.

2. In a small saucepan, combine sugar and cornstarch. Gradually whisk in water until smooth. Stir in 1-1/2 cups blueberries. Bring to a boil; cook and stir for 1-2 minutes or until thickened. Stir in the lemon juice, peel and remaining blueberries. Cool completely.

3. In a small bowl, beat cream until it begins to thicken. Add confectioners' sugar; beat until soft peaks form. Fold in marshmallows. Spread over crust. Top with blueberry mixture. Cover and refrigerate until set, about 45 minutes. **Yield:** 9 servings.

Lime 'n' Spice Peach Cobbler

Mary Ann Dell, Phoenixville, Pennsylvania

This was my grandmother's favorite recipe to make when fresh peaches were in great abundance. Now I bake it frequently during the summer when peaches are ripe.

✓ This recipe includes Nutrition Facts.

- 8 **medium peaches, peeled and sliced**
- 3 **tablespoons sugar**
- 3 **tablespoons brown sugar**
- 2 **tablespoons minced crystallized ginger**
- 4-1/2 **teaspoons cornstarch**
- 1 **tablespoon lime juice**
- 2 **teaspoons ground cinnamon**
- 1/2 **teaspoon grated lime peel**
TOPPING:
- 1/4 **cup packed brown sugar**
- 2 **tablespoons sugar**
- 3 **tablespoons butter, softened**
- 1 **cup cake flour**
- 1/2 **teaspoon baking powder**
- 1/4 **teaspoon salt**
- 2 **tablespoons cold water**
- 1/4 **cup chopped pecans**
- 2 **tablespoons buttermilk**
- 1 **egg yolk**

1. In a large bowl, combine the first eight ingredients. Transfer to an 8-in. square baking dish coated with cooking spray.

2. For topping, in a small bowl, beat sugars and butter until crumbly, about 2 minutes. Combine the flour, baking powder and salt; gradually add to butter mixture. Beat in water just until moistened (mixture will be crumbly). Stir in chopped pecans. Crumble over fruit mixture.

3. Combine buttermilk and egg yolk; drizzle over topping. Bake at 375° for 35-40 minutes or until filling is bubbly and topping is golden brown. Serve warm. **Yield:** 8 servings.

Nutrition Facts: 1 serving equals 275 calories, 8 g fat (3 g saturated fat), 38 mg cholesterol, 155 mg sodium, 51 g carbohydrate, 3 g fiber, 3 g protein.

Peach 'n' Pear Crisps

Prep: 20 min. **Bake:** 20 min.

Susan Wilson, Milwaukee, Wisconsin

I have such a sweet tooth that even when I'm trying to cut calories, it's tough to skip dessert. So I adapted one of my favorite peach pie recipes to make this light, no-crust delight.

- **1 medium peach, peeled and chopped**
- **1 medium ripe pear, chopped**
- **1 tablespoon honey**
- **2 teaspoons all-purpose flour**
- **1-1/2 teaspoons lemon juice**
- **1/4 teaspoon ground cinnamon**
- **1/8 teaspoon ground allspice**
- **TOPPING:**
  - **1 tablespoon all-purpose flour**
  - **1 tablespoon reduced-fat butter, melted**
  - **1 tablespoon honey**
  - **1/8 teaspoon ground allspice**
- **Dash ground cinnamon**
  - **1/3 cup old-fashioned oats**
  - **2 tablespoons coarsely chopped almonds**

1. In a small bowl, combine the first seven ingredients. Divide between two 8-oz. ramekins coated with cooking spray.

2. For topping, in a small bowl, combine the flour, butter, honey, allspice and cinnamon; stir in oats and almonds. Sprinkle over fruit mixture.

3. Bake at 375° for 18-20 minutes or until bubbly and golden brown. Serve warm. **Yield:** 2 servings.

Plum Good Crisp

Prep: 20 min. **Bake:** 30 min. + standing

Peter Halferty, Corpus Christi, Texas

This is a great crisp that goes well with any meal, but you can also serve it as a breakfast treat or snack. It combines such interesting flavors. I like it best served warm—can't be beat!

> ✓ This recipe includes Nutrition Facts.

- **4 cups sliced fresh plums (about 1-1/2 pounds)**
- **3 medium nectarines, sliced**
- **1-1/2 cups fresh blueberries**
- **3 tablespoons brown sugar**
- **2 tablespoons cornstarch**
- **1/4 cup maple syrup**
- **2 tablespoons lemon juice**
- **1/4 teaspoon ground ginger**
- **1/8 teaspoon ground nutmeg**
- **TOPPING:**
  - **1/2 cup all-purpose flour**
  - **1/2 cup old-fashioned oats**
  - **1/4 cup packed brown sugar**
  - **1/4 teaspoon salt**
  - **4 teaspoons unsweetened apple juice**
  - **4 teaspoons canola oil**
- **1-1/2 teaspoons butter, melted**

1. In a large bowl, combine the plums, nectarines and blueberries. Combine the brown sugar, cornstarch, syrup,

lemon juice, ginger and nutmeg until smooth; drizzle over plum mixture and toss to coat. Transfer to an 11-in. x 7-in. baking dish coated with cooking spray.

2. For topping, in a small bowl, combine the flour, oats, brown sugar and salt. Stir in the apple juice, oil and butter until crumbly. Sprinkle over fruit mixture.

3. Bake, uncovered, at 400° for 28-32 minutes or until bubbly and topping is golden brown. Let stand for 15 minutes. Serve warm. **Yield:** 9 servings.

Nutrition Facts: 1 serving equals 216 calories, 4 g fat (1 g saturated fat), 2 mg cholesterol, 78 mg sodium, 46 g carbohydrate, 3 g fiber, 3 g protein.

Cranberry Walnut Tart

Prep: 30 min. + chilling **Bake:** 20 min. + cooling

Patricia Harmon, Baden, Pennsylvania

Both attractive and delicious, this flaky tart combines a tender golden brown crust with a sweet filling that might remind you of baklava. It's a holiday favorite at our house.

2-1/2 cups all-purpose flour
    1 cup cold butter, cubed
1/4 cup sugar
    2 egg yolks
    3 tablespoons cold water
    1 tablespoon lemon juice
1/2 teaspoon grated lemon peel
FILLING:
    1 cup sugar
1/4 cup butter, cubed
1/4 cup water
2/3 cup heavy whipping cream
    3 tablespoons honey
1/2 teaspoon salt
    2 cups chopped walnuts
1/2 cup dried cranberries
    1 egg white, lightly beaten
    1 teaspoon coarse sugar

1. Place the flour, butter and sugar in a food processor; cover and process until mixture resembles coarse crumbs. Add the egg yolks, water, lemon juice and peel; cover and process until dough forms a ball. Divide dough in half; wrap in plastic wrap. Refrigerate for 1 hour or until firm.

2. In a small saucepan, bring the sugar, butter and water to a boil; cook and stir for 1 minute. Cook, without stirring, until mixture turns a golden amber color, about 7 minutes.

3. Remove from the heat; gradually stir in cream. Return to heat; stir in honey and salt until smooth. Stir in walnuts and cranberries. Bring to a boil. Reduce heat; simmer, uncovered, for 5 minutes. Remove from the heat; cool to room temperature.

4. On a lightly floured surface, roll out one portion of dough into an 11-in. circle. Transfer to an ungreased 9-in. fluted tart pan with a removable bottom; trim pastry even with edge. Add filling.

5. Roll out remaining dough to fit top of tart; place over filling. Trim and seal edges. Cut slits in pastry.

6. Brush with egg white; sprinkle with coarse sugar. Bake at 400° for 20-25 minutes or until filling is bubbly. Cool on a wire rack. **Yield:** 10-12 servings.

Taffy Apple Pizza

Prep: 10 min. **Bake:** 15 min. + cooling

Melissa Beachy, Guthrie, Kentucky

This sweet treat has something for everyone. With peanut butter, apple, peanuts, caramel topping and a sugar cookie crust, this pleasing pizza is a sheer delight.

- 1/2 cup refrigerated sugar cookie dough
- 3 ounces cream cheese, softened
- 2 tablespoons brown sugar
- 2 tablespoons creamy peanut butter
- 1/4 teaspoon vanilla extract
- 1/2 medium tart apple, thinly sliced
- 1 tablespoon chopped unsalted peanuts
- 1/4 teaspoon ground cinnamon
- 2 tablespoons caramel ice cream topping, warmed

1. Pat cookie dough onto a 7-1/2-in. pizza pan coated with cooking spray. Bake at 350° for 12-14 minutes or until lightly browned. Cool.

2. In a small bowl, beat the cream cheese, brown sugar, peanut butter and vanilla. Spread over crust.

3. Arrange apple slices on top. Sprinkle with peanuts and cinnamon; drizzle with caramel topping. Cut into wedges. **Yield:** 4 servings.

Pumpkin Cheesecake Dessert

Prep: 25 min. **Bake:** 40 min. + chilling

Cathy Hall, Phoenix, Arizona

With its gingersnap crust and maple syrup drizzle, this rich pumpkin dessert is chock-full of fall's finest flavors!

✓ This recipe includes Nutrition Facts.

- 32 gingersnap cookies, crushed (about 1-1/2 cups)
- 1/4 cup butter, melted
- 5 packages (8 ounces *each*) cream cheese, softened
- 1 cup sugar
- 1 can (15 ounces) solid-pack pumpkin
- 1 teaspoon ground cinnamon
- 1 teaspoon vanilla extract
- 5 eggs, lightly beaten

Dash ground nutmeg
Maple syrup

1. In a small bowl, combine gingersnap crumbs and butter. Press into a greased 13-in. x 9-in. baking dish; set aside.

2. In a large bowl, beat cream cheese and sugar until smooth. Beat in the pumpkin, cinnamon and vanilla. Add eggs; beat on low speed just until combined. Pour over crust; sprinkle with nutmeg.

3. Bake at 350° for 40-45 minutes or until center is almost set. Cool on a wire rack for 10 minutes. Carefully run a knife around edge of baking dish to loosen; cool 1 hour longer. Refrigerate overnight.

4. Cut into squares; serve with syrup. Refrigerate leftovers. **Yield:** 24 servings.

Nutrition Facts: 1 serving (1 piece) equals 143 calories, 7 g fat (4 g saturated fat), 60 mg cholesterol, 122 mg sodium, 17 g carbohydrate, 1 g fiber, 3 g protein.

Strawberry Fudge Torte

Prep: 30 min. **Bake:** 20 min. + chilling

Pat Stewart, Lees Summit, Missouri

We love strawberries and chocolate at our house, so I developed this fudgy, fruity torte out of two recipes we've enjoyed in the past. Fresh raspberries, along with raspberry cream cheese and yogurt make tasty substitutes in this simple but impressive dessert.

1 tube (16-1/2 ounces) refrigerated chocolate
  chip cookie dough
1 carton (6 ounces) strawberry yogurt
1/2 cup spreadable strawberry cream cheese
2 teaspoons lemon juice
1/8 teaspoon almond extract
2 cups confectioners' sugar
2 cups whipped topping
1 cup hot fudge ice cream topping, warmed,
  divided
1-1/2 cups sliced fresh strawberries
1/4 cup sliced almonds

1. Let dough stand at room temperature for 5-10 minutes to soften. Press into an ungreased 9-in. springform pan. Bake at 350° for 18-20 minutes or until golden brown. Cool on a wire rack.

2. In a small bowl, beat the yogurt, cream cheese, lemon juice and extract until smooth. Beat in confectioners' sugar; fold in whipped topping.

3. Remove sides of springform pan; place crust on a serving plate. Spread 3/4 cup fudge topping over crust to within 1/2 in. of edges; top with cream cheese mixture. Arrange strawberries on top; sprinkle with almonds. Refrigerate for 1 hour or until set.

4. Drizzle with remaining fudge topping. Serve immediately. **Yield:** 12 servings.

Editor's Note: Torte is best served immediately after removing from the refrigerator.

Chocolate Peanut Butter Dessert

Prep: 40 min. + freezing

1-1/4 cups packed dark brown sugar
1 cup heavy whipping cream, *divided*
3 egg yolks
1-1/4 cups creamy peanut butter
6 tablespoons butter, softened
GLAZE:
1-1/2 cups heavy whipping cream
2 tablespoons butter
4 teaspoons dark corn syrup
12 ounces bittersweet chocolate, chopped
1/4 cup coarsely chopped dry roasted peanuts

1. In a small saucepan, combine the brown sugar, 1/2 cup cream and yolks. Cook and stir over medium heat until mixture reaches 160° and is thick enough to coat the back of a metal spoon. Cover and refrigerate for 3 hours or until thickened.

2. Line an 8-in. x 4-in. loaf pan with plastic wrap; set aside. In a large bowl, cream peanut butter and butter until light and fluffy. Add brown sugar mixture; beat until smooth. In small bowl, beat remaining cream until stiff peaks form. Fold into peanut butter mixture. Spoon into prepared pan. Cover and refrigerate.

3. For glaze, in a large heavy saucepan, bring the cream, butter and corn syrup to a boil, stirring frequently. Remove from the heat. Add chocolate; whisk until smooth. Set aside 1/3 cup of glaze to cool. Place remaining glaze in a microwave-safe bowl; cover and refrigerate overnight. Spread cooled glaze over loaf; cover and freeze overnight.

4. Using plastic wrap, lift loaf out of pan. Place chocolate side down in a 15-in. x 10-in. x 1-in. pan; place on a wire rack. Discard plastic wrap.

5. In microwave, warm refrigerated glaze; stir until smooth. Pour over loaf; spread with a metal spatula to completely cover top and sides. Sprinkle with peanuts. Freeze for 1 hour or until the glaze is set. **Yield:** 10-12 servings.

CHRISTINE MONTALVO WINDSOR HEIGHTS, IOWA

When I want to splurge on a rich dessert, I whip up this chocolate-glazed frozen peanut butter mousse. It's so decadent, even a thin slice will satisfy. And it's worth every luscious calorie!

GRAND PRIZE WINNER

Mango Fruit Crisp

Prep: 20 min. **Bake:** 30 min.

Judy Schatzberg, Livingston, New Jersey

For many years, this was one of my most delicious summer standbys. To make it a bit more healthy, I recently started substituting whole wheat flour—and it's still a favorite!

    4 medium peaches, peeled and sliced
    3 medium mangoes, peeled and chopped
 1/3 cup sugar
 1/4 cup orange juice
    2 tablespoons whole wheat flour
    1 tablespoon lemon juice
 1/2 teaspoon salt
TOPPING:
 1/2 cup whole wheat flour
 1/3 cup packed brown sugar
    3 tablespoons cold butter
 1/2 cup granola without raisins

1. In a large bowl, combine the first seven ingredients. Transfer to an 11-in. x 7-in. baking dish coated with cooking spray.

2. For topping, in a small bowl, combine flour and brown sugar. Cut in butter until crumbly; stir in granola. Sprinkle over fruit mixture.

3. Bake at 375° for 30-35 minutes or until topping is golden brown and fruit is tender. Serve warm. **Yield:** 8 servings.

Festive White Chocolate Cheesecake

Prep: 30 min. **Bake:** 35 min. + chilling

Mary Alice Graves, Kempton, Indiana

A buttery shortbread crust, creamy white chocolate filling and tangy cran-raspberry sauce create this showstopping dessert.

    2 cups crushed shortbread cookies
 1/4 cup butter, melted
FILLING:
    2 packages (8 ounces *each*) cream cheese, softened
    1 cup white baking chips
 2/3 cup sour cream
 3/4 cup sugar
    1 tablespoon grated orange peel
    1 teaspoon vanilla extract
    3 eggs, lightly beaten
SAUCE:
    1 cup whole-berry cranberry sauce
 1/2 cup seedless raspberry jam
 1/2 teaspoon grated orange peel
TOPPING:
    2 cups heavy whipping cream
 1/4 cup confectioners' sugar

1. In a small bowl, combine cookie crumbs and butter. Press onto the bottom of a greased 9-in. springform pan; set aside.

2. In a large bowl, beat the cream cheese, chips, sour cream, sugar, orange peel and vanilla until smooth. Add eggs; beat on low speed just until combined. Pour over crust. Place pan on a baking sheet.

3. Bake at 350° for 35-40 minutes or until center is almost set. Cool on a wire rack for 10 minutes. Carefully run a knife around edge of pan to loosen; cool 1 hour longer. Refrigerate overnight.

4. In a small saucepan, combine sauce ingredients. Cook and stir over medium heat until blended. Cool.

5. Just before serving, remove sides of springform pan. Spoon sauce over cheesecake to within 1 in. of edges. In a small bowl, beat cream and confectioners' sugar until stiff peaks form. Pipe over sauce. Refrigerate leftovers. **Yield:** 12 servings.

Crunchy Peach-Blueberry Crisp

Prep: 20 min. **Bake:** 20 min.

Lillian Charves, New Bern, North Carolina

A friend of mine gave me this fresh, fruity recipe. To make it healthier, I cut down a bit on the butter in the topping and switched in fat-free vanilla frozen yogurt. No more guilt!

✓ | This recipe includes Nutrition Facts.

3 medium peaches, peeled and sliced
1 cup fresh blueberries
1 tablespoon cornstarch
2 tablespoons orange juice
2 teaspoons lemon juice
TOPPING:
  1/4 cup Grape-Nuts
  1/4 cup quick-cooking oats
    3 tablespoons brown sugar
    1 tablespoon butter, melted
  1/8 teaspoon salt
  1/8 teaspoon ground cinnamon
    1 cup fat-free vanilla frozen yogurt

1. In a small bowl, combine the peaches, blueberries and cornstarch. Transfer to an ungreased 1-qt. baking dish. Combine juices; drizzle over fruit.

2. For topping, in a small bowl, combine the Grape-Nuts, oats, brown sugar, butter, salt and cinnamon. Sprinkle over fruit mixture.

3. Bake at 375° for 20-25 minutes or until topping is golden brown and fruit is tender. Serve warm with fat-free frozen yogurt. **Yield:** 4 servings.

Nutrition Facts: 1 serving with 1/4 cup frozen yogurt equals 226 calories, 4 g fat (2 g saturated fat), 8 mg cholesterol, 184 mg sodium, 46 g carbohydrate, 4 g fiber, 5 g protein.

Tropical Macadamia Custard Dessert

Prep: 15 min. **Bake:** 40 min. + cooling

Brenda Melancon, Gonzales, Louisiana

My husband's co-workers always love my desserts, especially the cookies and bars. So I often use them as my "guinea pigs." They nominated these bars for a recent contest entry.

    1 package (16 ounces) ready-to-bake refrigerated white chip macadamia nut cookie dough, *divided*
    3 eggs
    1 can (20 ounces) unsweetened crushed pineapple, well drained
    1 can (12 ounces) evaporated milk
    1 package (7 ounces) dried tropical fruit bits
  1/3 cup packed brown sugar
    2 tablespoons all-purpose flour
1-1/2 teaspoons rum extract
Whipped topping and maraschino cherries

1. Let dough stand at room temperature for 5-10 minutes to soften. Press nine portions of dough into a greased 9-in. square baking pan. Bake at 350° for 10 minutes or until set. Let stand for 2 minutes.

2. Meanwhile, in a bowl, combine the eggs, pineapple, milk, dried fruit, brown sugar, flour and extract. Pour over crust. Crumble the remaining dough over filling.

3. Bake for 30-35 minutes or until top is golden brown. Cool on a wire rack. Cut into squares; garnish with whipped topping and cherries. Refrigerate leftovers. **Yield:** 12 servings.

Banana Cheesecake

Prep: 45 min. **Bake:** 55 min. + chilling

Sera Smith, West Palm Beach, Florida

We have banana trees in our backyard that bear fruit virtually all year. After making banana bread, muffins and cookies, I still had some of our bountiful crop left, so I decided to try this recipe.

- 3/4 cup all-purpose flour
- 3/4 cup finely chopped pecans
- 3 tablespoons sugar
- 2 tablespoons brown sugar
- 1-1/2 teaspoons vanilla extract
- 6 tablespoons butter, melted

FILLING:
- 1 cup mashed ripe bananas
- 2 tablespoons lemon juice
- 2 packages (8 ounces *each*) cream cheese, softened
- 1-1/4 cups sugar
- 1 cup (8 ounces) sour cream
- 2 tablespoons cornstarch
- 1-1/4 teaspoons vanilla extract
- 1/8 teaspoon salt
- 3 eggs, lightly beaten

TOPPING:
- 1 cup (8 ounces) sour cream
- 1/4 cup sugar
- 1/4 teaspoon vanilla extract
- 1 cup assorted fresh fruit

1. Combine the first five ingredients; stir in melted butter. Press onto the bottom of a greased 9-in. springform pan; place on a baking sheet. Bake at 350° for 10 minutes or until lightly browned. Cool on a wire rack.

2. Combine bananas and lemon juice; set aside. In a large bowl, beat cream cheese and sugar until smooth. Beat in the sour cream, cornstarch, vanilla and salt. Add eggs; beat on low speed just until combined. Fold in banana mixture. Pour into crust. Place pan on a baking sheet.

3. Bake at 350° for 50-60 minutes or until center is almost set. Let stand for 5 minutes. Combine sour cream, sugar and vanilla; spread over top of cheesecake. Bake 5 minutes longer.

4. Cool on a wire rack for 10 minutes. Carefully run a knife around edge of pan; cool 1 hour longer. Refrigerate overnight. Garnish cheesecake with assorted fresh fruits. **Yield:** 12-14 servings.

Lemonade Dessert

Prep: 30 min. + freezing

Margaret Linder, Quincy, Washington

Here's a tasty way to chill out after any summer barbecue. Adults and kids will stand in line for this easy-to-make treat!

1-1/2 cups all-purpose flour
3/4 cup packed brown sugar
3/4 cup cold butter, cubed
3/4 cup chopped pecans
1/2 gallon vanilla ice cream, softened
1 can (12 ounces) frozen pink lemonade
   concentrate, thawed

1. In a small bowl, combine flour and brown sugar; cut in butter until crumbly. Stir in pecans. Spread in a single layer into a greased 15-in. x 10-in. x 1-in. baking pan. Bake at 375° for 9-12 minutes or until golden brown, stirring once. Cool on a wire rack for 10 minutes.

2. In a large bowl, beat ice cream and lemonade until blended. Sprinkle half of the crumbles into a greased 13-in. x 9-in. dish. Spread with ice cream mixture; sprinkle with remaining crumbles. Cover and freeze overnight. Remove from the freezer 15 minutes before serving. **Yield:** 12-15 servings.

Ultimate Fruit Pizza

Prep: 30 min. **Bake:** 15 min. + chilling

Peggy Galyen, Tilden, Nebraska

This classic dessert makes a refreshing snack any time of year. We also made smaller individual pizzas at school with our junior-high students, and all of them enjoyed choosing their favorite fruits to make the pizzas and then eating them. This is a fast, fun party idea for kids of all ages!

1 tube (16-1/2 ounces) refrigerated sugar
   cookie dough
1 package (8 ounces) cream cheese, softened
1/2 cup confectioners' sugar
1 teaspoon lemon juice
1 can (21 ounces) cherry pie filling
1-1/2 cups pineapple tidbits, drained
3/4 cup mandarin oranges, drained
3/4 cup green grapes, halved
3/4 cup fresh strawberries, halved
GLAZE:
1 tablespoon sugar
2 teaspoons cornstarch
1 can (5-1/2 ounces) unsweetened apple juice

1. Let dough stand at room temperature for 5-10 minutes to soften. Press onto an ungreased 12-in. pizza pan. Bake at 350° for 15-20 minutes or until deep golden brown. Cool on a wire rack.

2. In a small bowl, beat the cream cheese, confectioners' sugar and lemon juice. Spread over crust. Top with pie filling; arrange the pineapple, oranges, grapes and strawberries over filling.

3. In a small saucepan, combine sugar and cornstarch. Gradually stir in apple juice. Bring to a boil; cook and stir for 1-2 minutes or until thickened. Cool; brush over fruit. Refrigerate for at least 1 hour before serving. **Yield:** 10-12 servings.

GENERAL RECIPE INDEX

This handy index lists every recipe by food category, major ingredient and/or cooking method, so you can easily locate recipes to suit your needs.

✓ RECIPES INCLUDE NUTRITION FACTS AND/OR DIABETIC EXCHANGES

ALPHABETICAL RECIPE INDEX

This handy index lists every recipe in alphabetical order,
so you can easily find your favorite recipes.

✓ RECIPES INCLUDE NUTRITION FACTS AND/OR DIABETIC EXCHANGES

✓Lemon Yogurt Bread, 142
Lemonade Dessert, 227
Lemony Chicken Soup, 58
✓Lemony Vegetables and Pasta, 120
✓Lime 'n' Spice Peach Cobbler, 218

M

Macadamia-Crusted Tilapia, 117
Mango Fruit Crisp, 224
✓Mango Jicama Salad, 22
Maple Cream Meringue Pie, 184
Maple Walnut Rolls, 82
✓Maple-Ginger Root Vegetables, 155
Marinated Mozzarella, 18
Marshmallow Puffs, 163
Marvelous Chicken Enchiladas, 104
✓Mediterranean Vegetable Pasta , 130
Melt-in-Your-Mouth Pot Roast, 100
Mexican Lasagna, 94
✓Minestrone with Italian Sausage, 53
✓Mini Ham 'n' Cheese Frittatas, 76
Mint-Chocolate Ice Cream Cake, 194
Mixed Nut Chocolate Tart, 203
Mocha Nut Torte, 192
Mock Apple Pie Squares, 202
✓Mushroom Burgers, 47
✓Mushroom Rice Medley, 152
Mushroom Tomato Bisque, 57

N

✓Next-Generation German Potato Salad, 27
✓Northwest Cherry Salsa, 19
Nutcracker Bread, 147

O

✓Oat Pancakes, 83
Old-Fashioned Glazed Ham, 117
Onion-Beef Muffin Cups, 90
✓Orange and Jicama Salsa, 9
Orange Gelatin Pretzel Salad, 35
Orange-Mascarpone Breakfast Rolls, 65
Over-the-Top Mac 'n' Cheese, 116

P

✓Parmesan Herb Loaf, 148
✓Peach Almond Bars, 170
✓Peach Blackberry Cobbler, 204
Peach 'n' Pear Crisps, 219
Peanut Butter Brownie Bars, 164
Peanut Butter Chocolate Cupcakes, 182

Peanut Butter 'n' Jelly Bars, 171
Peanut Butter Pudding Dessert, 203
Peanut Butter S'more Bars, 165
Peanut Ice Cream Delight, 215
✓Pecan Caramels, 168
Pecan Chicken with Chutney, 96
Pecan Sour Cream Cake, 183
Pesto Chicken Lasagna, 106
✓Pina Colada Slush, 15
Pineapple Upside-Down Cupcakes, 189
✓Plum Good Crisp, 219
Popcorn Chicken Salad, 24
Praline Chocolate Dessert, 211
Prosciutto Provolone Panini, 42
Puff Pancake with Blueberry Sauce, 68
Pumpkin Cheesecake Dessert, 221

R

✓Ranch Turkey Burgers, 49
✓Raspberry Greek Salad, 27
Raspberry Patch Cream Pie, 185
✓Raspberry Patch Crumb Bars, 170
Raspberry Peach Cupcakes, 198
✓Raspberry Poppy Seed Dressing, 32
Raspberry Truffle Brownies, 172
Raspberry-Chocolate Mini Muffins, 83
Red, White and Blue Slaw, 35
✓Refried Bean Soup, 44
Rhubarb Dessert Cake, 188
✓Roast Beef Roll-Ups, 60
✓Roasted Beet and Potato Salad, 35
✓Roasted Cumin Cashews, 15
✓Roasted Pepper Chicken Penne, 99
✓Roasted Pepper Chicken Sandwiches, 46
Roasted Vegetable Lasagna, 130
✓Roasted Yellow Pepper Soup, 52
Rosemary Chicken with White Beans, 104
Rustic Caramel Apple Tart, 202
Rustic Nut Bars, 166

S

✓Saucy Pork Chops, 126
Sausage Wonton Cups, 16
✓Savory Apple-Chicken Sausage, 65
Shrimp Salad-Stuffed Avocados, 25
Skillet Sea Scallops, 123
✓Skillet Tacos, 98
Slow 'n' Easy Barbecued Chicken, 107
✓Slow-Cooked Pork Tacos, 115
Slow-Cooked Sausage Dressing, 148
Smoked Chops with Cherry Sauce, 110
So-Healthy Smoothies, 69
✓Sour Cream Loaves, 134